Dream! Create! Sustain!

Mastering the Art and Science of Transforming School Systems

Francis M. Duffy
With contributions by
Zengguan Chen, Pratima Dutta,
Nathan D. P. Powell, Charles M. Reigeluth,
Kurt B. Richter, Sunkyung Lee Watson, and
William R. Watson

ROWMAN & LITTLEFIELD EDUCATION
A division of
ROWMAN & LITTLEFIELD PUBLISHERS, INC.
Lanham • New York • Toronto • Plymouth, UK

Published by Rowman & Littlefield Education
A division of Rowman & Littlefield Publishers, Inc.
A wholly owned subsidary of The Rowman & Littlefield Publishing Group, Inc.
4501 Forbes Boulevard, Suite 200, Lanham, Maryland 20706
http://www.rowmaneducation.com

Estover Road, Plymouth PL6 7PY, United Kingdom

British Library Cataloguing in Publication Information Available

Library of Congress Cataloging-in-Publication Data

Duffy, Francis M. (Francis Martin), 1949–
  Dream! create! sustain! : mastering the art and science of transforming school systems / Francis M. Duffy ; With contributions by Zengguan Chen . . . [et al].
    p. cm.
  Includes bibliographical references and index.
  ISBN 978-1-60709-852-2 (cloth : alk. paper)—ISBN 978-1-60709-853-9 (pbk. : alk. paper)— ISBN 978-1-60709-854-6 (electronic)
  1. School improvement programs—United States. 2. School districts—United States. 3. Educational leadership—United States. I. Title.
  LB2822.82.D817 2010
  371.2'070973—dc22   2010010657

My wife, Marcia, and I have three wonderful grandchildren—Logan, Ella, and Reagan. I dedicate this book to these lovely children who have given new meaning to our lives. I pray that the ideas in this book will transform the school systems that will be responsible for educating our grandchildren, and your children and grandchildren, too, so that they will be well prepared to succeed and prosper in our nation's twenty-first-century society. They deserve no less!

Contents

Prologue to Revolution

Though we often prefer to believe that nothing can be done about the . . . problems we face, there comes a time when we have to take on the system because the system needs to change. There comes a time when we need to "just do it."

—Robert E. Quinn, *Deep Change: Discovering the Leader Within* (1996)

The historical chronicles of the United States of America are replete with examples of episodic revolutions. One of those revolutions was enacted by arms-bearing revolutionaries seeking freedom from tyranny (the American Revolution, 1776). Other revolutions in our history were driven by frame-breaking innovative ideas and technologies (e.g., airplane flight, computers, and the Internet). Even the field of education experienced a revolution in the eighteenth century when the Agrarian Age paradigm for educating children shifted to the Industrial Age paradigm, a paradigm that still controls the design, performance, and outcomes of school systems.

The societies of most modernized countries and their organizations and institutions have moved far into a new societal era—an era commonly referred to as the Information Age, the Knowledge Age, or the Conceptual Age. The name of this era notwithstanding, one thing is clear: this era is significantly, substantively, and qualitatively different from the Industrial Age.

Because the requirements for success in the Knowledge Age are so different from the requirements for success in the Industrial Age, America's children deserve and need an education that prepares them to succeed in this new age. An education cast in the mold of the Industrial Age cannot and will not help America's children succeed in our twenty-first-century society.

An education cast in the mold of the Industrial Age does and always will leave children behind.

DRIVING OUT FOUR INDUSTRIAL AGE PARADIGMS

Providing America's children with an education that satisfies the requirements of our twenty-first-century Knowledge Age requires a paradigm-shifting revolution that drives out four old interconnected Industrial Age paradigms that influence the design and performance of America's school systems. The four paradigm shifts are:

Paradigm 1: the way teachers teach and how children learn (shift from group-based, teacher-centered instruction to personalized, learner-centered instruction); and transforming the way academic and nonacademic support services are designed, managed, and delivered (redesigned to ensure that these services are aligned with the requirements of personalized learning);

Paradigm 2: the design of the internal social infrastructure of school systems (shift from a mechanistic, bureaucratic organization design to an organic, participative design; and transforming organization culture, the reward system, job descriptions, and so on, to align with the requirements of the new core and support work processes;

Paradigm 3: the way school systems interact with external stakeholders (move from a crisis-oriented, reactive approach to an opportunity-seeking, proactive approach); and

Paradigm 4: the way in which educators create change (shift from piecemeal change strategies to whole-system change strategies).

There are several reasons why a revolution in thinking, believing, and working in school systems is needed (rather than relying on evolution, or depending on the continuous improvement of the status quo). The reasons are:

- The existing four paradigms that control the field of education are hammered in hard and are extraordinarily resistant to change.
- The existing four paradigms are locked in place by popular mental models, change-resistant mind-sets, and careers and reputations built on the old paradigms and mental models.
- The existing four paradigms are protected by institutionalized policies, procedures, laws, reward systems, tradition, the organization design of school systems, and organization culture.

If America's children are to receive the education they deserve and need to succeed in our twenty-first-century society, then the four old paradigms need to be driven out, not tweaked, not continuously improved, and not fixed piecemeal. Driving out these old paradigms requires a revolution and requires revolution-minded change leaders.

REVOLUTION REQUIRES POLITICAL ADVOCACY, COURAGE, PASSION, AND VISION

Although a revolution to drive out the old paradigms requires muscular political advocacy, if you step forward to lead or join this revolution on the front lines of change you will require much more than political advocacy. Fighting this revolution requires significant courage, passion, and vision. You must have courage to stand and fight for what you believe in. You need passion to give you the emotional energy and resilience you need to persevere. And you must have a vision to serve as your North Star to keep you and your school system moving in the right direction. Further, these three traits—courage, passion, and vision—must be simultaneously present in each change leader. A change leader can have courage, but lack passion and vision. A change leader can have a powerful vision, but lack the courage to fight for it. A change leader can have courage and a vision, but lack the passion to pursue the vision relentlessly. All three traits must be present all at once in each man and woman who steps forward to lead this revolution.

THE FAILURE OF PIECEMEAL CHANGE

Many education reformers have left (and continue to leave) a legacy of failed or unsustainable change in the field of education. Although well-intentioned, their efforts failed (and are failing) because of the dominant paradigm (the fourth paradigm that must be driven out of the field of education) controlling how they seek to create and sustain change in school systems. That change paradigm is pejoratively characterized as "fix the broken parts," or as "fix one school, one classroom at a time," or more commonly as "piecemeal change."

Piecemeal change is driven by a powerful need for the "quick fix." Quick fixes produce temporary results, but more often than not the original problem that was fixed returns and returns with a vengeance (see Kim & Anderson, 2007). Fixing the broken parts is a failed change strategy, yet, almost inconceivably, reformers continue to use that strategy with the hope—the one last, desperate hope—that this time, this one last time, it will work. But, it won't! It can't! Quick fixes don't work because problems they attempt to solve are a complex web of cause-and-effect loops that resemble elaborate Celtic knot work. Quick fixes also don't and can't create transformational change because the four old paradigms have reached the upper limits of their performance ceiling (Branson, 1987; Handy, 1998), and no amount of tinkering with the old paradigms can create significant improvements. Breaking through the constraining performance ceilings requires the creation of whole new systems—school systems transformed to meet the requirements of the twenty-first-century Knowledge Age—and creating whole new systems is a revolutionary proposition.

THE PAST BEFORE US IS NOT THE FUTURE

Our society cannot afford to carry its old education paradigms forward. It does no good to dream of an idealized future for education if that future is just a projection and continuation of the past. Instead, change-minded revolutionaries should imagine that the four paradigms controlling the design and performance of school systems were destroyed last night and now they must invent four new paradigms. What would be the main features of those new paradigms? How could educators change the mental models supporting the old paradigms? And, importantly, how can they design new school systems driven by the four new paradigms and the new mental models required by the paradigms?

For years, progressive thinkers have called for systemic transformational change in America's school systems. And for the same amount of time the dominant paradigms have not yielded their control of education. I think there are at least five reasons for this stubborn resistance to change:

1. Some educators, consultants, and policymakers do not understand the meaning of systemic transformational change.
2. Some educators, consultants, and policymakers have a difficult time "seeing" school districts as intact systems, instead viewing them as a confederation of loosely coupled schools.
3. Those educators, consultants, and policymakers who do understand the meaning of systemic transformational change and those who do see school districts as intact systems are uncomfortable with the complexity and messiness of transformational change.
4. Those educators, consultants, and policymakers who do understand the meaning of systemic transformational change and who do see school districts as intact systems are uncomfortable with the amount of time it takes to create and sustain transformational change.
5. Those educators, consultants, and policymakers who do understand the meaning of systemic transformational change and who do see school districts as intact systems do not know how to create and sustain transformational change, so they avoid doing it.

Given the above five reasons for resisting transformational change, creating and sustaining a revolution to drive out the four controlling paradigms will require change leaders who are masters of transformational change. Masters of transformational change influence the design, performance, and outcomes of their school systems by making innovative but feasible choices about how to teach children, about how children learn, about how to treat the professionals who work in their systems, about how their systems interact with the external environment, and about how to create and sustain transformational change. Masters of transformation possess knowledge, skills, and dispositions that are organized into three broad competency sets:

- Mastery of Awareness
- Mastery of Deliberate Intention
- Mastery of Methodology

THE ORGANIZATION OF THIS BOOK

The book is organized into five sections. Section 1 offers information that provides a foundation for mastering transformational change. Sections 2 through 4 focus on the three mastery areas listed above. Section 5 offers ideas for shaping the future of change leadership in the United States.

Finally, because of space limitations, there is information about important change leadership knowledge and skills that could not be included in the book. For example, knowing about organization culture and how to change it is an important competency. Learning how to retool a school system's reward system is a key skill set. And, the ability to use interpersonal and group skills with grace, elegance, and skill is a nonnegotiable element of a change leader's skill set. Fortunately, there is an abundant amount of literature about these and other important topics, and learning more about these areas should be part of your personal professional development plan to become a master of transformational change.

Acknowledgments

Writing and publishing a book is not a solitary task. It requires substantial collaboration and cooperation by and from many people. I would like to acknowledge this help.

First, my heartfelt thanks to Dr. Thomas Koerner, vice president and editorial director for Rowman & Littlefield Education. I have had a professional relationship with Tom for several years now. Without his encouragement, support, and understanding, this book and the series of which it is a part would not exist. Through our professional relationship, we have also become good friends and I value that friendship immensely.

Next, I want to express my sincere gratitude to my colleagues who contributed important ideas to this book in several of the chapters. Specifically, Dr. Charles Reigeluth, Dr. Kurt Richter, Dr. Sunkyung Lee Watson, Dr. William Watson, Ms. Pratima Dutta, Ms. Zengguan Chen, and Mr. Nathan D. P. Powell.

Although I do not know these people personally, the graphic artist staff, the editing staff, and the production staff of Rowman & Littlefield Education are the professionals who take an author's words and transform them into books. Although I do not know them, I value their knowledge and skills.

Finally, I want to acknowledge Gallaudet University, the Graduate School and Professional Programs, and the Department of Administration and Supervision. I have been a faculty member at Gallaudet since 1982. Throughout all those years, my deans and Dr. William Marshall, my department chairman, have provided substantial encouragement for and the time to do my research, writing, and publishing.

I

FOUNDATIONAL KNOWLEDGE FOR TRANSFORMING SCHOOL SYSTEMS

1

Honoring the Past While Moving toward the Future

OVERVIEW

The way in which America's school systems educate children is controlled by a paradigm of education that emerged at the dawn of the Industrial Revolution, and which continues to control the teaching and learning processes in school systems. That paradigm—known as the Industrial Age paradigm—served this country exceedingly well throughout the Industrial Age. The Industrial Age, however, has been supplanted by what sociologists call the Knowledge Age, and to be aligned with the requirements of the Knowledge Age, America's school systems must also evolve—but they have not.

In this chapter, you will read about the dominant Industrial Age paradigm for educating children and learn why it needs to be replaced with a new paradigm—one commonly referred to as the Learner-Centered paradigm. Ten points will be articulated to document the need for paradigm change.

There are three additional paradigms that influence the design and performance of school systems that also must be replaced. These are: (1) the paradigm that influences the design and functioning of a school system's internal social infrastructure; (2) the paradigm that influences a school system's relationship with its external environment; and (3) the paradigm that guides how educators in a school system create and sustain change. Several fundamental principles for creating and sustaining all four paradigm shifts are also presented in this chapter.

3

Chapter 1

AMERICA'S DOMINANT PARADIGM
FOR EDUCATING CHILDREN

The design and performance of America's more than fourteen thousand school districts have not changed much since the beginning of the Industrial Age. As the Industrial Age displaced the Agricultural Age and took control of American society, America's school systems were confronted with the challenge of educating millions of new immigrant children. To meet this challenge, factory-size school systems were created to deliver the group-based, classroom-situated, fixed-content, fixed-time approach to teaching and learning (which replaced the one-room schoolhouses and church-run schools that dominated the Agricultural Age). This approach allowed school systems to educate large numbers of immigrant children to prepare them to work in the mills and factories of the Industrial Age.

The Industrial Age paradigms guiding the field of education have served the United States effectively. A country in its adolescent years with extraordinary needs to educate masses of immigrant children, the United States delivered education services on a grand scale. The country needed men and women with a fairly good basic education so that they could help drive the Industrial Revolution to create and sustain a country unlike any other in the history of the world.

Although the Agricultural Age paradigm for educating students was appropriate for its time, as America's society began to transform into the Industrial Age, thought leaders of that era began to recognize the need to transform the education paradigm. That "something different" became the Industrial Age paradigms for designing and managing school systems that still exist today.

Our society is once again undergoing a significant paradigm shift—one that is moving our institutions away from the requirements of the Industrial Age toward the requirements of the Knowledge Age. This societal paradigm shift is large and pervasive, and it is affecting all of our society's institutions as they coevolve to create more customized, personalized approaches to organization design, serving customers, and providing services. A few examples of changes in the design of organizations are shown in table 1.1 below.

TEN POINTS TO DOCUMENT THE NEED
FOR FOUR PARADIGM SHIFTS IN EDUCATION

There is a significant need for four new paradigms to guide the design and performance of school systems in the United States. Some evidence documenting this need is presented in the following ten points.

Table 1.1. Examples of Paradigm Change in American Organizations

Industrial Age Organization Design	Shift to	Information Age Organization Design
Bureaucratic design	→	Team design
Autocratic leadership	→	Distributed leadership
Centralized control	→	Autonomy with accountability
Compliance by employees	→	Initiative by employees
Forced conformity	→	Managed diversity
Compartmentalization	→	Holism
(Division of labor, vertical communication)		(Integration, coordination, horizontal communication)

Point 1: American school districts were designed to respond to the needs of the Industrial Age. Given that students learn at different rates, by forcing all students to learn the same content in the same amount of time, our educational system is designed for sorting students rather than for learning, which was appropriate in the Industrial Age when we needed to separate the laborers from the managers. However, in the Knowledge Age, we need citizens who are educated to succeed in our knowledge-driven society. This societal need requires school systems to evolve by shifting to: (1) a paradigm of teaching and learning that is better suited to requirements of our twenty-first-century society; (2) a paradigm for designing school systems that recognizes the nature of school districts as organic systems with knowledge workers as employees; (3) a paradigm that allows districts to interact proactively and positively with their external environments; and (4) a paradigm that replaces piecemeal change with systemic transformational change. Unfortunately, our school systems are not making this transformation. This "coevolutionary imbalance" (Banathy, 1992b) between education and society places our society in great peril.

Point 2: After more than thirty years of applying the traditional approach to school improvement (one school, one program at a time), very little has changed in how America's children are educated in school systems. The one-school-at-a-time approach, while important and still needed if it is part of a whole-system transformational change process, is inherently insufficient when used in a nonsystemic way because it disregards the nature of school districts as intact, organic systems governed by classic principles of system functioning. Further, the one-school-at-a-time approach often fails because changes to one part of a system makes that part incompatible with the rest of the system, which then works to change it back to its prechange state. Therefore, the piecemeal approach to change is insufficient when whole-system transformational change is required.

Point 3: Given the insufficiency of the one-school-at-a-time approach, change efforts are being scaled-up to the level of the whole school district, but the whole-district improvement methodologies currently being used are failing to create and sustain desired transformational change.

Point 4: There is a growing recognition of the need for local communities and state departments of education to become partners with local school systems as they engage in paradigm change. Barber and Fullan (2007) call this concept "tri-level development." The "three paths to transformation" metaphor explained later in this chapter (Duffy, 2006) is my way of recognizing this same need.

Point 5: There is definitional confusion about the meaning of "system" and "systemic change" (see chapter 2 for a discussion of this confusion). Many approaches to change that are characterized as systemic are not; for example, high school reform is not systemic change (although principles of systemic change can be used to reform a high school); developing a new curriculum is not systemic change; and introducing new instructional technology is not systemic change. These kinds of initiatives can be part of a systemic change effort, but by themselves they are not systemic.

Point 6: Not all systemic change efforts aim to create transformational change. For example, some systemic change efforts aim to make systemic (i.e., system-wide) improvements to a system's current operations (improvements to its existing paradigm). Making system-wide improvements to current operations is called continuous improvement, and this does not create transformational change. Transformational change, on the other hand, seeks organizational reinvention rather than change by replication of best practices, discontinuity rather than incrementalism, and true innovation rather than periodic reordering (Lazlo & Laugel, 2000, p. 184).

Point 7: Transformational change requires substantial change in how a district functions, how it is designed, and how it is managed. An example of a paradigm change for how a school system is designed and functions would be for educators in a school system to transform the Industrial Age design of their system (mechanistic and hierarchical) to a Knowledge Age design (i.e., organic and participative).

Point 8: Transformational paradigm change requires simultaneous improvements along three change paths: path 1—transform the system's core and support work processes; path 2—transform the system's internal social infrastructure; and path 3—transform the system's relationship with its external environment. Only one contemporary approach to improving school systems (described in chapter 12) follows these three paths.

Point 9: Now that knowledge work predominates in our society, America needs school systems that have as their purpose to ensure that every child who enters public education leaves having mastered a variety of important knowledge and skills so they can succeed in the twenty-first-century Knowledge Age.

Point 10: A paradigm of teaching and learning that meets the requirements of the Knowledge Age (see chapter 9) would not hold time constant, which forces achievement to vary; instead, it would hold achievement constant so that students can attain required learning standards. Within this new paradigm, each student would be given as much time as he or she needs to master each standard. Further, to enrich their learning, students would benefit from having opportunities to select and study topics of their own choosing or engage with others in community projects in which they would have opportunities to apply the content-related standards that are guiding their learning. The current reforms that predominate in education, however, fail to do this. Instead, these reforms leave the old teaching and learning paradigm intact, and therefore these reforms cannot and will not meet the needs of our Knowledge Age society. Therefore, we must transform rather than reform our school districts.

FUNDAMENTALS FOR SHIFTING EDUCATION PARADIGMS

There are ten fundamental principles upon which a paradigm shift in education is based (Duffy & Reigeluth, 2007):

Principle 1: Four paradigm shifts are required. Four complimentary paradigm shifts must be achieved to transform entire school systems for success in the twenty-first century (Duffy, 2003). The following paradigm shifts are made as educators think along three change paths, which were identified in point 8 above:

- Paradigm Shift 1: Transform the district's core and support work processes. The core work process—teaching and learning—must be transformed to a paradigm that is customized to learners' individual needs and is focused on attainment of proficiencies (Reigeluth, 1994), and the support work processes (academic support and nonacademic support) also must be transformed to best support the primary work processes. This shift is made along Change Path 1—transform the system's core and support work processes.
- Paradigm Shift 2: Transform the school system's "internal social infrastructure" (which includes organization culture, communication practices, job descriptions, reward systems, and so forth). The organization design and other elements of the social infrastructure must be transformed from a mechanistic, command-and-control organization design to an organic, participatory organization design with the goal of creating a good fit between the core and support work processes and the internal social infrastructure. This shift happens along Change Path 2—transform the system's internal social infrastructure.
- Paradigm Shift 3: Transform the district's relationship with its external environment. The relationship between the school system and its sys-

temic environment must be transformed from an isolated, crisis-oriented, and reactive stance by the school system to a collaborative, opportunity-seeking, and proactive stance. This shift happens by thinking along Change Path 3—transform the system's relationship with its external environment.

- Paradigm Shift 4: Transform the way in which educators create and sustain change in their districts. The dominant paradigm for improving school districts is the piecemeal, one-school-at-a-time paradigm. To create and sustain transformational change, the paradigm must shift from the piecemeal, one-school-at-a-time paradigm to a transform-the-whole-system paradigm.

Principle 2: The district is the unit of change. If paradigm change only happens in one part of a school district (e.g., in one school), that part becomes incompatible with the rest of the system, which then exerts powerful forces to change it back. Therefore, transformational change must view the whole school district as the unit of change.

Principle 3: Mind-set change is required (see chapter 5). A mind-set is a hardened attitude toward some object, idea, or proposal for change. Educators have well established mind-sets about the four dominant paradigms (described earlier) that influence their work behaviors and about the collection of mental models that help them comply with the requirements of those paradigms. If four new paradigms are to replace the existing paradigms, then the first step toward those shifts is to open educators' minds (that is, their mind-sets must become "open") to what the new paradigms offer. Opening minds requires mind-set change because mind-sets act as locks on people's hearts and minds. If the mind-sets don't change, then educators will resist new paradigms and mental models. Therefore, the paradigm change process must place top priority on helping educators and their systems' stakeholders unfreeze their mind-sets about how to best educate children, how to best design the internal social infrastructure of their systems, how to best interact with their external environments, and how best to create and sustain change.

Principle 4: Paradigm shifting is a customized invention process. The Knowledge Age paradigm of education is at the "Wright brothers" stage of development. Pieces of the four new paradigms identified earlier have been developed, but how to assemble all the pieces so newly redesigned systems can function effectively and efficiently still needs to be determined using design-based research methodologies (Dede, 2005; Reigeluth & Frick, 1999). Furthermore, elements of the new paradigms will differ from one school system to another because each school system is a unique entity. For both the previously stated reasons, it is futile to try to replicate a "comprehensive school design" developed by another school district. Instead, the four new paradigms must be implemented in ways that are tailored to the unique characteristics of each school system by using principles of idealized design (see chapter 7). Only after a variety of designs have proven effective in many school systems will it be possible for educators to adopt and replicate paradigmatic changes implemented by other districts.

Principle 5: Paradigm change requires broad stakeholder ownership. Because mind-set change is so important to successful paradigm change, stakeholders must be involved in the paradigm change process, for it is only through participation that mind-sets evolve. Also, the invention process described under principle 4, above, is a powerful tool for helping stakeholders to evolve their mind-sets about education. Furthermore, diverse perspectives enhance the creativity and effectiveness of the invention process. But simple involvement is insufficient. Stakeholders must develop a sense of ownership of the change process because that "sense of ownership" engenders true commitment, greatly reduces resistance to the four new paradigms, and enhances the sustainability of the changes that are being created.

Principle 6: Paradigm change requires a consensus-building process. Stakeholders have different mental models and mind-sets about what is important for educating children. Empowering stakeholders can generate discord and increase divisiveness unless a consensus-building process is used, along with a consensus-sustaining process.

Principle 7: Paradigm change requires participatory leadership. Stakeholder ownership and the consensus-building style of decision making both require a different paradigm of leadership from the common "command-and-control" style of management. A leadership style that empowers key stakeholders to be leaders, supports them in their work, and provides professional development whenever needed is required for transformational change (see chapter 3).

Principle 8: Paradigm change requires experienced outside facilitators. The journey of designing an idealized school system in accordance with the requirements of the four new paradigms identified earlier is a treacherous one, and stakeholders typically have a long history of disagreements, factions, animosities, rivalries, and such. Therefore, it is essential to have facilitators who are experienced in the systemic transformation process and who have experience implementing the principles listed above. Furthermore, the facilitators must be viewed as neutral and impartial by all stakeholder groups. They must also be readily available to facilitate the district's transformation journey until the district develops the internal capacity for engaging in transformational change.

Principle 9: Paradigm change is a time-intensive process. Mind-set change takes time, and the more mind-sets to be changed, the more time that will be needed. This is because mind-sets change primarily through exposure to new ideas and plentiful small-group discussion (e.g., see Kegan & Lahey,

2001). Unless individuals' time can be bought or otherwise freed up, the transformation process will take many years and be less likely to succeed. This makes external funding crucial.

Principle 10: Paradigm change requires capacity building. Empowerment of stakeholders requires building their capacity to lead the paradigm change process and to build participatory leadership skills. Such capacity includes Senge's (1990) five disciplines of a learning organization (systems thinking, team building, personal mastery vision, and mental models), as well as systems design, consensus-based decision making, sustainability, and much more.

CONCLUSION

The Agricultural Age paradigm that controlled the design and performance of schooling in America served our country well, but as our society transformed into the Industrial Age, so did America's approach to educating children. The Industrial Age design has also served us well for hundreds of years. However, our society is transforming once again—transforming into the Knowledge Age. Most of America's organizations have transformed in response to the needs and opportunities presented by the Knowledge Age. The organizations not making that transformation are America's school districts, yet they must transform or run the risk of becoming obsolete and irrelevant in America's Knowledge Age society.

Just as the Agricultural Age paradigm for educating students transformed into the Industrial Age paradigm, it is now time for the Industrial Age paradigm to transform into a Knowledge Age paradigm for educating students and for designing and managing school systems as learning organizations. But creating those kinds of paradigm shifts is extraordinarily difficult because the shifts are being resisted by those who are intentionally or unintentionally defending the status quo.

So, how should Knowledge Age school systems be designed? How would Knowledge Age school systems be different from the current design of school systems? The remaining chapters in this book will provide answers to these questions.

2

Strapping Wings on a Caterpillar and Calling It a Butterfly: When Systemic Change Is Not Systemic

OVERVIEW

This chapter begins with an idealized vision for the future of schooling in twenty-first-century America. Achieving this vision requires the transformation of entire school systems. Some of us who are advocates of transforming school systems believe that whole-system transformation requires four new interlocked paradigms: one for teaching and learning; another for how school systems are designed and perform as systems; a third for how districts interact with their external environments; and a fourth for how to create and sustain change (these paradigms are discussed later in this chapter).

The chapter continues with a discussion of common misperceptions about the meaning of systemic change in school districts, misconceptions fed by confusion about the definition of the term "systemic change." Following the discussion of the definitional confusion, core principles of systemic change are presented, and a comparison between piecemeal and systemic change is drawn. Next, a more comprehensive definition of systemic change is offered—a definition characterized as "systemic transformational change." Systemic transformational change is required if paradigm change is desired for a school system. The expanded definition provided in this chapter includes a discussion of why the current design of school systems cannot get us to where we need to be; explains why transformational change is complex and messy; clarifies why piecemeal change is inappropriate when transformational change is required; explains how a system's performance ceiling requires transformational change if a system wants to break through that ceiling; points out how dysfunctional system dynamics require transformational change in response to the dysfunction; and describes three paths to systemic transformational change that must be followed to create and sustain the four required paradigm shifts. The chapter concludes with a brief discussion of how leadership for transformational change requires living with paradoxical situations (chapter 3 offers more insights to transformational leadership).

THE FUTURE OF SCHOOLING IN AMERICA

Richter and Reigeluth (2007) build a powerful case for systemic transformational change in American school systems. The core premise of their argument is that the current paradigm for schooling in America is driven by the needs of the Industrial Age, but our society is well into the Knowledge Age, which has different requirements for educating students. The essential elements of their argument are presented below (see chapter 10 for a more in-depth exposition of their views).

CHANGES IN SOCIETY MAKE THE DESIGN OF CURRENT SCHOOL SYSTEMS OBSOLETE

As the United States evolves deeper into the Knowledge Age, our society's needs and problems are changing dramatically. Richter and Reigeluth suggest that these dramatic changes in our society require comparable dramatic and deep systemic changes in how school districts deliver education services to students. However, the typical response in school districts to this growing mismatch between our society's needs and how children are educated is the piecemeal, "fix-the-broken-part" approach to change. A reading program does not work well, so remediation is offered. Test scores fall, so yearly statewide testing is increased. A middle school is failing, so a "heroic principal" is brought in to save the day. A school system is underperforming, so the school year is extended and the school day is made longer. These changes are made by school systems in response to symptoms of systemic distress—distress caused by dysfunctional system dynamics created by applying principles of piecemeal change when principles of systemic change are required.

Richter and Reigeluth also believe that the fundamental paradigm that guides teaching and learning in America's school systems needs to be transformed to satisfy the requirements of the Knowledge Age. For example, regarding "time to learn," it is known that different students learn at different rates (Mayer, 1999), yet educators typically require all students to learn the same amount of content in the same amount of time. By holding time constant, educators force achievement to vary.

According to Richter and Reigeluth, the current design of school systems was intended for sorting students rather than for learning, which was appropriate in the Industrial Age because we did not need to and could not afford to educate large numbers of students to high levels. But the Knowledge Age, with its predominance of knowledge work (a term coined by Peter Drucker, 1959) and demand for higher-order thinking skills, makes learning a much higher priority than sorting.

In the Knowledge Age paradigm, according to Richter and Reigeluth (2007, p. 2), it is no longer acceptable to promote learners to the next grade-level simply because they have spent a year at the previous grade-level. It is no longer acceptable to emulate the factory model and to teach all children at the same rate. In the Knowledge Age paradigm, they argue, we need to educate more children to their potential. Faster learners must no longer be forced to waste time until the class is ready to move on, and slow learners must no longer be forced to move on before they have mastered the content, thereby forcing them to accumulate learning deficits that make it exceedingly more difficult to learn future material that builds on that content.

KEY MARKERS FOR THE INDUSTRIAL AGE COMPARED WITH THOSE FOR THE KNOWLEDGE AGE

Richter and Reigeluth identified and compared key markers illustrating differences between the Industrial Age and Knowledge Age paradigms. The markers are shown in table 2.1.

Richter and Reigeluth began their comparison of the key markers by noting that coevolution happens when systems evolve in ways that satisfy the

Table 2.1. Key Markers of the Industrial Age and the Information Age

Industrial Age	Information Age
Standardization	Customization
Bureaucratic organization	Team-based organization
Centralized control	Autonomy with accountability
Adversarial relationships	Cooperative relationships
Autocratic decision making	Shared decision making
Compliance	Initiative
Conformity	Diversity
One-way communications	Networking
Compartmentalization	Holism
Parts oriented	Process oriented
Planned obsolescence	Total quality
CEO or boss as "king"	Customer as "king"

Source: Reigeluth, 1999, p. 17. Used with permission.

needs and requirements of their external environment (see chapter 6). They discuss how coevolution has already happened for our society and its institutions; for example, our contemporary society has evolved from the Agrarian Age (in which agricultural activities formed the backbone of society) to the Industrial Age (in which the assembly line and mass production created products and goods for consumption by the public). America's school systems also coevolved with those societal changes.

Our society has now evolved into the Knowledge Age, in which knowledge work has replaced manual labor as the predominant form of work. Most of America's organizations are coevolving to meet the requirements of the Knowledge Age. The institutions that are not coevolving to meet the needs of the Knowledge Age are America's school systems.

As can be seen in table 2.1, the key markers of the Knowledge Age portray a paradigm that is significantly different from the Industrial Age paradigm. The Knowledge Age markers focus on teams over bureaucracy, on autonomy over control and command, and on initiative over compliance. In the same way, the needs of our Knowledge Age society now require school systems to create and commit to using substantially different criteria for evaluating their success as systems—criteria that correspond closely with the Knowledge Age key markers. Richter and Reigeluth conclude that to be relevant and meet the needs of our twenty-first-century society, school systems must seek to evolve in ways that correspond with the needs and requirements of the Knowledge Age.

IN THE BEGINNING THERE WAS CONFUSION

Some of us in the field of education believe that the future of education in America, as described above, requires the total transformation of America's school systems—a transformation that will shift school districts from the Industrial Age–influenced paradigms to four new Knowledge Age paradigms for designing, organizing, and managing school systems. These paradigms are discussed later in the chapter.

Creating and sustaining four paradigm shifts requires revolutionary transformational change, not piecemeal change. Yet piecemeal change is the dominant approach used to improve schooling. Piecemeal change is also often mistakenly characterized as "systemic change." This mischaracterization reminds me of a question I have addressed repeatedly in my writing, teaching, and speaking about systemic change in school districts over the past quarter century: "When is systemic change not systemic?"

There are many often conflicting definitions of systemic change (described below). The definitional uncertainty still baffles practitioners and policymakers today, and I see this confusion appearing in publications on school improvement; for example,

- when I see articles about building-level change that are characterized as systemic change;
- when I read books about systemic change that only focus on improving student performance on achievement tests; and
- when I listen to presentations claiming that curriculum improvement is an example of systemic change.

All of the above changes can be part of a systemic change initiative, but, by themselves, they are not examples of systemic change. Calling these kinds of changes systemic is analogous to strapping wings on a caterpillar and calling it a butterfly.

Definitional Confusion

There are several different definitions of "systemic change" used in the school improvement literature. This definitional confusion was identified by Squire and Reigeluth (2000). Reigeluth and Duffy (2006) commented on these different definitions and added one definition to the mix. They are:

Statewide policy systemic change. Systemic change used in this context creates statewide changes in tests, curricular guidelines, teacher-certification requirements, textbook adoptions, funding policies, and so forth that are coordinated to support one another (Smith & O'Day, 1991). This meaning is how policymakers typically think of systemic change.

District-wide systemic change. From this perspective, systemic change produces changes in curriculum or programs instituted throughout a school district. This meaning is how P–12 educators typically think of systemic change.

Schoolwide systemic change. People holding this view of systemic change focus on what happens inside individual school buildings. Systemic change in this context is any change or program instituted throughout a school. This meaning is how educators participating in groups such as the Coalition of Essential Schools typically think of systemic change.

Ecological systemic change. From this point of view, systemic change is based upon a clear understanding of interrelationships and interdependencies within the system of interest and between the system of interest and its external systemic environment. Change leaders subscribing to this view recognize that significant change in one part of their system will require changes in other parts of that system. Of necessity, this meaning of systemic change subsumes all the other three meanings, and it is how systems thinkers view systemic change (see, e.g., Ackoff, 1981; Banathy, 1996; Checkland, 1984; Emery & Purser, 1995; Senge, 1990).

The first three definitions apply principles of systemic change, but they are not truly systemic. The fourth definition is an example of systemic change, but it does not always create transformational change. Thus, the one definition of systemic change not included in Squire and Reigeluth's original compendium of definitions is one for systemic transformational change. Before exploring this special instance of systemic change I will first present additional information about systemic change.

PRINCIPLES OF SYSTEMIC CHANGE AND WHY IT IS IMPORTANT

Russell Ackoff (1981, 1999, 2001) is an early pioneer of systemic change in organizations. He tells us that it is pure folly to improve parts of a system (as in focusing improvement only on a school building or a level of schooling like high school reform). He says that not only will the entire system fail to improve by improving the parts, but it is likely that this piecemeal focus will actually cause the system's performance to deteriorate. Ackoff (1999, pp. 6–8) also offers eight characteristics of systems that enlighten us about why piecemeal change fails to improve whole systems. The eight characteristics adapted for school systems are:

1. The whole system (e.g., a whole school system) has one or more defining properties or functions; for example, a defining function (i.e., a system's main purpose) of a school district is to educate students.
2. Each part in the system (e.g., each school in a district) can affect the behavior or properties of the whole; for example, a couple of low performing schools in a district can drag down a whole school district.
3. There is a subset of system parts that are essential for carrying out the main purpose of the whole system, but they cannot, by themselves, fulfill the main purpose of the system; for example, teachers and classrooms in a single school building are essential parts of a school system and they are necessary for helping a school system fulfill its main purpose, but these "parts" cannot and never will be able to do what the whole system does.
4. There is also a subset of parts that are nonessential for fulfilling the system's main purpose, but are necessary for other minor purposes (e.g., in a school system these important but nonessential parts include school and community relations, pupil personnel services, among others).
5. If a system depends on its environment for the importation of "energy" (i.e., human, technical, and financial resources), then that system is said to be an "open system." A school district is an open system. Its environment consists of its community, individuals, groups, the state and federal governments, and society in general. The part of a

school district's environment that it can influence, but not control, is called its "transactional" or "task" environment. That part of the environment that a school district is affected by but cannot influence nor control is called its "contextual" or "general" environment. To succeed, school systems need to improve their relationships with their transactional environments and become skilled at anticipating influences from their contextual environments.

6. The way in which an essential part of a system affects the whole system depends on its interaction with at least one other essential part; for example, the effect a single school has on the whole district depends on the interaction that school has with other schools in the district. For example, let us say that a school district is organized prekindergarten–12th grade. This means the work process for that district is thirteen steps long (preK–12th grade). Now let us say that district leaders are concerned about the performance of their high school (which represents a subset of the system). The high school contains grades 9–12. Then let us say that the performance of that high school is dragging down the overall performance of the district on state assessments. According to Ackoff's systems principles, it would be a mistake to focus improvement efforts only on the high school, because that high school's performance is affected by at least two other subsets of schools (i.e., the elementary and middle schools that "feed" kids into those high schools). Since all essential parts of a school system interact and affect each other, it would be reasonable and "systemic" to examine and determine how these parts are affecting the performance of the high school. Focusing improvement only on the high school would be a nonsystemic and, therefore, piecemeal approach to improvement.

7. A system is a whole entity that cannot be divided into its individual parts without loss of its essential properties or functions. For example, the dominant approach to school district improvement is called school-based or site-based improvement. This approach has had the consequence of deconstructing school systems into their aggregate parts (individual classrooms, schools, and programs). Further, individual classrooms, schools, and programs do not and never will provide children with a total education; they only provide children with a partial education represented by the curriculum for the grades embedded in a particular school or level of schooling. When efforts are made to improve a school system in this way—by disaggregating it into its individual parts—a system's effectiveness deteriorates rapidly.

8. Because a system derives its effectiveness from the synergistic interaction of its parts rather than from what the parts do independent of the system (i.e., the whole is always greater than the sum of its parts), when efforts are taken to improve the individual parts separate from

the system (as in school-based improvement), the performance of the whole system, according to Ackoff, deteriorates and the system involved may be significantly weakened. This is one reason why I believe that school-based improvement and piecemeal change have generally failed to improve schooling to the degree that it needs to improve.

So, the answer to my earlier question, "When is systemic change not systemic?" is "When it focuses on anything less than the whole system."

PIECEMEAL CHANGE VERSUS SYSTEMIC CHANGE IN SCHOOL DISTRICTS

Piecemeal change. Ever since John Goodlad proclaimed in 1984 in *A Place Called School* that the school building was the appropriate unit of change for improving schooling, that approach—improving one school at a time—has dominated efforts to improve schooling in America. So, why, after applying that philosophy over all these years, has so little changed? It is because that approach, while important and still needed if it is an element of a systemic transformational change process, is by itself inherently insufficient, because it disregards the nature of school districts as intact, organic systems governed by powerful principles of complex adaptive systems (e.g., Dooley, 2004; Olson & Eoyang, 2001). It is also insufficient because it is a piecemeal approach that fails to comply with systems principles like those identified and described by Ackoff (described above).

Despite a strong desire of some educators to transform their school systems, they have been unable to do so because of the inherent deficiencies of the one school, one-program-at-a-time approach to improvement. Given this insufficiency of the traditional approach to school improvement, there is an extraordinary need for transforming, not reforming, school systems.

WHAT SYSTEMIC TRANSFORMATIONAL CHANGE MEANS TO ME

In the field of organization development, the alternative to piecemeal change is systemic change. Systemic change has a mysterious sound to it. Some people have a hard time getting their minds around the idea, and they cannot envision a school district as a system. All they see is a collection of unconnected or loosely coupled individual schools, classrooms, and programs. Some people catch a glimpse of a district as a system, but cannot hold onto the image because it disappears like a ghost floating into a bank of clouds. Still others define a school system as a classroom inside a school inside a cluster of schools inside a district inside a community inside a state inside a region inside the country inside the world inside the universe. This mental model is often referred to as a "nested system" (e.g., Bronfenbrenner, 1977, 1979). Although theoretically correct, the nested system mental model is notably useless for informing the practice of school district transformation. How can anyone change a system that complex? Instead, the "system to be changed" is everything inside what is commonly called a school district, and everything outside that system is its external environment (see Emery & Purser, 1995). Then, efforts are made to change the system inside the circle and to improve the system's relationship with its external environment.

There is an important problem with the concept of systemic change; that is, not all systemic change results in the transformation of a system. This fact requires an additional definition of systemic change—one for systemic transformational change.

I would like to share a few thoughts with you about what systemic transformational change means to me. Let me begin with a quote by Nevis, Lancourt, and Vassallo (1996, pp. 11–12). They said,

> To transform something is to change its fundamental external form or inner nature. . . . In the world of nature, a caterpillar is transformed into a butterfly; its DNA remains unchanged, but its form and properties are fundamentally different. A butterfly is not a caterpillar with wings strapped on its back.

Eckel, Hill, and Green (1998, p. 3) define systemic transformational change as a process that:

1. alters the culture of the system by changing select underlying assumptions and institutional behaviors, processes, and products;
2. is deep and pervasive, affecting the whole system;
3. is intentional; and
4. occurs over time.

I added the following two requirements to the above definition:

5. creates a system that continuously seeks an idealized future for itself; and
6. creates a future system that is substantially different than the current system; that is, the system must be transformed to perform within a different paradigm.

Retired Vice Admiral Arthur Cebrowski, who headed a task force to transform the armed forces of the United States, defines transformational change as follows:

Transformation is foremost a continuing process. It does not have an end point. Transformation is meant to create or anticipate the future. Transformation is meant to deal with the coevolution of concepts, processes, organizations and technology. Change in any one of these areas necessitates change in all. Transformation is meant to create new competitive areas and new competencies. Transformation is meant to identify, leverage and even create new underlying principles for the way things are done. Transformation is meant to identify and leverage new sources of power.

THE CURRENT DESIGN OF SCHOOL
SYSTEMS CANNOT GET US TO WHERE WE NEED TO BE

Systemic transformational change creates a substantially different organizational reality in a school system. It does not focus on fixing the parts of the system. Here is a metaphor that reinforces that point. If you have good car (your current system) that gets a flat tire (a broken part) you might ask, "Why not just fix the flat and keep moving on?" Fixing the flat is an example of piecemeal change. The "fix" works if your goal is to keep your current "good car" and if the car gets you to where you need to go. But what if your "good car" cannot take you where you need to go? What if instead of a car you need an airplane? If you need an airplane, fixing the flat tire and continuing on your way in your good car will not get you to where you need to go. To get to where you need to go you need a completely different system. And no matter how many parts you fix or replace in your good car, that car will never be an airplane, so you will never get to where you need to go, and you will continue to suffer from not having the airplane that you need.

The above metaphor captures the conundrum we face in education. The old paradigms controlling the design and performance of school systems cannot get us to where we need to go. Fixing the parts of school systems designed for success in the Industrial Age will not get us to where we need to be in the twenty-first century; that is, we need to design whole new school systems that are totally aligned with the needs and requirements of the Knowledge Age.

TRANSFORMATIONAL CHANGE IS COMPLEX AND MESSY

Creating and sustaining transformational change in school systems is complex and messy. One of the reasons for this condition is that within each school district there are multiple realities encased in the mental models and mind-sets (see chapter 5) of the educators working in those districts; not to mention in the mental models and mind-sets of key external stakeholders who think they know what is best for a school system. Effective transformation requires influencing and expanding the existing multiple realities to create a shared reality of an idealized future for a school system.

Another reason for the complexity and messiness of transformational change is that it is simply insufficient to create an idealized vision of a desirable future for a school system. Action must be taken to implement that vision, and the transition from the present to the future is always challenging; in fact, most large-scale change efforts fail because of insufficient transition management. Further, the transition must help people in organizations to change the way they think and act along three change paths (which are identified below, but described in more detail later in this chapter):

- Path 1—transform their system's core and support work processes
- Path 2—transform their system's internal social infrastructure (which includes organization culture, the organizational mental model, organization design, job descriptions, reward system, and so on)
- Path 3—transform their system's relationship with its external environment

Transformational change is also complex and messy because educators not only must create change along the three paths identified above, but, if they want to create and sustain systemic transformational change, they also need to make four paradigm shifts as they move along the three change paths. The four paradigm shifts are:

- *Paradigm Shift 1*: Shift from the current paradigm of teaching and learning (the Industrial Age paradigm) to a new paradigm (the Learner-Centered, Knowledge Age paradigm; see chapter 9), and include the support work processes in a school system within this shift (this is done by moving along Path 1—transform the system's core and support work processes).
- *Paradigm Shift 2*: Shift from a mechanistic, hierarchical organization design to an organic, participatory organization design (this is accomplished by moving along Path 2—transform the system's internal social infrastructure, which requires changes to organization culture, the organization's mental model, communication practices, job descriptions, reward systems, and other elements of the social infrastructure).
- *Paradigm Shift 3*: Shift from a reactive stance in response to the external environment to a proactive stance (this shift is made by moving along Path 3—transform the system's relationship with its external environment).
- *Paradigm Shift 4*: Shift from a piecemeal approach to change to a systemic transformational approach to change (this shift is made by following the three change paths identified above and by abandoning the piecemeal approach to change).

An early challenge for managing the complexity and messiness of transformational change is to convince educators that transformational change is needed. Telling them that this kind of change is needed is inadequate. They have heard these kinds of calls for change before. They must be provided with compelling data that not only point out the need for change, but also shine a bright floodlight on the opportunities that systemic transformational change provides them, their students, their districts, and their communities. "Need data" push people toward change. "Opportunity data" draw people toward change. Both kinds of data are critical for motivating educators to allow their mental models to become malleable and therefore capable of considering previously unconsidered possibilities for transforming their school systems.

Data, alone, however, are insufficient for motivating people to engage in complex and messy change processes. Data only communicate with the head. To inspire people to engage in transformational change, you must also communicate with their hearts. You communicate with people's hearts by creating an inspiring idealized vision for the future of your school system that uses powerful and compelling metaphors that capture your system's core values and beliefs. When calls for change talk to the head and the heart, people tend to join you in moving toward the idealized vision.

WHEN TRANSFORMATIONAL CHANGE IS REQUIRED, PIECEMEAL CHANGE IS INAPPROPRIATE

When systemic transformation is required, piecemeal change to create that transformation is an approach that at its worst does more harm than good and at its best is limited to creating pockets of "good" within school districts. When it comes to transforming school systems, however, doing more harm than good is immoral, and creating pockets of good in a district is not good enough. To create excellence within school districts, change leaders must help their systems create and sustain four paradigm shifts (described above).

An additional reason for the inappropriateness of piecemeal change when transformation is required is that transforming a single school (or program) makes that school incompatible with its system. When a changed part is incompatible with its system, the unchanged parts of the system will strive to overwhelm it and force it to revert back to its prechange status. For example, the Saturn School of Tomorrow in St. Paul, Minnesota (Bennett & King, 1991), overcame great odds to establish a learning-focused, attainment-based paradigm in that school. But that new paradigm was, of course, incompatible with the controlling Industrial Age paradigm of its school system, which then exerted powerful forces to kill the innovations.

Failed school-based transformation efforts like the Saturn School of Tomorrow provide ample evidence that paradigm change requires systemic transformational change. Only with district-wide transformation that creates four paradigm shifts can unparalleled improvements in student, faculty and staff, and whole-system learning be created and sustained.

ONE MORE REASON WHY SCHOOL DISTRICTS NEED TO TRANSFORM

Handy (1998) conceptualized the Sigmoid Curve (or S-curve) to describe the life cycle of organizations as systems. The Sigmoid Curve is a biological metaphor to help us understand the need for organizational transformation. The curve is "S"-shaped, as shown in figure 2.1.

The bottom-left tail of the S-curve in figure 2.1 represents the birth of a system. The steep upward slope is the system's growth phase. A system's growth phase begins to level off as it enters a maturity phase and approaches its performance ceiling.

Once a system hits its performance ceiling, no amount of tinkering with the system will push it through that ceiling. In other words, the system has reached the upper limits of its potential to improve, and no amount of tinkering with the existing system will create significant improvement.

System's Performance
Ceiling

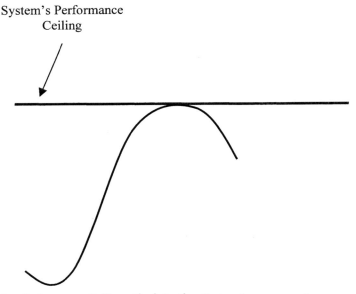

Figure 2.1.   Performance Ceilings Block Further System Improvement

Branson (1987) supports the conclusion that school systems cannot improve because they have reached the upper limits of their performance capacity. He suggests that traditionally designed school systems have attained about 97 percent efficiency. There is, in other words, simply almost no room for improvement in school systems that are designed for the Industrial Age.

As a district skirts along the bottom edge of its performance ceiling (a practice that can go on for years), what worked in the past to make that system successful no longer works. Eventually, after many failed attempts to push through the performance ceiling and failing to do so, a system will enter a prolonged slow-fade toward mediocrity or obsolescence, which is represented as the downward tail of the S-curve shown in figure 2.1.

During the period of decline (which also can last for many years because systems never crumble in a day), educators begin experiencing significant negative emotions that constrain or diminish their ability to solve problems, seek a desirable future for their system, and collaborate for change. Leaders lose their credibility, their emotional energy is low, fear and anxiety are their motivators, and their resources for managing their systems are depleted or may disappear all together.[1]

Yet, almost inconceivably, in this slow-fade toward mediocrity or obsolescence, educators in those declining systems continue to hang onto their old mental models, mind-sets, behavioral strategies, programs, and approaches to change with the irrational hope that the next quick-fix—the next "silver bullet"—the next "flavor of the month" change—will reverse their systems' slow decline. They work harder and harder, do increasingly more with increasingly less, try to control declining quality with ever-increasing mandates and policies (e.g., ratcheting-up assessments, making accreditation standards more stringent, and "fixing" the No Child Left Behind Act), and, despite all of these piecemeal, quick-fix efforts, their school systems fail to break through their performance ceilings.[2] While seeking quick fix after quick fix, their systems' performance continues sliding downwards while scapegoats are identified and blamed for the systems' declining performance.

Unable to understand why they cannot improve their systems, educators stubbornly keep using piecemeal improvement strategies designed to tweak or tinker with their school systems' status quo with the hope that this time—this one last desperate time—the promise of significant improvement will become a reality. But it does not become a reality and it cannot, because the old systems are up against their performance ceilings and life at the top of the S-curve is inescapably suppressed by the systems' performance ceiling; or, the old systems are descending the downward tail of their S-curves, thereby making significant improvement exceedingly difficult. And, the emotional toll that this deteriorating situation takes on educators in those systems is significant as they swim in a turbulent emotional sea of anger, frustration, and, in some cases, despair as their efforts to improve their systems fail year in and year out.

But there is a way to escape the downward slide toward mediocrity and obsolescence. The escape occurs by breaking through the system's old performance ceiling to reach new performance heights. Breakthrough is achieved by starting a new S-curve before the system hits its performance ceiling and enters a period of decline; that is, the best time to launch a systemic change effort is at point "A" shown in figure 2.2. In other words, as Burke (2007) tells us, the best time to introduce significant change to a system is when it is doing well.

Point A is an arbitrary point that will vary from school system to school system, but ideally, for all school systems, point A should be positioned somewhere along a system's upward climb toward its performance ceiling.

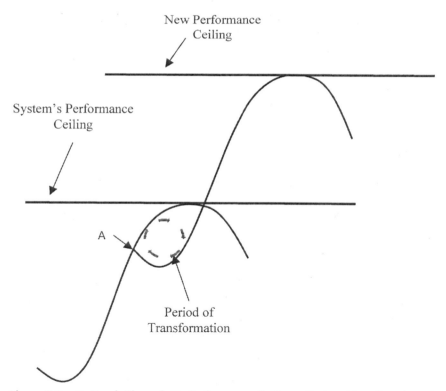

Figure 2.2. **To Break Through Its Performance Ceiling a System Must Transform by Creating a New S-Curve**

If point A, however, is on the downward slope of a system's performance curve, then creating and sustaining transformational change will be more challenging for the reasons discussed above.

Further, the second S-curve must create and sustain a system that is significantly different from what it was in the past (see Nevis, Lancourt, & Vassallo, 1996); that is, the new S-curve must transform the system by creating and sustaining the four paradigm shifts identified earlier. If the second S-curve does not create and sustain those four paradigm shifts, then all that educators do is create a clone of the old system with all of its old and wicked unsolvable performance problems. And a new system that is a clone of its old self is doomed to fail in exactly the same ways as the old system did; or, as Albert Einstein (and others) once observed, "If you keep doing what you're doing, you'll keep getting the results you've been getting."

Because educators cannot completely shut down their school systems to transform them, their new system (their new S-curve) is first created as a parallel organization (e.g., see Fisher & Brin, 1991; and see chapter 13 for a brief explanation of how this is done); that is, the new system is created as change leaders and their colleagues envision their idealized new system, adopt a transformational change methodology and tools (e.g., the School System Transformation Protocol described in chapter 10), create a change structure to support and guide the transformation of their system, define the operational characteristics of their ideal system, and finally, implement their plans for creating and sustaining their idealized system. At a point that will vary from district to district, the parallel organization and the current system will merge, and the old system will be displaced as the nascent system emerges.

In figure 2.2, the period of systemic transformation where the new system replaces the old is in the space created by the intersection of the old S-curve with the beginning of the new S-curve. This period of transformation is complex, ambiguous, and messy. Moving a system successfully through that transformation phase requires change leaders who are masters of the art and science of transforming school systems and who possess significant courage, passion, and vision.

DYSFUNCTIONAL SYSTEM DYNAMICS REQUIRE TRANSFORMATIONAL CHANGE

Throughout this chapter the term "systemic transformational change" has recurred. Over the past decade the notion of systemic transformational change has emerged as an approach that is needed to significantly change all kinds of organizations; for example, consider the following excerpt from an article by Amy Zegart in the *Washington Post* on Sunday, July 8, 2007, about the failures of the intelligence system in the United States to prevent the ghastly September 11, 2001, attack. She said that the FBI and the CIA missed twenty-three potential opportunities to disrupt the September 11 attack. She identified the causes of this failure as:

1. agency cultures that led officials to resist new ideas, technologies, and missions;
2. promotion incentives that rewarded the wrong things; and
3. structural weaknesses that hampered those agencies and prevented them from working as a unified team. (p. B5)

With regard to the structural deficiencies of the FBI, she said, "Individuals were not the problem. The FBI was. The bureau's highly decentralized structure . . . meant that what should have been a nationwide effort was instead the focus of a few people" (p. B5).

It does not require a very big stretch of our ability to recognize similar patterns of behavior to see how what Zegart said about the failures of the U.S. intelligence system also applies to school systems; for example, the struggles of many U.S. school systems have root causes anchored in:

1. school-system cultures that motivate faculty and administrators to resist new ideas, technologies, and missions;
2. incentives that reward the wrong things; and
3. structural weaknesses such as over-decentralization (as in school-based management where each school essentially is its own system) and piecemeal approaches to change that hamper a school system from working as a coherent, unified system.

School districts, like the U.S. intelligence system, can benefit from systemic transformational change. But systemic transformational change in education requires educators in school systems to break free of their controlling mental models for how their systems perform so they can create and sustain substantially different systems for delivering education services to students—systems transformed to meet the requirements of the twenty-first-century Knowledge Age.

THREE PATHS TO SYSTEMIC TRANSFORMATIONAL CHANGE

Earlier, three change paths that must be followed simultaneously to create and sustain systemic transformational change were identified. In this section, additional details about those three paths are offered.

Over the past fifty years a lot has been learned about how to improve entire systems (e.g., Ackoff, 1981; Banathy, 1996; King & Frick, 1999, Pas-

more, 1988; Pava, 1983a, 1983b; Reigeluth, 1994). One of the core principles of whole-system transformation that emerges from this literature is
that three sets of key organizational variables must be transformed simultaneously (e.g., see Ackoff, 2001; Duffy, 2003a; Duffy, Rogerson, & Blick,
2000; Pasmore, 1988). I characterize these three sets of variables as change
paths.[3] Each of these change paths is explored briefly below.

Path 1: Transform a district's core and support work processes. Core work is the
most important work of any organization. In school districts, the core work
is teaching and learning conjoined with student learning supports (see
Adleman & Taylor, 2006, for more about student learning supports).

Core work is maintained and enriched by support work. In school districts, there are two kinds of support work: academic and nonacademic.
Academic support work roles include instructional technologists, school-
and district-level administrators, instructional supervisors, education specialists, and school librarians, among others. Nonacademic support work
includes cafeteria workers, janitors, bus drivers, and others. Support work is
important to the success of a school district, but it is not the most important
work. Classroom teaching and learning is the most important work, and it
must be elevated to that status if a school system wants to increase its overall effectiveness.

When transforming a school system, both the core and support work processes must be redesigned. Further, entire work processes must be examined
and transformed, not just their parts (e.g., not just the language arts curriculum, or not just the high school program). One of the reasons that entire
work processes must be transformed is because of a system improvement
principle expressed as "upstream errors flow downstream" (Pasmore, 1988).

The "upstream errors flow downstream" principle reflects the fact that if
mistakes are made early in a work process and not corrected, the mistakes
flow downstream, are compounded, and create more problems later on in
the process; for example, Hoover (2002, p. 1) points out that "we know that
if the child is not making progress in reading by the third grade, there is very
little likelihood that she will ever, regardless of the intervention used, be able
to read at the same level as her same-age peers." Upstream errors always flow
downstream and learning deficits always accumulate if not corrected!

While transforming a school system's core work process is absolutely
critical for the future success of a school district, focusing only on improving student learning is a piecemeal approach to transformation. A teacher's
knowledge, literacy, and skills are probably some of the most important
factors influencing student learning (e.g., see Sanders & Rivers, 1996a, to
learn more about what happens to students when they have two or three
ineffective teachers in succession). So, taking steps to improve teacher
knowledge, literacy, and skills must also be part of any school district's effort to transform its core work processes.

Further, while improving student and teacher learning are two important goals of improving the core work process in a school district, this is also a piecemeal approach to improving a school district, because a school system is a knowledge-creating organization and it is, or should be, a learning organization. Professional knowledge must be created and embedded in a school district's operational structures, and organizational learning must occur if a school district wants to develop and maintain the capacity to provide children with a high-quality education and provide faculty and staff with a motivating and satisfying work life. So, school system learning (i.e., organizational learning) must also be part of a district's transformation strategy.

Path 2: Transform a district's internal social infrastructure. Improving core and support work processes to improve learning for students, faculty and staff, and the whole school system is an important transformation goal, but it is still a piecemeal approach to change. It is possible for a school district to have a fabulous curriculum with extraordinarily effective instructional methodologies supporting it but still have an internal social infrastructure (which includes organization culture, organization design, communication patterns, power and political dynamics, reward systems, and so on) that is demotivating, dissatisfying, and demoralizing for teachers and staff. Demotivated, dissatisfied, and demoralized teachers cannot and will not use a fabulous curriculum in remarkable ways. Demotivated, dissatisfied, and demoralized support staff cannot and will not perform their duties in value-adding ways. So, in addition to improving how the work of a district is done, transformation efforts must focus simultaneously on improving a district's internal social infrastructure.

The social infrastructure of a school system needs to be redesigned at the same time the core and support work processes are redesigned because it is important to ensure that the new social infrastructure and the new work processes complement each other. The only way to ensure this complementarity is to make simultaneous improvements to both elements of a school system.

Path 3: Transform a district's relationship with its external environment. A school district is an open system. An open system, according to organization theory (e.g., see Daft, 2006), is one that interacts with its environment by exchanging a valued product or service in return for needed resources. If change leaders want to transform their districts to become learner-centered, knowledge-creating school systems, they need to have a positive and supporting relationship with stakeholders in their districts' external environment. They need positive and supporting relationships to make important changes within their districts, so they have to transform their districts' relationships with key external stakeholders.

Hopefully this three-path metaphor makes sense, because the principle of simultaneous improvement along the three paths is absolutely essential for effective systemic transformational change (e.g., see F. E. Emery, 1977; Pasmore, 1988; Trist, Higgin, Murray, & Pollack, 1963). In the literature on systems improvement this principle is called joint optimization (Cummings & Worley, 2001, p. 353). This systemic approach to transforming school systems, while considerably more challenging than piecemeal change, is possible and is indeed being carried out successfully in all kinds of organizations, including the Metropolitan School District of Decatur Township, Indiana.[4] Furthermore, I believe it is the only approach that can help school districts break through their performance ceilings by creating and sustaining a new S-curve—a significantly different system transformed to meet the needs of our twenty-first-century society.

LEADING SYSTEMIC TRANSFORMATIONAL CHANGE REQUIRES LIVING WITH PARADOX

The world of systemic transformational change is one colored by paradoxical dilemmas. The color of paradox is grey. The world of systemic transformational change is covered by a diaphanous veil that must be lifted by the artful application of change leadership skills to expose, examine, and cope with the paradoxes beneath. As Richard Farson observed in Duffy (2006),

> As people make their way up the management ladder, they deal less and less with problems and more and more with what the late philosopher Abraham Kaplan called predicaments—permanent, inescapable, complicated, paradoxical dilemmas. Problems can be solved, but predicaments can only be coped with. (p. 180)

Leading systemic transformational change is an exercise in solving paradoxical dilemmas and tolerating ambiguity (see chapter 3). This kind of leadership demands change leaders who are masters of the art and science of transforming school systems and who have extraordinary courage, passion, and vision. Mastering the art and science of transformation requires mastery of three sets of competencies (Duffy, 2009):

- *Mastering Awareness* (see the chapters in section 2): becoming skillful in collecting, analyzing, interpreting, and reporting need data (which push people toward change) and opportunity data (which draw people toward change)
- *Mastering Deliberate Intention* (see the chapters in section 3): becoming skillful in creating and communicating a compelling and emotionally powerful vision of a desirable future for a school system
- *Mastering Methodology* (see the chapters in section 4): becoming skillful in using a methodology especially designed to create and sustain systemic transformational change and the tools that are part of that methodology

CONCLUSION

Despite the paucity of real-life examples of systemic transformational change in school districts, it is strongly advocated. An example of advocacy for systemic transformational change is found in an initiative launched by the Association for Educational Communications and Technology (AECT) called FutureMinds: Transforming American School Systems (see chapter 14).

The FutureMinds initiative has an inspiring and far-reaching change agenda. It aims to train teams of professionals in selected state departments of education to lead the creation and sustainment of transformational change in local school systems in their states. The ultimate goal of this transformational change initiative is to help school systems create and sustain transformational change that results in the four paradigm shifts that were described earlier.

Substantial evidence documents a robust interest in systemic transformational change in school systems (e.g., see Burney, 2004; Houlihan & Houlihan, 2005; Simmons, 2006; Wright, 2004; the report by the New Commission on the Skills of the American Workforce titled "Tough Choices or Tough Times"; the Educational Commission of the States' report, "Bending without Breaking"; and the National Education Commission on Time and Learning's 1994 report, "Prisoners of Time").

The interest in whole-system transformational change is also validated by highly visible and powerful groups such as Ohio's Transformational Dialogue for Public Education (TDPE). The TDPE is a dialogue group composed of high-level state leaders including the chancellor of higher education, the state superintendent of schools, the governor's education policy advisor, and the first lady of Ohio. The TDPE was formed by the KnowledgeWorks Foundation Institute for Creative Collaboration headed by Dr. Jillian Darwish. The TDPE is facilitated by Daniel Kim of MIT and Diane Cory, and, as a group, they are exploring what it will take to reconceptualize the system of public education in Ohio. The initiative helps state leaders to place the system of public education and the student within that system at the center of their conversations and transcend their particular organizational interests to focus on the common good of educating their state's citizens for the twenty-first century.

Initiatives like Ohio's TDPE and AECT's FutureMinds recognize that America's school systems need to be transformed—not tweaked, not tinkered with, not improved one building or one program at a time—if these systems are to become something fundamentally different than what they are today. These groups fully understand that the caterpillar needs to transform into a butterfly, not have wings strapped to its chrysalis.

NOTES

1. These conclusions are derived from the literature on organizational theory and design; see Daft (2006).

2. For information about the failures of quick fixes please see the references for Braun (2002) and Gibson, Levine, and Novak (2006).

3. These change paths should not be conceived of as physical paths that are traversed one step at a time. Rather, they should be thought of as cognitive pathways that are "thought along" simultaneously.

4. You may visit their website at www.indiana.edu/~syschang/decatur/the_change_effort.html. The change effort is being facilitated by Dr. Charles Reigeluth of Indiana University.

3

Leadership for
Transformational Change

OVERVIEW

Transforming an entire school system requires courageous, passionate, and visionary leadership (Duffy, 2003a). This leadership is not limited to one person; rather, it is required from people at all levels of a school system—from the superintendent to the receptionist, from the teachers to the cafeteria workers. Transforming a school system is a challenge for everyone in that system and it requires multilevel, multidirectional leadership. This chapter offers insights into the leadership challenges that educators will face as they lead the transformation of their school systems.

THE POWER OF VISION

The power of a vision is essential for the ongoing success of any organization because it sets the stage, frames the actions, and directs the energy of the people in the organization (see chapter 7). Senge (1990) believes that people must be committed to the vision, not just compliant with it. Commitment releases human potential and energy. Effective change leadership develops this commitment and sustains school improvement.

Fullan (1993) articulated the developmental nature of vision-building. He said "under conditions of dynamic complexity one needs a good deal of reflective experience before one can form a plausible vision. Vision always emerges from, more than it precedes action. Even then it is always provisional . . . [a] shared vision, which is essential for success, must evolve through the dynamic interaction of organizational members and leaders" (p. 28).

LEADERSHIP FOR INNOVATION

Leadership for innovation is absolutely critical to the success of a school system's transformation journey. Some important leadership concepts and principles for creating and sustaining innovation are presented below. Mastering these concepts and principles is important for the success of a transformation effort.

Creating innovative ideas to transform a district's core and support work processes, its internal social infrastructure, and its environmental relationships is a challenging task. This task cannot be undertaken without many change leaders all following the same script—a script defined by the school system's strategic framework (which includes a new mission, vision, and strategic plan) that will guide its transformation.

Transformational Leadership

A specific type of leadership is required to create and sustain school district transformation. In the past, leadership was associated with "getting things done" or "leading people somewhere." To transform a school system, change leaders need to guide their colleagues through a change process that will simultaneously transform three sets of key school system variables (which were identified as change paths in the previous chapter): the district's core and support work processes, its social infrastructure, and its relationship with its external environment. This kind of leadership is called "transformational leadership" (Burns, 1978; Leithwood, 1992).

Transformational leadership motivates followers to work for long-term goals instead of short-term self-interests, and to work toward achievement and self-actualization instead of emotional security (Bass & Avolio, 1993). Transformational leadership is inspirational because it redirects the energies and potential of people to achieve a vision. Transformational leadership taps into the emotional energy of people and provides them with meaning and a sense of personal value. People inspired by transformational leaders no longer "go to work"; instead, they work for a "cause." There is a sense of excitement, adventure, and enthusiasm that emerges as people realize they can do more than they ever thought possible.

Transformational leadership factors emerged from Bass's (1985) research. He identified five factors that describe transformational leaders. These are:

- Charisma—the ability to instill values, respect, and pride and to articulate a vision

- Individual attention—paying attention to followers' needs and assigning meaningful projects so followers grow personally
- Intellectual stimulation—helping followers rethink rational ways to examine situations and encouraging followers to be creative
- Contingent reward—informing followers about what must be done to receive the rewards they prefer
- Management by exception—permitting followers to work on tasks without being interrupted by the leader unless goals are not being accomplished in a reasonable time and at a reasonable cost

Avolio, Waldman, and Yammarino (1991) described the "Four Is of Transformational Leadership": (1) idealized influence; (2) inspirational motivation; (3) intellectual stimulation; and (4) individual consideration. Bass and Avolio (1993) added depth to these "Four Is" by suggesting that "transformational leaders integrate creative insight, persistence and energy, intuition and sensitivity to the needs of others to 'forge the strategy-culture alloy' for their organizations" (p. 113).

An essential element of transformational leadership is its focus on vision. Making explicit the core values that support the vision, modeling behaviors and attitudes that reflect those core values, and coaching and facilitating the development of individuals in the adopting of these core values are important tasks of transformational leadership.

Another fundamental aspect of transformational leadership is an astute understanding of the interconnectedness of all aspects of a school system. This understanding is a hallmark of systems thinking. Systems thinking is also an essential element of organization learning (Senge, 1990). Change leaders who want to transform school systems must be well versed in the principles of systems thinking. Systems thinking helps change leaders see their school system as a whole and to see interrelationships, interdependencies, patterns, and relationships. Change leaders also use systems thinking to determine where small but powerful changes in their district might result in the greatest improvements. These small but powerful change points are examples of what system designers call high-leverage change points (Reigeluth, 2006b).

Transformational leaders also have an informal personal style with people. They approach their tasks from a collaborative orientation reflected in statements such as "We are in this together, so let's see what we can do to be creative and solution-oriented." Transformational leaders see their role focusing on coaching and facilitating, rather than on directing or commanding. Building relationships, inspiring creativity and humor, demonstrating optimism, solution-finding, and dogged persistence are important characteristics of those who want to transform entire school systems into high-performing organizations of learners.

LEVELS OF LEADERSHIP FOR
TRANSFORMING SCHOOL SYSTEMS

Transformational leadership provides the context for four levels of leadership required for effective transformation. These four levels are: Strategic Leadership, Tactical Leadership, Team Leadership, and Self-Leadership (see figure 3.1). These levels of leadership are required for the School System Transformation (SST) Protocol described in chapter 12.

Strategic Leadership. Strategic leadership focuses on the big picture, the vision, the core values, and on the strategy for achieving the vision. For a school system's transformation effort, a Strategic Leadership Team (SLT), which includes the superintendent, provides strategic leadership. The SLT is also the primary "vision keeper." In this role, members of the SLT ask questions such as: "Who are we as a school district?" "Where are we going?" and "What do we need to do to get there?" This team frequently monitors the external environment, the school system's culture, and the morale of people in the school system to determine what needs to be done to achieve the district's vision more effectively.

Nicholls (1999) described two important tasks of strategic leadership: path-finding and culture-building (p. 20). A vision statement is directly

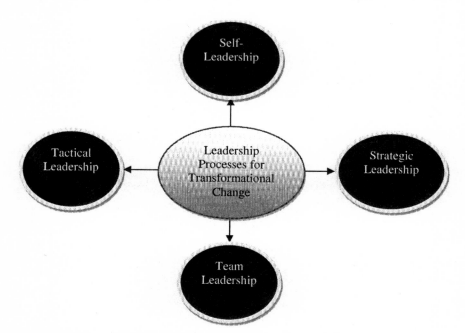

Figure 3.1.   Four Leadership Processes for Transformational Change

related to path-finding. Culture-building, which supports the vision, depends upon the quality and articulation of the core values. Leaders engage in these path-finding and culture-building tasks so that their school system can move toward higher levels of performance. When strategic leadership is functioning properly,

> [t]here is a unity of purpose throughout the [school system] in accord with a clear and widely understood vision. This environment nurtures total commitment from all employees. Rewards go beyond benefits and salaries to the belief "we are family" and "we do excellent work." (Scholtes, 1992, section 1, p. 12)

The SLT also aligns school district policies, procedures, and reward systems with the emerging transformed district so that an organization culture of participation and collaboration can take root and thrive. The SLT removes obstacles, creates metaphors to facilitate organization learning, finds and distributes resources, and models appropriate behaviors while also encouraging others to do the same. They are skilled systems thinkers who diligently anticipate problems, challenge assumptions that could hinder progress, and explore the effects of policies and procedures.

Tactical Leadership. Tactical leadership focuses on daily leadership tasks to keep teams focused and productive. This leadership responsibility is entrusted to a senior level district leader; for example, an assistant superintendent for reinvention.[1] This senior level leader is the primary tactical leader who guides his or her district's transformation journey on a daily basis. The leaders of the various transformation teams that are distributed throughout a school system also provide tactical leadership in concert with this senior change leader.

Scholtes (1992) describes the tactical leadership role as follows:

> The team leader is the person who manages the team: calling and facilitating meetings, handling or assigning administrative details, orchestrating all team activities, and overseeing preparations for reports and preparations. The team leader should be interested in solving the problems that prompted this project and be reasonably good at working with individuals and groups. Ultimately, it is the leader's responsibility to create and maintain channels that enable team members to do their work. (section 3, p. 8)

It is important to note that the senior tactical leader does not have unilateral responsibility to resolve issues that arise during his or her district's transformation. Rather, this change leader has the responsibility to ask the district-wide transformation teams to address certain issues as they arise, to facilitate team members in a search for solutions, and to realign or adjust their activities to support the vision and strategic direction of the school system.

Team Leadership. School system transformation requires the involvement of several change leadership teams. These teams must also provide tactical leadership to create and sustain transformational change throughout their district, especially in classrooms, schools, and clusters of schools within a district. Team leadership responds to the issues, opportunities, and concerns upon which each team focuses. Each team's mission must be aligned with the goals of their buildings, their clusters, and with the strategic direction of the entire school system.

The various change leadership teams reframe everyday problems and challenges of the workplace. For example, they consider other ways of perceiving certain "symptoms" in the teaching and learning process, they explore curricular and instructional issues from broad perspectives, and they search for ways to balance the long-term and the short-term needs of the school district, students, and classroom teachers. The teams also explore various aspects of the school system's core and support work processes and social infrastructure to identify what's happening in lower grade-levels that might flow "downstream" to affect upper grade-levels. The transformation teams must also decide when to take action to correct any problems they identify or seize any opportunities that present themselves.

Self-Leadership. Self-leadership is required of all change leaders during a transformation journey. Self-leadership is a process of personal growth, self-development, stretching, learning, and exploring beyond the confines of one's comfort zone. It requires risk-taking, challenging assumptions, reforming perceptions, and changing personal beliefs. It also requires individuals to become familiar with "self." In a world that rewards "busy-ness," social activities, and productivity, it is often difficult for people—especially smart people—to take time for personal reflection.

Self-leadership is truly self-initiated learning. The individual who devotes time and energy to self-development will constantly learn about the way he or she interacts with the environment, with workplace situations, with other people, and in response to personal needs, dreams, and goals. Confidence, commitment, risk-taking, creativity, and communication are enhanced when people engage in self-development activities.

Self-leadership is an evolutionary process. It unfolds over time as people test themselves in the new situations that are being created as their districts transform. Those who engage in self-leadership processes are also more likely to be self-starters and understand the concept of personal accountability.

One of the important outcomes of self-leadership is the release of "previous dependency on superior authority" (Manz & Sims, 1995, p. 218). Dependence on authority figures in organizations is a psychological problem described by Argyris (1957). When this problem exists, people in organizations are reluctant to take initiative, and instead wait for directions from superiors about what to do and when to do it. For transformational change to occur, this kind of dependence must be driven out of the system.

LEADERSHIP STAGES FOR TRANSFORMING SCHOOL SYSTEMS

Transforming an entire school system requires four levels of leadership (described above). Within each level, there are four leadership stages that contribute to the overall effectiveness of a district's transformation journey. These stages are: gathering, choosing, mastering, and renewing (Duffy, Rogerson, & Blick, 2000).

Each of the four stages has two key leadership tasks. The four stages parallel the five phases of the School System Transformation Protocol described in chapter 12. The Gathering Stage correlates with Phase 1: Prepare; the Choosing Stage is connected to Phase 2: Envision; the Mastering Stage relates to Phase 3: Transform and Phase 4: Sustain; and the Renewing Stage connects with Phase 4 and Phase 5: Evaluate. The four stages are shown in figure 3.2, and their respective subtasks are described below in more detail.

Stage 1: Gathering

Preparing to launch a transformation journey is a challenging leadership task. Activities designed to gain political support begin prior to launching

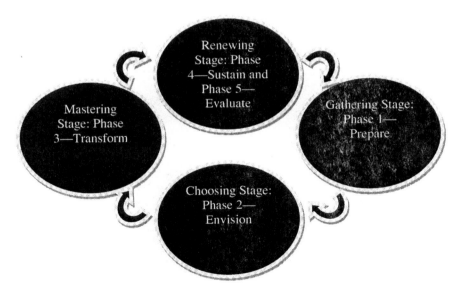

Figure 3.2. Leadership Stages for Transforming School Systems

the transformation effort. Without broad and deep political support from influential members of the school system and the community, there is little chance that transformation activities will begin, never mind survive. This support must be powerful and continuous. This means that administrators, teachers, parents, students, legislators, and other education professionals need to look for ways to solve the transformation puzzles that arise, rearrange the pieces of those puzzling situations, experiment with new approaches, and work to transform their district.

Leadership Task 1.1: Keeping Hope Alive. The primary leadership task for the Gathering Stage is to "Keep Hope Alive." John Gardner (1969) first used this notion to convey the importance of the encouragement aspect of the leader's role. Moving into new territory, embarking on a great journey, or finding ourselves in a seemingly endless wilderness of change requires a continuous reminder of a vision or end result. The primary task that Moses had with his Israelite wanderers was to keep their sights and hearts on the "land of milk and honey" so that they wouldn't get discouraged by the hardships and endlessness of the desert trek. In the television series *Wagon Train*, Ward Bond, as the wagon master, continuously helped his would-be settlers keep their focus on the Willamette Valley or other lush and green destinations. He had his scout go out in search of encouraging signs: water, resting places, landmarks, and so on. These were efforts to "keep hope alive."

As vision keepers, leaders must also have a clear sense of their school system's idealized vision for the future of their school system (see chapter 7). They must describe and transmit that vision, along with a clear sense of mission, every step of the way toward higher levels of performance. It is important to note that it isn't the leaders who define the specifics of a vision; rather, the leaders' job is to provide a "big picture" description of the vision and then inspire individuals to create the specifics.

Leaders must also embody a sense of service. A sense of service means that leaders see themselves as providing a service rather than receiving power and status for their efforts. In a culture of participation and collaboration, servant leadership, a term coined by Greenleaf (1973) and expanded upon by others such as Block (1993) and Greenleaf, Spears, and Covey (2002), is a required correlate of transformational leadership. Effective leaders are constantly attending to the needs of their followers (J. W. Gardner, 1990, p. 143).

Leadership Task 1.2: Leading Change. Kotter (1996) described eight errors made by change leaders. When describing these errors he reminded readers of an important lesson about change: it is important not to skip steps in the change process. Skipping steps brings about the illusion of speed, but only slows down the process in the long run and often results in failed organization improvement efforts.

Kotter (1996) converted the eight errors into positive statements describing what change leaders can do to increase the effectiveness of their organization improvement efforts. Kotter's principles influenced the design of the SST Protocol described in chapter 12.

1. Create a sense of urgency. People need to have a reason to change. Kotter recommended that leaders identify a rallying point around which people can coalesce. This sense of urgency is created prior to beginning a transformation journey.
2. Create a powerful, guiding coalition. In the SST Protocol described in chapter 12, the Strategic Leadership Team is the guiding coalition. It is powerful because it includes the superintendent, one or two of his or her trusted subordinates, influential building-level administrators and teachers chosen by their colleagues to serve on this team, and others. The SLT is formed during Phase 1: Prepare of the SST Protocol.
3. Develop and recognize the power of a vision and a strategy. Vision and strategy evolve during Phase 2: Envision of the SST Protocol. It becomes the task of leaders to articulate this vision clearly to people throughout the school system and the community. In addition, the change strategy, in this case the SST Protocol, needs to be clearly articulated.
4. Communicate the new vision. Kotter argued that there can never be too much communication about the vision and the strategy. Every channel of communication must be engaged, including face-to-face, written, visual, and electronic communications. Kotter, however, suggested that people often underestimate the time needed to communicate the vision by a factor of ten. Kotter also emphasized the importance of the adage "walk your talk." He said, "Nothing undermines change more than behavior by important individuals that is inconsistent with the verbal communication" (p. 10). Communicating about the vision occurs throughout all five phases of the SST Protocol.
5. Remove obstacles (policies, procedures, and people) that act as barriers to the new vision. "Whenever smart and well-intentioned people avoid confronting obstacles, they disempower employees and undermine change" (p. 10). People in leadership roles must learn how to identify and evaluate the nature of the obstacles that prevent progress toward the vision. Obstacles to innovation should be removed continuously throughout the life of a school system.
6. Generate short-term wins. Celebrating success is very important. During times of change, some people make the mistake of postponing celebrations until everything is finished. The problem is that being "finished" is a relative term when implementing innovative ideas. By

celebrating little milestones, people generate the energy and enthusiasm needed to continue onto more challenging milestones. Short-
term wins are created during phases 3 and 4 of the SST Protocol.

7. Consolidate gains and produce more change. Kotter warned against
   declaring victory too soon. People will lose their edge and stop push-
   ing toward the vision if victory is declared before the entire redesign
   process is completed. Gains are consolidated and used as a spring-
   board for further innovation. This consolidation occurs during phase
   4 of the SST Protocol.

8. Anchor changes firmly into the corporate culture. Leaders must understand the puissant role that organization culture plays in inhibiting or
   enhancing opportunities for innovation and change. In addition,
   leaders must have the ability and the courage to reconstruct and redi-
   rect organization culture in ways that support desired changes. An-
   choring also occurs during phase 4 of the SST Protocol.

Stage 2: Choosing

With increased confidence and competence, people also increase their
readiness to explore new ways of working. In the SST Protocol this exploration occurs during Phase 2: Envision and Phase 3: Transform. Redesigning
a school system's core and support work processes, social infrastructure, and
its environmental relationships creates many choices. The faculty and staff
in every school and support unit in a district must consider choices appropriate to the design and functioning of their schools and support units.
Each individual school needs to consider choices directed to finding solutions that make teaching and learning more effective in the classrooms in
that building. Each person must choose behaviors and attitudes that facilitate the accomplishment of critical job tasks. Everyone must choose to align
themselves with the district's new mission, vision, and strategic framework.
There are many choices to be made.

Leadership Task 2.1: Releasing Potential. An acorn has the potential to
become an oak tree. A caterpillar has the potential to become a butterfly.
Students and teachers have the potential to become self-directed, lifelong
learners. A traditional school system has the potential to become a dazzling
community of learners characterized by participation and collaboration.
Each potential must be unlocked, channeled, and nurtured by making appropriate and effective choices.

Potential means the capacity to become. There are many obstacles in
complex school systems that hinder or prevent achievement of potential.
Structural and procedural barriers funnel people and teams down the path
of least resistance where genuine, long-lasting change rarely occurs. More
often it is the road that must be hewn out of the dense forest of longstand-

ing mind-sets or blasted out of the hard granite of tradition found in the system's controlling mental models and change-resistant status quo that leads to significant change and improvement.

To release potential, leaders must ensure that the work of individuals and teams actually supports the vision and the core values of the school system. Accomplishing this requires the application of seven principles described by Walter (1995):

- Know each person as an individual.
- Understand what each person values as a reward or expects in terms of recognition.
- Model equity and apply fairness.
- Learn what motivates and frustrates each member of the team.
- Encourage and develop both internal locus of control and self-efficacy.
- Repeatedly clarify and articulate the vision and the core values.
- Connect all actions, projects, and strategies to the vision.

The nature of these principles is a reminder that transformational leadership is a personal style of leadership. In fact, transformational leadership won't work in an organizational culture that treats people impersonally. In a high-performance work environment, a learning environment, or a culture that embodies the process of transformation, the personal touch works. Equity and fairness, for instance, in traditional organizations are designed around the principle that everyone is treated the same (a basic tenet of egalitarianism). Treating everyone the same amounts to treating them impersonally and thus without regard to their individual needs, interests, abilities, goals, and values.

Flexibility, patience, and persistence. Releasing potential is also influenced by other leadership actions, specifically by practicing flexibility, patience, and persistence, and by helping people overcome feelings of learned helplessness. Cutting a path through the wilderness of change also requires leaders to be flexible, patient, and persistent in helping people achieve the district's vision through systemic transformation. With the vision and the core values as a compass, individuals and teams who are redesigning their school system must be willing to learn and model appropriate attitudes and behaviors that support systemic improvement.

Classic behavioral models of leadership (Blake & Mouton, 1964; Fiedler, 1967; Hersey & Blanchard, 1988; Likert, 1961; Stogdill & Coons, 1957; Tannenbaum & Schmidt, 1957) address the need for leaders to apply structure or to allow autonomy depending upon the readiness, competence, or commitment of followers. However, this notion of designated leaders making these kinds of decisions is incompatible with the organization culture required by school systems designed for success in the twenty-first-century Knowledge Age—a culture of participation and collaboration.

Even though autonomy, decision making, and creative freedom are built into the change leadership teams that are part of the SST Protocol, a school district cannot and must not throw control and order out the window. "The result would be complete anarchy and total chaos—as people would be working at cross-purposes with each other. There would be no sense of alignment or social cohesiveness" (Purser & Cabana, 1998, p. 37). Thus, as the level of autonomy and creativity is raised, the level of control and order must also be raised to prevent the system from spinning out of control. This results in a school system that has top-down guidance modified by bottom-up realities. The requisite top-down guidance, however, doesn't come from the old hierarchical, authoritarian, command-and-control paradigm; instead, it comes from the development of working partnerships and trust within a school system.

Overcoming learned helplessness. Overcoming organizationally induced helplessness (McGrath, 1994) is essential for releasing potential in individuals and teams. Organization-induced helplessness evolves as individuals learn that their ideas are not valued and that they have little or no control over events and decisions affecting them. This helplessness is manifested in their inability and unwillingness to initiate action, participate in efforts to empower people, and failure to exercise personal power. Helplessness can also be the motivation behind efforts to sabotage the district's transformation journey, because the helpless have a cynical belief that there is no future for the desired changes.

Kankus and Cavalier (1995) described two simple but powerful methods for reducing feelings of helplessness. First, they suggested that people be encouraged to identify areas of their work that they do have control over and then identify things that they would like to change. McGrath (1994) also suggested that continuous reinforcement and encouragement will help people overcome feelings of helplessness.

To increase the potency of transformational change, it is important for leaders to address organizationally induced helplessness. Hoy (1998) stated that "unless people believe they can make a difference through their actions, there is little incentive to act" (p. 153). This behavior is based in the concept of self-efficacy described by Bandura (1997). Hoy outlined four of Bandura's broad categories and related them to the development of self-efficacy. These four categories also form the basis for creating "learned optimism" (Seligman, 1990). The categories are personal attainment, vicarious experience, receiving encouragement or feedback, and the energized emotional and physiological states brought about by anxiety and excitement. Hoy, Bandura, and Seligman believed that helplessness is a learned behavior and, thus, can be unlearned.

Leadership Task 2.2: Defining and Shaping Culture. The transformation of a school system's culture is essential to the redesign of an entire school system. Schein (1985) described the creation and management of culture as the only important thing leaders do. Culture provides the context for everything that happens inside a school district. Bass (1985) concurred with this assertion when he said "transformational leaders change their culture by first understanding it and then realigning the organizational culture with a new vision and a revision of its shared assumptions, values, and norms" (p. 112).

Along with articulating the district's vision, leaders assist faculty and staff in the identification of those beliefs and assumptions that are most important to them as members of the district. Shared values are the basis of a learning community. They bind people together and provide the foundation for decision making and for aligning people to the vision.

Stage 3: Mastering

In the SST Protocol, mastery emerges during Phase 3: Transform and Phase 4: Sustain. As the school system and its redesign teams become more and more confident that transformational change will succeed, and when the richness of their various choices becomes clear, they enter the Mastering Stage. "Mastering" means that a high level of competence is achieved. At this stage, the various changes made by using the SST Protocol are integrated in varying degrees into the daily thinking and behavior patterns of the faculty and staff. The focus is no longer on "How do we work with this new idea?" It is now on "How can we perfect this new idea?" Mastery is the understanding of what needs to be done to make high performance more than an abstract goal statement. Mastery reflects an ongoing process of improvement that becomes a routine part of a school district's culture.

With mastery comes an increased comfort level for working in teams, for collaboration, and for rewarding individual and team efforts. Prior to moving into the Mastering Stage, performance standards for the system, teams, and individuals are described and processes are installed to assist the various change leadership teams in evaluating their success.

Leadership Task 3.1: Management of attention. One of the most significant leadership processes is the "management of attention" (Bennis & Nanus, 1985). Management of attention means that leaders have the responsibility and the prerogative to declare the "subject of the day." Just as the agenda of the president of the United States in the political arena manages the attention of the people who work around him, leaders in school systems manage the attention of people working in the system.

During a transformation journey, change leaders need to help individuals and teams align themselves with the district's new strategic framework that is composed of the district's new mission, vision, and strategic goals. Much of this can be accomplished through reframing. Reframing implies that it isn't a specific event that is important; rather it's the interpretation of that event that matters. The lenses through which people perceive events create personal and shared mental models and mind-sets (see chapter 5 for more about mental models and mind-sets). These lenses can be based upon goals and needs, or upon educational, religious, or political orientations. They also can be based upon personal preferences, occupational disciplines, ethics, pragmatism, or expediency.

Bolman and Deal (1997) described a variety of frames for organization decision making including: political, caring, structural, and symbolic or cultural. They believe leaders can enhance the success of their organizations by reframing events using multiple frames, thus enabling richer solutions and decisions. Senge (1990) also reminds us that part of the journey to personal mastery is the ability to assign as many interpretations to an event as possible, thus seeing it from many angles (i.e., reframing). Reframing also results in the reassignment of energy, resources, and priorities. Interpretations of events are reinterpreted so leaders can keep hope alive and release potential.

Leadership Task 3.2: Creating and disseminating knowledge. Creating and disseminating knowledge is an outgrowth of the Mastering Stage. Once the redesign teams become accustomed to the SST Protocol process, they learn how to create and disseminate knowledge. In this way, information, innovations, and good ideas are shared widely among clusters of schools, between and among schools within clusters, and even across school districts. Much of this can be accomplished through the selection of special computer-based groupware that encourages the sharing of information in the form of electronic bulletin boards, web pages, and "listservs" (see Duffy, 2002).

Breakthroughs in thinking and problem-solving occur by combining ideas, situations, and context information in new ways. Without the types of information exchanges referred to above, which Pava (1983b) calls deliberations, it will be extraordinarily difficult to create district-wide professional knowledge.

Stage 4: Renewing

In the SST Protocol, renewing occurs during Phase 4: Sustain and Phase 5: Evaluate. At this stage, the transformational change activities become second nature. Individuals have begun to let go of their longing for the old ways and have come to believe that "this new way is a better way."

During the Renewing Stage, educators also reassess and customize the innovations they created to assure they are still effective. Renewing is an aspect of continuous improvement.[2] It is also important to remember that unless innovation recycles to generate new ideas and new choices (by recycling the SST Protocol to Phase 1: Prepare), the school system runs the risk of once again becoming entrenched in outdated and ineffective routines, procedures, and policies that no longer serve the needs of students, communities, and other stakeholders. Renewing prevents the unnecessary institutionalization of innovation.

Leadership Task 4.1: Scanning and interpreting boundaries. There are invisible but real boundaries between levels of schooling, between and among individual schools, between grades, between and among preK–12 clusters of schools in a district, and between the entire school system and its broader environment. All of these boundaries need to be managed during and subsequent to a district's transformation journey.

Steckler and Fontas (1995) developed a diagnostic tool for evaluating several boundary management behaviors that transformational leaders need to master. These behaviors include clarifying the expectations of outside stakeholders regarding team performance; sharing and disseminating information; gathering and using data to improve performance of teams, team members, and others in the school system; securing needed resources; and identifying and minimizing obstacles that prevent high performance.

Creating partnerships with key external stakeholders is another aspect of boundary management. Harrison and St. John (1996) referred to this process as bridging. "When environments are more complex and uncertain, webs of interdependencies are created among stakeholders. In these environments bridging (or boundary spanning) techniques are needed to build on interdependencies" (p. 6) rather than preventing the system from experiencing these kinds of relationships.

Harrison and St. John emphasized the importance of incorporating stakeholders as partners in the process of innovation rather than excluding them as interlopers. "Partnering activities allow firms to build bridges with their stakeholders, in the pursuit of common goals, whereas traditional stakeholder management techniques (buffering) simply facilitate the satisfaction of stakeholder needs and/or demands" (p. 6). In the SST Protocol, bridging and partnering are important examples of the improvements needed in the relationship between a school district and its broader environment. Bridging and partnering are also required between and among each subsystem of the district and their respective environments. It is the task of leadership to initiate and sustain the important processes of scanning, interpreting and bridging boundaries, and creating partnerships with stakeholders.

Leadership Task 4.2: Inspiring continuous learning. Continuous learning is an important process throughout a district's transformation journey, especially in the Renewing Stage, for it is here that the momentum needs to be increased to move the school system to the next round of innovation that begins by recycling the SST Protocol to Phase 1: Prepare. The ability to keep people asking questions, exploring ideas, and initiating periods of ·

frame-breaking, transformational change followed by continuous improvement is an essential task for change leaders to master.

Continuous learning is at the center of the learning organization, but learning is not simply the gathering and manipulation of information. Senge (1990) characterized the core feature of a learning organization as a shift of mind—from seeing ourselves as separate from the world to connected to the world, from seeing problems as caused by someone or something "out there" to seeing how our own actions create the problems we experience. A learning organization is a place where people are continually discovering how they create their reality (Senge, 1990).

With this approach people can continue to learn how to learn with each other. Each person needs to become aware of the value of challenging assumptions, introducing new ideas, drawing from the experts and the researchers in the field, and learning to use personal creativity and initiative to empower change and innovation in the school system.

The various transformation teams and the senior-level change leader using the SST Protocol provide tactical leadership on a daily basis using the following process of continuous learning throughout their district's transformation journey:

- Communicate the vision mission, core values, and strategic direction.
- Assist each change leadership team in defining its mission, objectives, corresponding values and performance expectations.
- Inspire the energy of a critical mass of people toward accomplishing the vision.
- Encourage and sustain the momentum of the various team and individual actions required to design and implement innovations and support continuous improvement efforts on the part of the teams.

Another important element of a school system that contributes to continuous learning is a district's central administration office. When this office is transformed into a Central Service Center (which happens by using the SST Protocol) that embraces and enacts principles of servant leadership, the staff in this center effectively and efficiently provide the financial, technical, human, and time resources needed to support continuous learning.

CHANGE LEADERSHIP CHALLENGES

Although transformational leadership is a powerful tool for creating and sustaining transformational change, navigating large-scale, district-wide transformational change is still challenging. Yet, there are examples of it happening; for example, in the Metropolitan School District of Decatur

Township in Indianapolis, Indiana, facilitated by Dr. Charles Reigeluth from Indiana University.[3] Navigating change at this scale requires change leaders who are courageous, passionate, and visionary, using power and political skills in ethical ways (Duffy, 2003a).

Change leaders focusing on whole-system transformation, their transformational leadership knowledge and skills notwithstanding, will inevitably face significant challenges during their district's journey toward a desirable new future—a future that captures extraordinary opportunities to improve student, faculty and staff, and whole system learning. Below, twenty-one key challenges that change leaders may face while leading transformational change in their districts are presented.

Challenge 1: Mastering Change Leadership Knowledge and Skills

One of the key reasons why large-scale change fails is that those trying to lead it sometimes do not have adequate theoretical knowledge and practical skills needed to lead this kind of change. Graduate programs preparing future school administrators ought to develop a specialty area in change leadership; for example, at Gallaudet University in Washington, DC, the faculty in the Department of Administration and Supervision retooled their Education Specialist Program to offer an education specialist degree in change leadership in education (see chapter 15 for an example of a design for this kind of program).

In the absence of formal graduate programs focusing on change leadership, educators (teachers as well as administrators) with an interest in leading change in their school systems could design and implement a personal learning plan. This plan would bring them to books, articles, and perhaps courses in graduate schools of business where they could learn what they need to know to lead change effectively.

Because foundational knowledge and skills are so important to effective change leadership, it would be a serious mistake for change leaders to launch a large-scale transformation journey without that knowledge and those skills. In fact, it can be predicted that if these leaders do not have prerequisite change leadership knowledge and skills, their change effort will fail.

Challenge 2: Becoming Systems Thinkers and System "Changers"

To transform an entire school system, change leaders in that system must know what a system is and how it functions; they must understand what it means to be a systems thinker; they must be able to define the system to be improved; they must understand the dynamics of critical system archetypes; and they must be skillful in using a set of systems thinking tools. And then they must use that knowledge to transform their school systems.

Challenge 3: Overcoming the System's History with Change

The field of education is littered with the debris of failed change efforts. When people working in a school district repeatedly experience failed change efforts, at best they become cynical about the newest change proposal. At worst, they become hard core guerrilla warriors working to undermine the latest "fad" that change leaders are trying to introduce to their systems.

When educators experience either a pattern of failed change efforts or frequent change brought on by each new superintendent, they become resistant to change, angry, depressed, burned out, or a combination of these emotions. If change leaders are in a system where these kinds of emotions are prevalent, then they must take time during phase 1 (prepare) of the SST Protocol to work with people to help restore hope and optimism and ultimately strengthen commitment to the change process that is being proposed—before launching the change effort. If change leaders try to launch a transformation journey without identifying these emotions and then taking steps to help their colleagues work through their feelings, I predict the change effort will fail.

Challenge 4: Becoming Willing to Break or Bend Rules

Rule-breaking or rule-bending is a hallmark characteristic of effective change leaders. It is only through the artful circumvention of carefully selected rules that true innovation can happen, because the rules almost always protect the status quo, and the status quo is a great wall of resistance to innovation.

The only rules that I know of that were sent directly from God are the Ten Commandments. All other rules were created by people. Of course, not all rules should be broken or bent, because the consequences of breaking or bending them are severe; for example, it is probably unwise to break rules associated with local, state, and federal laws, although there may be laws that should be protested and perhaps disobeyed if they are seriously flawed or inherently unfair.

Even though it is important to identify rules that can be circumvented, it is challenging for change leaders to do so. It is especially challenging for change leaders who like rules and believe in them. These people can make rule-breaking easier by using the principle of "outside-in analysis" (Beckhard, 1983). With outside-in analysis, change leaders identify those rules that are not required by law and that are defined as policies. They search for policies, especially within their school district, that are potential obstacles to change. Then they figure out ways to change the policies or to circumvent them. If these policies are not changed or circumvented, then when change ideas are proposed people will say, "We can't do that because the policy says. . . ."

Challenge 5: Unfreezing Mental Models and Mind-Sets

Systemic transformational change focuses on making four sets of simultaneous district-wide transformations: transform core and support work, transform the internal social infrastructure, transform relationships with the external environment, and transform the district's approach to creating and sustaining change. This kind of whole-system transformational change requires educators to unlearn the mental models that inform their work, influence their internal social infrastructure, and affect their external relationships. Then they must learn new mental models that support the four new paradigms identified in the previous chapter. Willingness to unlearn old mental models and learn new ones is a function of a mind-set, which is a hardened, change-resistant attitude toward some idea, proposal for change, or person.

Challenge 6: Creating Disequilibrium in the System

It's a fact—when a system is in a state of stable equilibrium, not much is changing. To create change, especially transformational change, that stable equilibrium must be disrupted to create what systems dynamics experts call a reinforcing loop. A reinforcing loop causes change to happen and happen quickly. The danger is that reinforcing loops are like neutral third parties—they don't care if the change is positive or negative. Either way, the loops will drive change quickly. Therefore, having a positive, idealized vision for the future of a school system to work toward will be important for influencing the direction of the reinforcing loops that must be created if systemic transformational change is desired.

Challenge 7: Managing Organizational Entropy

Entropy is a law of physics. Systems of all kinds, including our human bodies, consume and deplete energy. The "energy" used by school systems includes human energy, equipment, money, books, furniture, and other supplies. The depletion of this energy is called entropy.

In living systems, entropy cannot be stayed and always results in death. In organizations, entropy can lead to figurative death. However, entropy in organizations can be slowed or reversed by replenishing resources and human energy. This replenishment process is called negative entropy or negentropy. Change leaders must be aware of entropy and know how to create negentropy if they want to lead their school systems effectively toward desirable futures.

Challenge 8: Acknowledging That the Best Time to Change an Organization Is When It's Doing Well

"Deeply troubled companies don't usually seek help. And when they do, they have a hard time benefiting from it" (Farson, 1996, p. 95). Burke

(2002) says that "a paradox of organization change is that the peak of success is the time to worry and to plan for and bring about significant change" (p. 1). This suggests that the best time to transform a school system is when it is healthy and doing well, and the worst time to do this is when a school system is failing. Healthy, well-functioning school systems are potentially easier to improve that failing ones.

Challenge 9: Learning That the Path to the Future Is Not a Straight Line Upward and Forward

The traditional approach to change management assumes that change rolls out according to a rational plan that is relatively straightforward and sequential. Experience, however, serves as a powerful counterpoint. Change rolls out in illogical, paradoxical ways that resemble winding paths coursing their way toward a future. Burke (2002) provides examples of why change is nonlinear and messy. He says,

> The implementation process is messy: Things don't proceed exactly as planned; people do things their own way, not always according to the plan; some people resist or even sabotage the process; and some people who would be predicted to support or resist the plan actually behave in just the opposite way. In short, unanticipated consequences occur. (p. 2)

These unintended consequences are made even more complex because they often appear as paradoxes representing unknowable realities in human affairs (Farson, 1996). These paradoxes, according to Farson, cannot be controlled or managed. Effective change leaders engage these situations by tapping into the collective wisdom of the community inside their districts instead of relying on their own unique perspectives. Farson (1996) suggests that change leaders wrestling with paradoxes find their strength as leaders "not in control, but in their passion, sensitivity, tenacity, patience, courage, firmness, enthusiasm and wonder" (p. 35).

Challenge 10: Responding Quickly to the Unexpected Consequences of Change

The organization design of most school systems is mechanistic and bureaucratic. In turbulent times this mechanistic design (Daft, 2001) can create arthritic-like symptoms in a school district that prevent people from reacting quickly to seize unexpected opportunities or to protect the system from startling threats. A more appropriate organization design for today's school systems is what organization theorists call the organic design, which increases a school system's flexibility and speed in responding to opportunities and threats in its external environment.

Challenge 11: Working to Anticipate and Prevent Iatrogenic Effects

With transformational change, change leaders must be aware of iatrogenic effects. These dreadful effects are commonly found in the health care field and they are defined as physician induced, as when a patient dies of staphylococcal infection induced by a doctor not washing her hands before treating a patient; or the patient who becomes deathly sick with an infection caused by a surgical tool inadvertently left inside the patient's body by a surgeon. In school districts engaged in systemic change, with every big change there may be iatrogenic effects that are exactly the opposite of what is intended. Therefore, it is important to apply principles of systems thinking to anticipate unintended consequences of planned changes.

Challenge 12: Surviving Environmental "Tsunami"

Another source of unexpected consequences is found in a school district's external environment. Some external forces roll over a school district like a flooding tsunami, and it is very difficult, perhaps impossible, for people in the district to influence the direction of these forces or their consequences (for example, consider the impact of No Child Left Behind).

Challenge 13: Recognizing the Difference between Problems and Predicaments

Unexpected outcomes come in the form of paradoxes. Some of these will be problems to be solved and others will be true predicaments. While problems can be solved, predicaments cannot. Farson (1996) tells us that people can only muddle through predicaments. While problem-solving requires analytical thinking, muddling through predicaments requires interpretive thinking that puts a larger frame around the puzzling situation so that its complexity can be understood. In fact, according to Farson, predicaments worsen if they are treated as problems to be solved. Change leaders moving their districts toward transformational change will need to interpret and work their way through predicaments more than they solve problems.

Challenge 14: Accepting the Importance of Equifinality

Equifinality is a concept from the field of organization development (Cummings & Worley, 2001). In plain English, it means there is more than one acceptable way to achieve the same goal. Within the context of systemic transformational change, it means that given a strategic framework to work within, educators can be innovative in how they create desired changes within their district. But whatever innovations they imagine, changes must be aligned with the overall strategic direction of the district; that is, they must fit within the strategic framework.

The opposite of equifinality is found in those situations where senior administrators identify changes to be made, issue directives that must be obeyed about what must be changed, and then tell people exactly how to make the changes. Giving people freedom to innovate within specified boundaries (the strategic framework) is not an easy thing for control-minded change leaders to do, yet when equifinality is encouraged and supported, it gives people the delimited autonomy they need to innovate (complete autonomy, however, would move a system toward chaos and anarchy). Autonomy, by the way, is one of six psychological requirements for creating a motivating work environment (Emery & Thorsrud, 1976).

Challenge 15: Managing Human Relations

Effective human relations in school districts are like glue—they can hold things together. Ineffective human relations are like solvent—they can dissolve the connections between and among people. Whole-system transformational change in school districts requires glue, not solvent, because when change leaders are trying to transform their entire school district they need ways to bind people together in support of their district's new grand vision and strategic direction.

Effective human relations involve more than communicating better, although good communication is an important element of human relations. Effective human relations also create authentic district-wide opportunities for people throughout a district to participate actively and meaningfully in the transformation of their district instead of complying with directives to change. Effective human relations require change leaders to identify those who support change, those who object to it, and those who haven't made up their mind about the changes and then devise strategies for communicating effectively with these people. Effective human relations not only focus on people inside a district, but also on individuals and groups in the external environment. Finally, effective human relations help change leaders recognize, honor, and work through resistance to change. Several examples of important human relations that need to be managed are highlighted below in challenges 16–21.

Challenge 16: Enabling Others to Lead and Contribute

There is no question that the superintendent of schools, as the senior executive in a school district, must lead whole-system transformational change. Her leadership must be unequivocal and visible. However, her leadership alone is insufficient for creating and sustaining whole-system change. A superintendent's leadership is like a tree. But to succeed in the transformation of a school system, there must be a forest of leaders throughout a school district. Creating a forest of leaders will require a superintendent to have a change of heart and a change of mind about how to involve faculty and staff in her district's transformation journey.

Challenge 17: Working with Allies, Opponents, Adversaries, Bedfellows, and Fence-Sitters (see chapter 6)

Peter Block (1991) advises managers about how to use positive political skills to communicate more effectively with people in five political groups inside organizations. Block suggests that managers can use two dimensions when making political decisions about how to interact with people inside those five categories. The first dimension is "level of agreement." The second dimension is "level of trust." Each dimension runs from high to low. The intersection of the two dimensions creates four quadrants, one for each of the first four political groups, with the fifth group centered and straddling all four quadrants. The political groups are:

- Allies—this group is defined by high trust and high agreement. You trust them, they trust you, and you are in agreement about what needs to be done.
- Opponents—this group is defined by high trust, but low agreement. You trust them, they trust you, but you disagree about what needs to be done.
- Bedfellows—this group is defined by low trust and high agreement. You don't trust these people and they don't trust you, but you agree with what needs to be done.
- Adversaries—this group is defined by low trust and low agreement. You don't trust these people and they don't trust you. Further, you disagree on what needs to be done.
- Fence-sitters—this group is defined as the undecided, the uncommitted, or the "I can't make up my mind" people.

Block's "five group" model dovetails with another important change management principle—the principle of "critical mass." Critical mass is a physics concept given to us by Kurt Lewin (1951). It serves as metaphor for building political support for change. A critical mass is that "magical" number of people needed to launch and sustain successful change. The critical mass number seen most often in the literature on change is 25 percent; that is, change leaders need about 25 percent of their faculty and staff to be committed to and willing to support the change process (Block might call these people allies and bedfellows). About 50 percent of the faculty and staff will stand on the sidelines and observe what's happening, not yet ready to make a commitment one way or the other (these people might be called fence-sitters in Block's model). Another 25 percent will actively resist the change. Of that final 25 percent, some of those will be "opponents" whose minds and hearts can be changed and who may eventually support the change. The remaining people in that last 25 percent group are hard core "adversaries" who will probably never accept or support your change leadership and who may actively work to undermine the change process.

Identifying the 25 percent critical mass in support of change, communicating with the 50 percent fence-sitter group, and working to bring opponents into the ally camp are significant challenges that change leaders must meet before they launch system-wide change. This political work begins during Phase 1: Prepare of the SST Protocol and continues throughout the effort.

Challenge 18: Communicating with External Stakeholders (see chapter 6)

Earlier, I identified three paths that must be followed if you want to create and sustain whole-system transformational change in a school district. One of those paths is "improve environmental relationships." A school district's external environment has two parts: the general environment (the economy, world events, societal norms and values) that districts have no chance of influencing, and the task environment (those individuals and groups that a school district interacts with directly and therefore can influence). Key players in a district's external task environment include: local community groups, state departments of education, parent groups, competitors (private schools, both nonprofit and for-profit), critics, and suppliers (which not only include suppliers of text books, equipment, and so on, but also include colleges and universities that prepare future teachers and school administrators).

Change leaders need to improve their district's relationship with these and other key players. To do this, first they have to know who the key players are. Second, they must assess the nature of the relationship they have with the key players and develop strategies for working with each one. Third, they determine what the key players need, want, and expect. Fourth, they determine if, when, and how to respond to their needs, wants, and expectations. Fifth, they use strategic communication (see Duffy & Chance, 2007) that is timely, accurate, honest, simple, clear, and powerful and that is tailored to each key player (see chapter 6).

Challenge 19: Managing Resistance to Change

Sometimes people and systems don't change quickly. Their slow response is often perceived as resistance. There are four common reasons for resisting change. The first reason is that people frequently resist the efforts of other people to impose change on them. The second main reason is related to human psychology and the need for stability or equilibrium in our lives. The third reason is fear—fear of losing prestige, losing power, losing relationships, or losing a job. And, the fourth reason is related to an organization's reluctance to change. One of the most powerful ways to respond to all four sources of resistance is to offer authentic opportunities for employees and external stakeholders to participate in the process of shaping the future of their school systems (see chapters 7 and 8).

Challenge 20: Building Trust

One thing's for sure: if change leaders have the courage, passion, and vision to lead whole-system change, they will get nowhere if their teachers and professional staff don't trust them. Trust is the foundation for respect. Respect is the cornerstone of professional influence. Influence is the essence of leadership. No trust + no respect + no influence = less than effective change leadership.

Challenge 21: Maintaining Personal Energy and Commitment

System-wide change takes time. William Pasmore (1988) suggests it takes anywhere from eighteen to thirty-six months. John Kotter (1996) believes it can take between five to seven years. Block (2003) said that transformation takes more time than we could possibly imagine. Common sense suggests a pragmatic estimate of the required time, which is found in the planning principle "plan for the worst and hope for the best"; therefore, assume it will take your school system five to seven years to complete its transformation journey. If transformation takes five to seven years, then another challenge change leaders will confront is creating and deploying strategies for maintaining their personal energy and commitment, as well as the energy and commitment of their colleagues so that all of them can persist toward their transformation goals.

CONCLUSION

School districts are complex, organic, adaptive systems. Complex, organic, and adaptive systems are mysterious entities that confound some people as they attempt to create and sustain transformational change. Further, leading transformational change predictably raises significant challenges that come in the form of paradoxes and problems. Twenty-one key challenges that transformational leaders may face when trying to transform their school districts were presented in this chapter.

Clearly, to navigate a river of complex change made dangerous by the invisible currents of system dynamics (Kim & Anderson, 2007) flowing beneath the surface and marked by the visible class 5 rapids formed by resistance to change, you will need:

- a vehicle (a change methodology and tools to carry you and your colleagues along the river of transformational change);
- a map and compass (knowledge of systems theory, systems dynamics, complexity and chaos theory, and knowledge of what needs to change); and
- superior change navigation skills that include:
  ○ Mastery of Awareness—becoming skillful in collecting, analyzing, interpreting and reporting need data (that push people toward change) and opportunity data (that draw people toward change);
  ○ Mastery of Intention—becoming skillful in creating and communicating a compelling and emotionally powerful vision of an idealized future for a school system; and
  ○ Mastery of Methodology—becoming skillful in using a methodology especially designed to create and sustain transformational change and the tools that are part of that methodology.

Yet even though you have a change vessel, a map, and a compass, you still need to help people in your district along the river of transformational change and through the periodic rapids. Helping people choose to make the journey (rather than being directed to do so) will require your sophisticated and ethical use of power and political skills (Duffy, 2003).

If you use power and political skills unethically, people will not make the journey effectively or maybe not at all. They will despise you and not trust your motives. Their resistance to your leadership will increase and some of them will figure out creative ways to delay or abort the school district's transformation journey toward its idealized future.

NOTES

1. This is a position created in the Metropolitan School District of Decatur Township, Indiana, to provide tactical leadership for their district's transformation journey.

2. For transformational change, continuous improvement is practiced after the transformation journey is complete; it is not a replacement for transformational change. Continuous improvement as a replacement for transformational change is an example of piecemeal change that has not and never will create transformational change.

3. You can visit the website for their transformation journey at www.indiana.edu/~syschang/decatur/index.html.

4

Chaos Theory and the Sciences of Complexity: Foundations for Transforming Education

Charles M. Reigeluth

OVERVIEW

Chaos and complexity theories offer change leaders concepts and principles that can inform their efforts to transform their school systems. In this chapter, Charles Reigeluth of Indiana University offers readers a glimpse into the world of chaos and complexity theory and offers an explanation of how these theories can inform the practice of transformational change in school systems.

THE CONTEXT FOR APPLYING CHAOS AND COMPLEXITY THEORIES IN EDUCATION

Public education in the United States is an array of highly complex systems whose behavior, or causal dynamics, has proven difficult to understand. Similarly, the process of transforming a school system is highly complex and difficult to predict or control. Chaos theory and the sciences of complexity (Gleick, 1988; Holden, 1986; Kellert, 1993; Lorenz, 1995; Nowotny, 2005; Wheatley, 1999) are branches of systems theory that were developed to help understand highly complex systems. They recognize that beneath the apparently chaotic or unpredictable behavior of a complex system lie

An earlier version of this chapter was published as Reigeluth, C. M. (2008). Chaos theory and the sciences of complexity: Foundations for transforming education. In B. Despres (Ed.), *Systems thinkers in action: A field guide for effective change leadership in education.* Leading Systemic School Improvement Series. Lanham, MD: Rowman & Littlefield Education. Used with permission.

certain patterns that can help one to both understand and, especially in the context of the theme of this book, influence the behavior of the system. This chapter begins with a summary of some of the key features of chaos theory and the sciences of complexity and then explores the ways that these theories can inform systemic transformation (paradigm change) in K–12 education in the United States and other parts of the world.

WHAT ARE CHAOS THEORY
AND THE SCIENCES OF COMPLEXITY?

Some of the key features of chaos theory and the sciences of complexity include coevolution, disequilibrium, positive feedback, perturbation, transformation, fractals, strange attractors, self-organization, and dynamic complexity. Each of these is briefly discussed next and related to school systems.

Coevolution

For a system to be healthy, it must coevolve with its environment: it changes in response to changes in its environment, and its environment changes in response to its changes. Wheatley says, "We inhabit a world that coevolves as we interact with it. This world is impossible to pin down, constantly changing" (Wheatley, 1999, p. 9). A K–12 educational system exists in a community and larger society that are constantly evolving. But how are they evolving? Toffler (1980) has identified three major waves of societal evolution. Each has been accompanied by a fundamental change of paradigm in all of our society's systems, and they provide us with examples of coevolution between educational systems and their respective environments. During the Agrarian Age, the one-room schoolhouse was the predominant paradigm of education, with its focus on tutoring and apprenticeship. During the Industrial Age, the factory model of schools became the predominant paradigm of education, with its focus on standardization and teacher-centered learning. Now, as we evolve ever deeper into the Information Age, society is undergoing just as dramatic a change as during the Industrial Revolution, and this is putting greater pressure on our educational systems to coevolve through a similarly fundamental shift in paradigm.

As our communities and society evolve deeper into the Information Age, in which knowledge work is rapidly replacing manual labor and more and more children are being raised in poverty and single-parent or dual-income households, the need for coevolution in education has become ever more urgent (Reigeluth, 1994). Banathy (1991) has pointed to a large coevolutionary imbalance between education and society, which places our society in ill health and peril. Schlechty (1990), Caine and Caine (1997), and others have pointed out that our educational systems are doing a better job than ever at what they were designed to do, but that our society is increasingly calling on them to do things they were not designed to do. Therefore, our educational systems must coevolve to meet the changing educational needs of society.

To identify how an educational system should coevolve, there are two issues we must look at. One is how its environment has changed. This includes changes in the community's educational needs, in the tools it offers to educators, and in other community (and societal) conditions that impact education, such as drugs, violence, teen pregnancy, and latchkey children. However, an educational system is not just shaped by its community; it also helps shape its community. Thus, the second issue for identifying how an educational system should coevolve is the ways the community would like its educational system to change to better reflect the values of the community and thereby to help make the community more consistent with its values. Therefore, an educational system should coevolve based on the evolving values, beliefs, and visions of the community as well as on the evolving educational needs of the community.

This brings us to the all-important question: How can coevolution be fostered in our educational systems?

Disequilibrium and Positive Feedback

According to chaos theory and the sciences of complexity, coevolution is fostered by disequilibrium and positive feedback. Equilibrium is defined as "a condition in which all acting influences are canceled by others, resulting in a stable, balanced, or unchanging system" (American Heritage Dictionary, as quoted by Wheatley, 1999, p. 76). Systems can be in a state of equilibrium, in which case minor changes or adjustments to the system are all that is necessary; or systems can be in a state of disequilibrium, in which case they approach the edge of chaos. This might lead one to believe that disequilibrium is a bad thing. However, Wheatley (1999) makes the following points:

- "I observed the search for organizational equilibrium as a sure path to institutional death" (p. 76).
- "In venerating equilibrium, we have blinded ourselves to the processes that foster life" (p. 77).
- "To stay viable, open systems maintain a state of non-equilibrium. . . . They participate in an open exchange with their world, using what is there for their own growth" (p. 78).
- "Prigogine's work demonstrated that disequilibrium is the necessary condition for a system's growth" (p. 79).

Hence, disequilibrium is one important condition for coevolution. The other is "positive feedback," which has a particular meaning in systems theory.

Systems may receive both negative and positive feedback. Negative feedback provides information about deficiencies in attaining a system's goals, so that the system can adjust its processes to overcome those deficiencies. In contrast, positive feedback provides information about opportunities for a system to change the goals that it pursues. Thus, positive feedback is information from the environment that helps a system to coevolve with its environment. Often it takes the form of perturbations (or disturbances) that cause disequilibrium in a system.

Perturbation

A perturbation is any change in a system's environment that causes disequilibrium in a system. For example, as our society in the United States has evolved into the Information Age, a new educational need that has arisen is the need for lifelong learning. Rapid change in the workplace and the new reality of multiple careers during one's life require people to be lifelong learners. To help people become lifelong learners, schools must cultivate both the desire to learn (a love of learning) and the skills to learn (self-directed learning). However, our typical Industrial Age school systems do the opposite on both counts, thereby placing stress on the environment (coevolutionary imbalance) and causing the environment to put pressure (perturbation) on the educational system to undergo fundamental change, or transformation.

Transformation

Disequilibrium creates a state in which the system is ripe for transformation, which is reorganization on a higher level of complexity. Transformation occurs through a process called "emergence," by which new processes and structures emerge to replace old ones in a system. Transformation is paradigm change and stands in contrast to piecemeal change, which leaves the structure of a system unchanged. Piecemeal change often involves finding better ways to meet the same needs, whereas transformation entails modifying the structure of a system, usually in response to new needs. Piecemeal change usually changes one part of a system (albeit perhaps a part that exists in all schools within a district) in a way that is still compatible with the rest of the system, whereas transformation (or paradigm change) entails such a fundamental change that it requires changes in other parts of the system, because the other parts are not compatible with the change.

According to Duffy, Rogerson, and Blick (2000), transformation of an educational system requires simultaneous changes in the core work processes (teaching and learning), the social infrastructure of the system (organization design, organization culture, the reward system, communications, among other variables), and the system's relationships with its external environment.

Fractals and "Strange Attractors"

Transformation is strongly influenced by "strange attractors," which are a kind of fractal (Wheatley, 1999). Fractals are patterns that recur at all levels of a system, called self-similarity. In educational systems, they can be considered "core ideas" and values or beliefs (Banathy, 1991, 1996) that guide or characterize the design of the new (transformed) system. These recurring patterns can be structural and/or behavioral—that is, they can be patterns of form and/or function, and they strongly influence, and are influenced by, complex system dynamics (Senge, 1990). One example of a fractal in education is top-down, autocratic control. On the district level of an educational system, the school board typically controls the superintendent, who controls the principals. On the building level the principals control their teachers. And on the classroom level the teachers control their students.

Another example of a fractal in education is uniformity or standardization. On the district level all elementary schools are typically supposed to be the same (equal) in such key features as policies, curriculum, methods, and assessments. On the building level all teachers at the same grade level are supposed to teach the same content at the same time with the same textbooks, again to provide "equality." On the classroom level all students in a classroom are typically supposed to learn the same thing at the same time in the same way. And even for professional development, all teachers typically engage in the same professional development activities at the same time. Top-down control and uniformity are but two of many fractals that characterize our factory model of schools. While we are beginning to see changes in some of these patterns, few would argue that they were not typical of our Industrial Age educational systems, and they are still the predominant paradigm in educational systems today.

A strange attractor is a kind of fractal that has a powerful influence over the processes and structures that emerge in a system undergoing transformation. Fractals are similar to what Dawkins called "memes," which are ideas or cultural beliefs that are "the social counterpoints to genes in the physical organism" and have the power to organize a system in a specific way (Caine & Caine, 1997, p. 33). One example of a strange attractor, or meme, in education is stakeholder empowerment or ownership, which entails providing both the freedom to make decisions, and support for making and acting on those decisions. On the district level this takes the form of the school board and superintendent empowering each building principal to experiment with and adopt new approaches to better meet students' needs and to make other important decisions (hiring, budgeting, etc.). On the building level, the principal empowers each teacher to experiment with and adopt new approaches to better meet students' needs and to participate in school policymaking and decision making. On the classroom level, the teacher empowers each student to make decisions about how to best meet her or his needs. This form of leadership at all levels entails providing guidance and support to cultivate the ability to make good decisions and act effectively on them.

A second example of a strange attractor is customization or differentiation (or diversity). On the district level, each school has the freedom to be different from other schools. On the school level, each teacher has the freedom to be different from other teachers. And on the classroom level, each student has the freedom to be different from other students (with respect to both what to learn and how to learn it). A third example is shared decision making or collaboration. On the district level, the school board and superintendent involve community members, teachers, and staff in policymaking and decision making. On the school level, the principal involves parents, teachers, and staff in policymaking and decision making. And on the classroom level, the teacher involves the child and parents in decisions and activities to promote the child's learning and development.

To become an effective strange attractor for the transformation of a school system, the core ideas and values (or beliefs) must become fairly widespread cultural norms among the stakeholders most involved with making the changes. Once that status is reached, very little planning needs to be done for the transformation to take place. Appropriate behaviors and structures will emerge spontaneously through a process called self-organization.

Self-Organization

Self-organizing systems are adaptive; they evolve themselves; they are agile (McCarthy, 2003). They require two major characteristics: openness and self-reference (Wheatley, 1999). To be open with its environment, a system must actively seek information from its environment and make it widely available within the system.

The intent of this new information is to keep the system off balance, alert to how it might need to change. An open organization doesn't look for information that makes it feel good, that verifies its past and validates its present. It is deliberately looking for information that might threaten its stability, knock it off balance, and open it to growth (Wheatley, 1999, p. 83).

But the system must go beyond seeking and circulating information from its environment; it must also partner with its environment. As Wheatley

(1999) notes, "Because it partners with its environment, the system develops increasing autonomy from the environment and also develops new capacities that make it increasingly resourceful" (p. 84).

A second characteristic of self-organizing systems is the ability to "self-reference" on the core ideas, values, or beliefs that give the organization an identity. In this way, "When the environment shifts and the system notices that it needs to change, it always changes in such a way that it remains consistent with itself. . . . Change is never random; the system will not take off in bizarre new directions." (Wheatley, 1999, p. 85).

A third characteristic is freedom for people to make their own decisions about changes. Jantsch (1980) has noted a paradoxical but profound systems dynamic: "The more freedom in self-organization, the more order" (p. 40, as cited by Wheatley, 1999, p. 87). As long as the freedom is guided by sufficient self-reference, it will allow changes to occur before a crisis point is reached in the system, thereby creating greater stability and order. Paradoxically, the system is "less controlling, but more orderly" by being self-organizing (Wheatley, 1999, p. 87). Typically, coevolution occurs through self-organization, but complex system dynamics have a powerful influence on self-organization and any resulting systemic transformation.

Dynamic Complexity

According to Peter Senge (1990), social systems have detail complexity and dynamic complexity:

> When the same action has dramatically different effects in the short run and the long, there is dynamic complexity. When an action has one set of consequences locally and a very different set of consequences in another part of the system, there is dynamic complexity. When obvious interventions produce nonobvious consequences, there is dynamic complexity. (p. 71)

System dynamics are the web of causal relationships that influence the behavior of a system at all its various levels. They help us to understand how a change in one part of an educational system is likely to impact the other parts and the outputs of the system, and to understand how a change in one part of an educational system is likely to be impacted by the other parts of the system. Dynamic complexity is captured to some extent by Senge's "eleven laws of the fifth discipline" and his "system archetypes." The laws include such general dynamics as:

- The harder you push, the harder the system pushes back.
- The easy way out usually leads back in.
- The cure can be worse than the disease.
- Faster is slower.

- Cause and effect are not closely related in time and space.
- Small changes can produce big results—but the areas of highest leverage are often the least obvious.

Senge's (1990) system archetypes include:

- "Limits to growth," in which an amplifying process that is put in motion to create a certain result has a secondary effect (a balancing process) that counters the desired result.
- "Shifting the burden," in which the underlying problem is difficult to address, so people address the symptoms with easier "fixes," leaving the underlying problem to grow worse, unnoticed until it is much more difficult, if not impossible, to fix.
- "Tragedy of the commons," in which a commonly available but limited resource is used to the extent that it becomes more difficult to obtain, which causes intensification of efforts until the resource is significantly or entirely depleted.
- "Growth and underinvestment," in which growth approaches a limit that can be raised with additional investment, but if the investment is not rapid or aggressive enough, growth will be stalled and the investment will become unnecessary.
- "Fixes that fail," in which a fix that is effective in the short run has unforeseen long-term effects that reduce their effectiveness and require more of the same fix.

Senge's laws and archetypes identify high-level or general system dynamics, but it is also important to identify the complex system dynamics at play in a particular educational system. Those dynamics are complex causal relationships that govern patterns of behavior, explain why piecemeal solutions are failing, and predict what kinds of solutions may offer higher leverage in transforming a system to better meet students' needs.

HOW CAN CHAOS THEORY AND THE SCIENCES OF COMPLEXITY INFORM THE TRANSFORMATION OF EDUCATION?

The remainder of this chapter explores the ways that chaos theory and the sciences of complexity can inform the systemic transformation of education. They can do so in two fundamental ways. First, they can help us to understand the present system of education and how it is likely to respond to changes that we try to make. Second, they can help us to understand and improve the transformation process, which is itself a complex system that educational systems use to transform themselves.

Understanding the Present System

Chaos theory and the sciences of complexity can help us to understand our present systems of education, including when each is ready for transformation, and the system dynamics that are likely to influence individual changes we try to make and the effects of those changes.

Readiness for Transformation. Chaos theory and the sciences of complexity tell us that readiness for transformation is influenced by several factors. First, there must be sufficient impetus for transformation, which is created by perturbations from outside the system that produce a state of disequilibrium in the system. That disequilibrium may be caused by either of two kinds of changes in the environment (a school system's community): ones that create problems for the system (such as dysfunctional home environments and lack of discipline in the home), or ones that present opportunities to the system (such as the Internet or other powerful technologies to support learning). Second, there must also be sufficient enablers of transformation, which are created by factors inside the system, such as "participatory" (Schlechty, 1990) or "transformational" leadership (Duffy, Rogerson, & Blick, 2000; as opposed to the Industrial Age command-and-control form of leadership—or more appropriately, management), and sufficient levels of trust within and among stakeholder groups, such as the teachers association, administration, school board, and parents.

System Dynamics. System dynamics are complex sets of causes and effects that are largely probabilistic, meaning that a "cause" increases the chances that an "effect" will take place but does not require that it must take place. The complex sets of causes and effects are also highly interactive, meaning that the extent of influence of a "cause" on an "effect" is strongly influenced by other factors, including other causes. Regarding causes, system dynamics provide us with an understanding of aspects of the current system that will likely influence the viability and durability of any given change. For example, we come to learn that high-stakes tests that focus on lower levels of learning in Bloom's taxonomy (Bloom, Krathwohl, & Masia, 1956) are likely to reduce the viability and durability of attempts by teachers to develop higher-order thinking skills, because such efforts will necessarily reduce the amount of time the teachers spend on the lower-level content, causing a decline in the high-stakes test scores. Regarding the effects of any given change, system dynamics provide us with the ability to predict the effects a change is likely to have on the outcomes of the transformed educational system, such as levels of student learning. For example, as the Saturn School of Tomorrow found (Bennett & King, 1991), allowing students to be self-directed learners can cause a reduction in "time on task" to learn the important skills and understandings, resulting in a reduction in learning.

Understanding the Transformation Process. Chaos theory and the sciences of complexity can also help us to understand and improve the transformation process in which educational systems engage to transform themselves. The transformation process is itself a complex system comprised of many subsystems, processes, and dynamics. With research and experience, we can expect to learn much about the dynamics that influence the subsystems and processes that are most likely to foster systemic transformation, but chaos theory and the sciences of complexity tell us that we cannot hope to control the transformation process (Caine & Caine, 1997; Wheatley, 1999). Caine and Caine (1997) state that "the underlying belief is that we are in charge and can control the nature of change. All the reports on how difficult it has been to change education confirm the failure of this logic" (p. 12). Chaos theory and the sciences of complexity also tell us that we can hope to influence the process through the use of such tools as strange attractors and leverage points, and that we must constantly adjust and adapt the process to the emerging, ever-changing reality of a particular educational system and its environment (Caine & Caine, 1997; Wheatley, 1999).

Strange Attractors. The most powerful strange attractors are core ideas and beliefs like those described earlier: ownership or empowerment, customization or differentiation, and shared decision making or collaboration. These core ideas stand in stark contrast to those that characterize the Industrial Age mind-set about "the real school" (Tyack & Cuban, 1995): centralization and bureaucracy, standardization (or uniformity), and autocratic (or command-and-control) management. However, to have a powerful influence on the features that emerge in the system undergoing transformation, the core ideas and beliefs must become integral parts of the mind-sets or mental models held by a critical mass of participants in the transformation process, and, therefore, they must collectively comprise the culture of the transformation process as a system. This means that the major focus of a systemic transformation process in a school district must be on helping all stakeholders to expand their mind-sets about education and to develop a set of shared core ideas and beliefs about the ideal kind of educational system they would like to have (Banathy, 1991; Caine & Caine, 1997; Reigeluth, 1993). This entails helping people to uncover the mental models that often unwittingly control their views of education and then deciding whether or not that is the way they really want their educational system to be.

Leverage Points. Leverage points can greatly facilitate the systemic transformation of educational systems. An example of a leverage point is student assessment. Our Industrial Age schools reflect the belief that the purpose of student assessment is to compare students with each other. Hence we use norm-based tests, we grade on a curve, and students become labeled as winners and losers, successes and failures. In contrast, if we want all children to succeed (no children left behind), then the purpose of assessment should be to compare students with a standard of attainment, so that they may continue to work on a standard until it has been met. The current report card, with its list of courses and comparative grades, could be replaced by an "inventory of attainments" that are checked off as they are reached by each student. This one change could exert powerful leverage on other parts of the system, most notably the way teaching and learning occur in the classroom—leverage that might be more powerful than the forces that the rest of the system would place on the inventory of attainments to change it back to a sorting-focused assessment system. Furthermore, if appropriate strange attractors have been developed (e.g., enough stakeholders have expanded their mental models to encompass the belief that student assessment should be designed to inform learning rather than to sort students), those strange attractors will create a powerful force in support of such a compatible leverage point and against those aspects of the current system that would otherwise be working to change the assessment system back to what it was.

CONCLUSION

Just as the Industrial Revolution made the one-room school house obsolete, the information revolution has made our current factory model of schools obsolete. Our educational systems must transform themselves to better meet the dramatically changing needs of our children and communities. An understanding of chaos theory and the sciences of complexity (two recent developments in systems theory) is crucial to successfully navigate such systemic (or paradigmatic) transformation of our educational systems. Helpful concepts include coevolution, disequilibrium, positive feedback, perturbation, transformation, fractals, strange attractors, self-organization, and dynamic complexity. These concepts can help us to understand when a system is ready for transformation, and the system dynamics that are likely to influence individual changes we try to make and the effects of those changes. Furthermore, chaos theory and the sciences of complexity can help us to understand and improve the transformation process as a complex system that educational systems use to transform themselves. Strange attractors and leverage points are particularly important to help our educational systems to correct the dangerous evolutionary imbalance that currently exists.

II

MASTERING AWARENESS

The chapters in section 2 present key concepts and principles for developing competencies that will help you become masters of awareness. Mastering awareness means being aware of the paradigm, mental models, and mind-sets that influence the design and performance of your school system. You will read about paradigms, mental models, and mind-sets in chapter 5.

Mastering awareness also requires you to scan your district's external environment to identify key stakeholders, to assess their concerns about and aspirations for your school system, and to identify the essential characteristics of your district's external environment. The results of this scanning help you identify your district's strengths and weaknesses and to identify external opportunities and threats. The results of the scanning are then used to prepare your system to engage in transformational change. In chapter 6, you will read about how to scan your district's external environment.

5

Paradigms, Mental Models, and Mind-Sets: Triple Barriers to Transformational Change in School Systems

OVERVIEW

Paradigms are held solidly in place by accompanying mental models and mind-sets. Given the controlling paradigms, mental models, and mind-sets, people then devise behavioral strategies to comply with those phenomena. When enacted, the behavioral strategies create observable behavior that is rewarded when it supports the paradigms, mental models, and mind-sets, or punished when it does not. There are four dominant paradigms controlling the field of education (discussed later in this chapter) and they all need to be replaced with new paradigms better aligned with the requirements of our twenty-first-century Knowledge Age society.

Anyone with an interest in creating paradigm-shifting, frame-breaking change in America's school systems is probably familiar with the terms "paradigm," "mental models," and "mind-sets." But what exactly do those terms mean? Are they distinct phenomena? Are they interchangeable synonyms? How powerful are they? And, importantly, if they are triple barriers to transformational change, how can change leaders influence these phenomena to create a paradigm shift? This chapter offers some interpretations of the meaning of these terms and why I believe knowing how to work with them is so important for any effort to create transformational change in school systems.

PARADIGMS, MENTAL MODELS, AND MIND-SETS IN USE

Here's what we know about the four dominant paradigms controlling the field of education and their attendant mental models and mind-sets: for more than a century the American education system has been guided by four Industrial Age paradigms for how school systems are designed and for how these systems organize and deliver educational services to children. The paradigms are:

Paradigm 1: the way teachers teach and how kids learn (shift from group-based, teacher-centered instruction to personalized, learner-centered instruction), and the way support services are designed, managed, and delivered (redesigned to ensure that these services are aligned with the requirements of personalized learning);

Paradigm 2: the design of the internal social infrastructure of school systems (shift from an authoritarian, bureaucratic organization design to a collaborative, participative design; and transformation of organization culture, the reward system, job descriptions, and so on, to align with the requirements of personalized learning);

Paradigm 3: the way school systems interact with external stakeholders (move from a crisis-oriented, reactive approach to an opportunity-seizing, proactive approach);

Paradigm 4: educators' approach to change (shift from piecemeal change strategies to whole-system change strategies).

These paradigms and their allied mental models are stubbornly resistant to change. Yet there is an inescapable consequence of these paradigms, especially Paradigm 1. They leave some children behind—they always have and they always will.

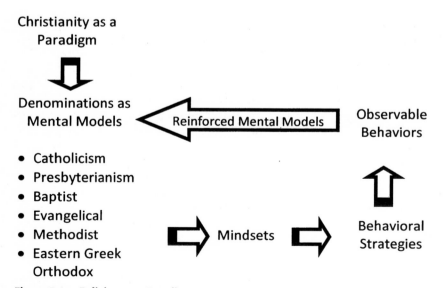

Figure 5.1.   Religion as a Paradigm

The world view alluded to above in paradigm 1 is called the Industrial Age paradigm. More derisively, it is called the factory model of teaching and learning. There is a growing movement in the United States to displace this world view—this paradigm—by replacing it with a world view of teaching and learning better suited to the demands of our twenty-first-century society and better suited to the learning needs, interests, and abilities of individual children. The new paradigm is sometimes called the Knowledge Age paradigm of teaching and learning. More commonly it is referred to as the Learner-Centered paradigm (see chapter 9). This new paradigm is built on the heartfelt belief that each student is one child with one mind who deserves a learning experience that is tailored to his or her personal learning needs, interests, and abilities so that he or she can achieve required standards of learning and become a successful and productive citizen in our society. Creating this kind of paradigm shift, however, is so challenging that it is quite a bit like trying to get an entire religious community to convert to a new religion.

CREATING A PARADIGM SHIFT IS LIKE CONVERTING AN ENTIRE RELIGIOUS COMMUNITY TO A NEW RELIGION

Christianity is a religious paradigm (refer to figure 5.1). Within that paradigm there are many different denominations (which are mental models); for example, Catholicism, Presbyterianism, and Evangelicalism are all Christian denominations. There are also other religious paradigms: Islam, Judaism, Hinduism, and so on.

As people practice their religious faith (their paradigm) in accordance with their denomination (their mental model), they make up their minds about how much they value their faith and their particular denomination; in other words, they develop mind-sets about their paradigm and mental model, how much they like or dislike other denominations, as well as other completely different religions (other paradigms).

Their attitudes (their mind-sets) toward their faith (their paradigm) and denomination (their mental model) motivate them to develop behavioral strategies for how to behave so that they can hold true to the tenets of their faith and denomination. As they implement their behavioral strategies, they can be observed practicing their faith and denomination in their chosen ways.

Creating a paradigm shift within this framework (paradigm, mental models, mind-sets, behavioral strategies, and observable behaviors) would require having an entire religious community (e.g., Christianity) shift to a new religion (e.g., to Islam). Can you imagine that happening? At best, it probably only would be possible to motivate individuals to change their mental models (e.g., to convert from Catholicism to Presbyterianism) or for individuals to convert to another religious paradigm (e.g., a person converting from Islam to Christianity). But getting an entire religious community to shift paradigms (to adopt a new religion) would be an extraordinary event.

Now, let's enter the world of education. The current dominant approach to designing and managing school systems in the United States is controlled by four paradigms, each of which is very much like a religion. Within the four dominant paradigms, there are various mental models that include, for example, group-based instruction; a bureaucratic organization design for school systems; a reactive, crisis-oriented approach to interacting with the external environment; and a nonsystemic, piecemeal approach to change.

As educators work within school systems designed in response to the four controlling paradigms and mental models, they make up their minds (that is, they create mind-sets) about the value of the paradigms and the mental models, and they develop mind-sets about the value or lack of value of other competing paradigms and mental models. Their attitudes (i.e., their mind-sets) toward their preferred and nonpreferred paradigms and mental models motivate them to create behavioral strategies for how to do their work in school districts. As they implement their behavioral strategies, they can be observed teaching, managing, leading, and so on, in ways that are aligned with the dominant paradigms and their preferred mental models.

Unlike a religious paradigm, it is probably easier to motivate the entire education community to convert to four new paradigms for designing and managing school systems; after all, it's happened before, when educators shifted from the Agrarian Age paradigm of schooling to the Industrial Age paradigm. Many reform-minded educators have long believed that it is time (actually, we believe it is long overdue) for the field of education to shift to the four new paradigms referred to earlier—shifts that will align school systems with the requirements of our Knowledge Age society. However, as with the religion paradigms, it may only be possible to help individual school districts break away from the prevailing Industrial Age paradigms and shift to the four new paradigms and accompanying mental models.

If we want the entire profession of education to adopt four new paradigms, this will require moving educators and policymakers toward a tipping point where the required changes gain unstoppable momentum. The field of change management suggests that tipping points are reached when about 25 percent of a population enthusiastically embraces proposed changes (Jones & Brazzel, 2006, p. 346; Rogers, 1995). Since there are more than 14,000 school systems in America, more than 3,500 of them would need to embrace the four new paradigms and their related mental models in order to reach a tipping point that would create and sustain the four required paradigm shifts for the entire field of education. Impossible? No. Challenging? Extraordinarily so!

PARADIGMS, MENTAL MODELS, AND MIND-SETS: THE ROCK-SOLID FOUNDATION OF RESISTANCE TO CHANGE

The literature on systemic change frequently includes information on paradigms, mental models, and mind-sets. The distinctions among these three phenomena, however, are unclear, and it is easy to become confused trying to sort out the meaning and importance of each one, especially since the terms are often misused as synonyms. I offer an interpretation of what these phenomena mean to me, why they are important, and how to change them. Having a clear understanding of their meaning, importance, and changeability is very important because as a single phenomenon each one is a powerful barrier to transformational change. As an interconnected triad, these phenomena can become an insurmountable and impenetrable barrier to change.

I am proposing that paradigms, mental models, and mind-sets are tightly interconnected but different. I also believe they interact to influence educators' behavioral strategies for how to succeed within their profession and in their school systems. The behavioral strategies result in observable behaviors that represent the core tenets of the controlling paradigm, mental models, and mind-sets. These three phenomena, therefore, represent theories of action (Argyris & Schön, 1978) for how to succeed within a profession, within a school district, within a team, and as individual professionals.

Paradigms, mental models, mind-sets, and behavioral strategies are what Argyris and Schön call "espoused theories of action," while observable behaviors are "theories of action in use." I also believe that paradigms, mental models, mind-sets, behavioral strategies, and observable behaviors can be organized as a hierarchy of nested theories of action as displayed in figure 5.2.

Within this nested framework, educators generate mental models that are aligned with the four dominant paradigms. This alignment reinforces and sustains the paradigms. As educators conform to the requirements of the paradigms and related mental models, they develop mind-sets (attitudes) about the value and effectiveness of the paradigms and the related mental models. The mind-sets influence educators' choice of behavioral strategies; that is, their attitudes toward the paradigms and mental models help them to devise strategies for how to do their work. As they implement their strategies, observable behavior is manifested. Successful behaviors are rewarded, which, in turn, reinforces the mind-sets, mental models, and the paradigms. This interconnectedness and reciprocal reinforcement is unavoidable and powerful.

Chapter 5

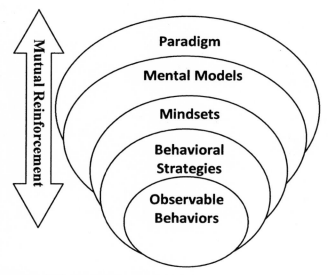

Figure 5.2. Nested Theories of Action

CLARIFYING MEANING

In the literature and in professional discourse there is often confusion about the meaning of paradigm, mental model, and mind-set. Frequently, the terms are used as interchangeable synonyms. I do not think that they are synonyms. I perceive them as distinct but interconnected phenomena. Below, I attempt to clarify the differences that I see among the phenomena.

Paradigms

Kuhn (1962) is credited with first using the term "paradigm" to characterize the dominant theories, core values, beliefs, assumptions, concepts, principles, and practices guiding the hard science professions of his time. He defined a paradigm as

> accepted examples of actual scientific practice, examples which include law, theory, application, and instrumentation together—[that] provide models from which spring particular coherent traditions of scientific research. . . . Men whose research is based on shared paradigms are committed to the same rules and standards for scientific practice. (p. 10)

Capra (1996) defined a paradigm as "a constellation of concepts, values, perceptions and practices shared by a community, which forms a particular vision of reality that is the basis of the way a community organizes itself" (p. 6).

For both of these definitions, a paradigm seems to be situated at the level of a profession, discipline, or field of study and serves as a powerful framework for helping practitioners make sense of the reality of their profession.

Barker (1992) provided another definition of paradigm. Although he defined a paradigm as "a set of rules and regulations (either written or unwritten) that does two things: (1) it establishes or defines boundaries, and (2) it tells you how to behave inside the boundaries in order to be successful" (p. 32), he seemingly situated his definition at the level of organizations and individuals. In my opinion, because of where Barker situated the concept of paradigm, his definition actually describes individual and organization-wide mental models.

In his book *The Third Wave*, Toffler (1980) described three types of societies based on the concept of "waves." Each wave pushes the older societies and cultures aside. Each "wave" was actually the dominant, controlling paradigm of its time.

- The First Wave emerged as the Agrarian Revolution replaced the Hunter-Gatherer Age. Schooling in America within the Agrarian Age paradigm was focused on learning reading, writing, and arithmetic to keep written records of planting and harvests, taxation, and barter. Advanced education was rare and usually reserved for society's elite.
- The Second Wave was the Industrial Revolution (which Toffler suggested emerged in the late 1600s and continued through the mid-1900s). Schooling in America during the Industrial Age saw the emergence of mass public education, large factory-like school systems, and group-based teaching and learning. Education during that era resulted in the emergence of an educated middle class. School systems had (and still have) a monopoly on teaching and learning for most of America's school-aged children. Academic subjects were (and still are at the secondary level) departmentalized in ways that mimicked factory assembly lines.
- Toffler described his Third Wave as the Postindustrial era. He posited that this era began in the late 1950s as most societies started moving away from the Industrial Age paradigm into the Postindustrial Age paradigm, or what he called the Third Wave Society. Other terms used to describe the Third Wave Society include Information Age, Knowledge Age, "Digital Age" (Head, 2005), and the "Conceptual Age" (Pink, 2006).

MENTAL MODELS

The concept of mental models was substantially defined by Craik (1943). He said, "the mind constructs 'small-scale models' of reality that it uses to anticipate events, to reason, and to underlie explanation" (cited in Johnson-Laird, Girotto, & Legrenzi, 1998, introduction, para. 1). Johnson-Laird (1983) is another of the foremost authorities of mental model theory. He believed that people construct cognitive representations of what they learn and what they think they know. He called these representations "mental models." Senge (1990) described mental models as "deeply ingrained assumptions, generalizations, or even pictures or images that influence how we understand the world and how we take action" (p. 8).

There are four paradigms currently controlling the field of education: (1) the Industrial Age paradigm guiding teaching and learning, (2) the Industrial Age mechanistic, bureaucratic organization design of school systems, (3) reactive, crisis-oriented relationships with the external environment, and (4) nonsystemic, piecemeal change. Given these paradigms, practitioners search for or construct mental models to guide their work in ways that conform to each paradigm. These models are held by individuals, groups, and entire school systems. Examples of mental models for each of the four paradigms are provided below.

- Examples of mental models in the field of education within the Industrial Age paradigm of teaching and learning (paradigm 1) include group-based teaching and learning, presenting a fixed amount of content in a fixed amount of time, teachers working center stage in classrooms, and so on.
- Examples of the controlling mental models for designing the internal social infrastructure of school systems (paradigm 2) include treating teachers as employees that need close supervision, centralized administrative services, an organization culture that punishes innovation and excellence, an organization design that is mechanistic and bureaucratic, and reward systems that reinforce mediocrity.
- Examples of the dominant mental models in education for interacting with the external environment (paradigm 3) include crisis-oriented school public relations, not allowing direct telephone calls or e-mail correspondence to senior line administrators, and perceiving external stakeholders as nuisances rather than as resources.
- Examples of the prevailing mental models for creating change in school districts (paradigm 4) include high school reform, curriculum reform, and a mixed bag of other "quick-fixes." The most famous, or perhaps infamous, mental model for change in contemporary school systems in the United States is the No Child Left Behind law.

All of the above mental models, and others not identified, often have the unintentional outcome of preserving the four dominant paradigms, and they exert significant influence on the behavior of school systems and the educators who work in them. Further, because the four dominant paradigms are so pervasive and because their related mental models are so widely practiced, it is extraordinarily difficult for educators to think outside the boundaries formed by the paradigms and mental models.

Two Categories of Mental Models

I also believe that there are two categories of mental models: organization-wide and personal. A school district's organization-wide mental model is found in its mission and vision statements and in its organization culture. Organization-wide mental models are often manifested as "groupthink" (Janis, 1972). Personal mental models are found in the minds of individual teachers, administrators, and support staff, and these are manifested in behavioral strategies and observable behaviors.

Organization-wide mental models. An organization-wide mental model is a collective representation of what a school system stands for and how it accomplishes its goals. An organization-wide mental model is embodied in a school system's internal social infrastructure (which includes organization design, organization culture, reward systems, job descriptions, and communication patterns). It is also reflected in its relationships with the outside world. The essential elements of a school system's controlling mental models are also captured in the district's mission and vision statements. Like their counterparts (individual mental models), organization-wide mental models are not easily described in words because some of what the models represent is at an intuitive level. Organization-wide mental models for school districts are usually constructed around three main themes:

- People served by the district (e.g., we educate the poorest students)
- The role of the school district (e.g., we provide a critically important educational and social service to parents)
- The nature of school district activities (e.g., we are the "drivers" of societal change)

Arango (1998) talked about the subtle but powerful role of organization-wide mental models. He said that outside an organization, there are many wonderful ideas, opportunities, needs, aspirations, and so on. Organization-wide mental models, according to Arango, filter all this information and . . .

- block it out all together—nothing gets in;
- let some of the information in, but only after modifying the information to support the existing organization-wide mental model; or
- let information get in unchanged only if it clearly fits the organization's existing mental model.

I believe there are four subcategories of organization-wide mental models. Each is briefly described below.

1. *Functional organization-wide mental models.* A functional organization-wide mental model, although flawed, is accurate enough to help an organization function effectively. An example of a functional organization-wide mental model would be found in a school district's management philosophy stating, "Our district is a system. In a system the various parts interact to produce outcomes. Some outcomes will be desirable and others will be undesirable. Undesirable outcomes should not be examined in isolation. Instead, we must examine the total system to identify multiple cause-and-effect relationships that contribute to the undesirable outcomes."

2. *Dysfunctional organization-wide mental models.* A dysfunctional organization-wide mental model is one that produces unintentional negative consequences. An example of a dysfunctional organization-wide mental model in a school district would be found in an organizational culture built upon the belief that "Teachers are employees who need close supervision, with very little autonomy to make decisions about how they do their work." This mental model is dysfunctional because it is intended to put managerial control into the hands of a few with the intention of increasing organizational effectiveness and efficiency, but often it unintentionally creates a climate of distrust, dissatisfaction, and demotivation among teachers and decreases organization effectiveness and efficiency.

3. *Incomplete organization-wide mental models.* An incomplete organization-wide mental model is one that has some correct information, but other important details are missing. An example of an incomplete organization-wide mental model would be found in a school district's vision statement where it is stated, "Our district is a learning community." This basic mental model may be correct, but it is insufficient because of its lack of details.

4. *Wrong organization-wide mental models.* A totally wrong organization-wide mental model would be found in a school board philosophy stating, "There is only one way to manage a school district." This mental model is wrong because, obviously, there are many different ways to manage a school district.

Personal mental models. An example of a personal mental model is found in a teacher's response to the statement "Effective classroom teaching is . . ." Every teacher should have a personal mental model that defines effective classroom teaching. Elements of this mental model might include communication skills, classroom management, and learning styles.

A teacher's mental model of effective classroom teaching guides his work. When asked to describe his mental model for effective teaching, a teacher may not be able to provide a detailed description of that model and will focus instead on its general features. The more abstract and vague the mental model is, the less likely it is that the teacher's mental model will be effective for guiding his work.

I also believe there are four subcategories of personal mental models: functional, dysfunctional, incomplete, and wrong. Each one is briefly described below.

1. *Functional personal mental models.* A functional personal mental model is one that, although flawed in some way, provides relatively effective guidance to a practitioner. An example of a functional mental model would be when a principal attends a training workshop on how to use clinical supervision with teachers. When she returns to her school she says to herself, "Okay, I know the stages of clinical supervision, I know what to do in each stage, and I know what to expect during the entire process." That knowledge represents her mental model of clinical supervision, and although it is probably not 100 percent accurate, it is sufficient for providing clinical supervision in a relatively effective way.

2. *Dysfunctional personal mental models.* A dysfunctional personal mental model is one that produces unintended negative outcomes. For example, a teacher says, "I don't have to worry about doing a detailed lesson plan. I have the big picture in mind and I know where I'm going with my lessons. Developing lesson plans is just an empty ritual with no real meaning." This is a dysfunctional mental model because it unintentionally results in inferior instructional planning, which in turn affects student learning.

3. *Incomplete personal mental models.* Incomplete personal mental models are partially correct, but lack other information that might be needed to make them more effective. For example, a curriculum specialist might think, "Whole-language reading instruction is a wonderful way for children to learn how to read and understand language [this would be the correct information]." But, what may be missing is knowledge of what it takes to use this approach effectively.

4. *Wrong personal mental models.* Wrong mental models are not incomplete and not dysfunctional. They are just plain wrong. For example, a teacher thinks, "Student misbehavior should be ignored. When I see it, I'll ignore it. It will pass and the children will like me for doing that." This is a totally wrong mental model for managing classroom behavior. Its use would result in serious negative consequences almost every time.

Changing Mental Models

Before educators and their school systems can learn new mental models, they have to unlearn what they think they already know. In some way, they have to come to the realization that they can no longer rely on their current knowledge, beliefs, and methods. People can unlearn what they think they know by engaging in structured and managed transformative learning activities.[1]

Transformative learning. Kegan (2000) identified two types of learning in adults—informative and transformative. Informative learning focuses on developing and deepening knowledge and skills. Transformative learning changes how we know—it creates a fundamental change in our world views. Transformative learning is a learning process of "becoming critically aware of one's own tacit assumptions and expectations and those of others, and assessing their relevance for making an interpretation" (Mezirow, 2000, p. 4). O'Sullivan (2003) defined transformative learning as involving: "a deep, structural shift in the basic premises of thought, feelings, and actions. It is a shift of consciousness that dramatically and irreversibly alters our way of being in the world."

When transformative learning occurs throughout an entire school system, it is called organization learning. Organization learning takes three forms: single-loop, double-loop, and deutero (Argyris & Schön, 1978). Single-loop learning happens when school system errors are detected and corrected, but the system continues with its present policies and goals. Double-loop learning happens when in addition to detecting and correcting errors, the school system questions and modifies its existing norms, procedures, policies, and objectives. Deutero-learning occurs when a school system learns how to engage in both single-loop and double-loop learning. Further, double-loop and deutero-learning focus on why organizations need to change, and on how to change them. Single-loop learning, on the other hand, focuses only on creating and accepting superficial change without questioning underlying assumptions and core beliefs.

Unlearning outdated mental models. Unlearning outdated mental models often begins when people can no longer rely on their current mental models (Duffy, 2003). The mental models influence their attitudes (mind-sets), and the mind-sets (discussed later in this chapter) blind people to other ways of interpreting events around them. People do not and will not cast aside their current mental models and mind-sets as long as the models and mind-sets seem to produce reasonable results (Kuhn, 1962). As Petroski (1992) argued, people tend to hold onto their theories until incontestable evidence, usually in the form of many successive failures, convinces them to accept new mental models. However, people and their organizations are notorious for sticking with their current mental models and mind-sets despite very poor and even disastrous results. Even after abject failure, some people will attribute their failures to some external event or person instead of recognizing the inadequacies of their own personal and organization-wide mental models and mind-sets.

Engaging in structured activities to uncover and explore mental models and mind-sets is essential if the current ones are obstacles to identifying and adopting new ones. Senge and colleagues (1994) reinforced this principle when they said,

> Because mental models are usually tacit, existing below the level of awareness, they are often untested and unexamined. They are generally invisible to us—until we look for them. The core task [for changing them] is bringing mental models to the surface, to explore and talk about them with minimal defensiveness—to help us see the pane of glass, see its impact on our lives, and find ways to reform the glass by creating new mental models that serve us better in the world. (p. 236)

Why Mental Models Are Difficult to Change

Antichange immune systems. According to Kegan and Lahey (2001), people have a built-in, antichange "immune system." I believe that this metaphor also applies to entire school systems. This immune system is dynamic and creates a powerful inclination to resist change. If this immune system can be unlocked and modified, people can then release new energy on behalf of new ways of thinking (a new paradigm and supporting mental models), believing (new mind-sets), and doing (new behavioral strategies and observable behaviors).

Kegan and Lahey believe that our internal antichange immune systems are powered by three significant forces: entropy, negentropy, and dynamic equilibrium. Each of these is briefly described below.

Entropy. Entropy is the process by which dynamic systems (such as people, organizations, mechanical systems, or solar systems) gradually fall apart and "die." Entropy is motion toward increasing disorder, randomness, and dissipation of energy (Kegan & Lahey, 2001, p. 3).

Negentropy. Mechanical and natural systems cannot stop or slow entropy. Human systems like school districts, however, do have limited potential to reverse the entropic degeneration of their systems by importing and using energy in the form of resources (human, technical, and financial). This increase in energy is the opposite of entropy, and physicists call it negative entropy, or more commonly negentropy. However, when systems engage in negentropy, it is usually for the purpose of preserving the status quo, also known as dynamic equilibrium.[2]

Dynamic equilibrium. One of the most powerful forces blocking a school district's path toward high performance is dynamic equilibrium. Dynamic equilibrium is an invisible force that tends to keep things pretty much the way they are. It is more commonly called the status quo. The forces of dynamic equilibrium play a large role in blocking change in individuals and organizations.

Dynamic equilibrium is not about standing in place or lack of motion. Dynamic equilibrium is about motion. But it is the motion of positive and negative forces working against each other, balancing each other out, and keeping everything basically locked in place. The consequences of dynamic equilibrium are reflected in the French adage, "The more things change, the more they stay the same." As most of us have experienced in our lifetimes, we produce change only to find ourselves reverting back to prechange conditions. We lose ten pounds and gain it back (along with a few extra pounds). Educators create a new vision for their school districts, and they march to the tune of the old vision. The competing forces for and against change balance each other out and keep educators and their school systems in a relatively stable state of existence.

Entropy, negentropy, and dynamic equilibrium create something in educators and their school systems that functions like an immune system in our bodies. Just as bodily immune systems fight off foreign substances, the metaphorical antichange immune system powered by entropy, negentropy, and dynamic equilibrium holds educators and their school systems in place and blocks change. This "immune system" is difficult to change because people are captives of their systems; or as Kegan and Lahey (2001) said, "We do not have them; they have us" (p. 6).

Social Infrastructure Blocks Change in Mental Models

A school district's social infrastructure is that collection of policies, procedures, organization culture, organization design, job descriptions, communication patterns, reward systems, among other things, that support (or constrain and undermine) life in an organization. Educators in school districts hold certain beliefs and specific mind-sets that are hardened by the district's internal social infrastructure. Educators then create and defend policies, procedures, decisions, and behaviors that support and reinforce their mind-sets. Further, as educators interact, all of these mind-sets are woven together to create a district-wide organization mind-set that reflects what they *think* their district stands for and how they *think* it should function as a system. This organization-wide mind-set then takes on a degree of rigidity that makes it very difficult for educators to think, believe, and do things in ways that do not align with the dominant mind-set (which is one of the key reasons why people resist innovative ideas). Change-minded educators working within a school system with this kind of internal social infrastructure often find it difficult to seek and implement innovative ideas, and it becomes challenging for them and their systems to create and sustain change.

Sometimes organizations change in spite of their internal social infrastructure. Tushman, Newman, and Romanelli (1986) commented on this phenomenon by observing that organizations develop over long periods of convergent, incremental change that are punctuated by brief periods of "frame-breaking change" (another term for transformational change). They suggested that frame-breaking change occurs in response to or in anticipation of major changes in an organization's environment. Starbuck (1996), however, believed that frame-breaking change happened differently. He suggested that big changes happen when people and organizations unlearn their old mental models and then suddenly undertake breathtaking change to enact their new mental models; that is, change is a revolutionary response to a dramatic and sudden disorienting dilemma that motivates people to examine critically their thinking, believing, and doing (Mezirow, 2000). This "revolutionary response" is also known as punctuated equilibrium (Eldredge & Gould, 1972).

A social infrastructure that supports unlearning, which is essential for transformational change to occur, can be intentionally and effectively designed. Starbuck (1996) identified the essential characteristics of an "unlearning environment." He believed that these unlearning environments should:

1. create dissatisfaction with the dominant mental models;
2. introduce new mental models as "experiments," which reduces the fear of failure;
3. state the desirable outcomes of exploring new mental models without expecting people to start applying the mental models "right now," which, again, reduces the fear of failure;
4. encourage and consider dissent and dialogue;
5. reconcile differences between old and new mental models by seeking commonalities and complementarities;
6. encourage and actively seek the views of "outsiders"; and
7. encourage people to be skeptical of all mental models, not just the old ones.

CONSTRUCTING NEW MENTAL MODELS

The process of constructing new mental models is a knowledge-creation process. Nonaka and Takeuchi (1995) described a knowledge-creation process for organizations. The core elements of their knowledge-creation process are what they called tacit and explicit knowledge. Tacit knowledge is difficult to describe using words. It is often situated at an intuitive level. For example, a teacher may be "famous" for her ability to manage classroom behavior. But when asked to describe in words how and why she is so successful she replies, "I don't know. I just do it." Explicit knowledge, on the other hand, is easily described using words. For example, when asked how to solve a quadratic equation, a mathematics teacher describes the formula and solution steps accurately and in detail.

Nonaka and Takeuchi's knowledge creation process, as noted above, was created for use by organizations. Their methodology for creating organization-wide knowledge begins by engaging individual experts in structured activities to make their tacit expertise (their tacit knowledge) explicit. The best of that explicit knowledge is then transformed into organization-wide explicit knowledge (in other words, it is shared throughout the organization). Then, steps are taken to embed that explicit organization-wide knowledge deep within the organization's memory, thus making it organization-wide tacit knowledge. The goal of this process is to create functional organization-wide mental models that are sustainable.

MIND-SETS

Given the four controlling paradigms in the field of education (described in earlier chapters and discussed once again in this chapter) and related mental models, individuals, teams, and entire school districts begin to make up their minds about what works and what does not work and about what has merit and value and what does not. "Making up one's mind" is another way of saying that a person's mind is set; in other words, a mind-set has been established. These mind-sets are, in fact, really attitudes hammered in hard by a school system's internal social infrastructure. These attitudes can be either positive or negative.

As a mind-set hardens it creates a predisposition to think, believe, and do things in a particular way. Mind-sets also create powerful incentives for individuals and groups to behave in ways that are congruent with the controlling paradigm and mental models.

Why Mind-Sets Need to Shift

When first-order change (piecemeal continuous improvement) is required, mind-sets can motivate people to resist those changes. When second-order change (discontinuous, paradigm-shifting, transformational change) is required, the change-resistant power of mind-sets increases exponentially. Increasing the malleability of hardened mind-sets requires the application of third-order change principles (D. Zimmerman, 1998).

Changing mind-sets can be particularly challenging for educators and policymakers who are successful within the old paradigm. These people, I believe, are some of the most resistant to discontinuous transformational change because that kind of change threatens to undermine and displace everything they know, believe, and do. This level of fierce resistance to shifting paradigms is captured in an observation by Yasuo (1993), who said,

> When the rise of a new theory suggests a change of direction in scholarship, history attests to a common pattern of reaction among the established intellectual community. There is often a flat dismissal or at best vehement attack in order to kill and bury that theory, especially if it signals an imminent as well as immanent possibility of shaking the secure and comfortable foundation upon which the existing paradigm of thinking rests. (pp. ix–x)

Starbuck (1996) also observed that professionals are among the most resistant to new ideas and to evidence that contradicts their current mental models. This kind of resistance has several sources. Professionals must specialize, and their specialized niches can lock people in place (Beyer, 1981). Because professionals accrue social status in organizations and, in some cases, earn high incomes, they have much to lose if there are significant changes in their fields of expertise. This state of being "blinds" them from seeing opportunities to create change (Armstrong, 1985).

Creating Conditions That Can Shift Mind-Sets

Howard Gardner (2004) described seven "levers" for changing mind-sets (see figure 5.3). These levers can be used to create communication strategies for persuading educators to open their minds to consider the four new paradigms for creating and sustaining breakthrough performance for their school systems. As a reminder, the four paradigm shifts, which were described earlier, are:

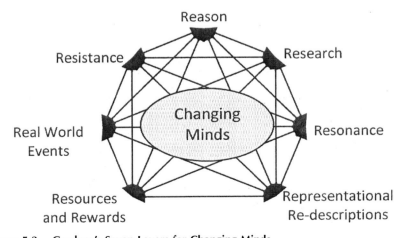

Figure 5.3.   Gardner's Seven Levers for Changing Minds

Paradigm Shift 1: Core work (shift from group-based teaching and learning to personalized teaching and learning) and support work (from isolated, disconnected services to a coordinated service orientation that is aligned with the new core work);

Paradigm Shift 2: Internal social infrastructure (shift from a mechanistic, bureaucratic organization design to an organic, participative organization design; and related shifts in organization culture, reward systems, job descriptions, and so on);

Paradigm Shift 3: Relationships with external stakeholders (shift from a reactive, crisis-oriented paradigm to a proactive, opportunity-seeking paradigm); and

Paradigm Shift 4: Approach to creating and sustaining change (shift from piecemeal change to whole-system change).

Here's a summary of each of Gardner's seven levers. He advises change agents to use all seven levers in concert because none of them are effective in isolation.

Lever 1: Reason—Reason involves using logic, analogies, and other rational processes to persuade others to consider new ideas. Rational explanations create a foundation for persuasive communication because they answer the question "Why should I change my mind?"

Lever 2: Research—The "Lever 1: reason" should always be backed up with data from research. Data offer proof of concept and also answer the question "Why should I change my mind?"

Lever 3: Resonance—Although reason and research create the foundation for persuasive communication, many people make their final decisions about changing their minds based on how they feel about a new idea. Resonance is about communicating with people at the "feeling" or intuitive level. While reason and research may be solid, it will be insufficient for changing people's minds if they do not care about what you want them to consider. It is not enough to convince people that they should open their minds to new ideas—they must also be inspired to open their minds.

Structuring communication to resonate with people is not limited to the content of the message. The people delivering the message must also resonate with the audience. It is very important to engage the service of messengers who are likable, credible, and who have a common bond with the audience.

Lever 4: Representational Redescriptions—This lever is Gardner's way of saying that you need to present information in a number of different ways using different media. Unknowingly, many advocates of transformational change structure their messages in ways that are best for them, and they do not think about the communication needs of their audience. This is a serious communication error because people have different learning preferences and language competencies. Communication breaks down quickly when there is a mismatch between the structure and content of a message and the audience's information processing and language needs.

One of the significant obstacles to structuring a message in a variety of ways is what Heath and Heath (2007, p. 20) call the "curse of knowledge." The curse of knowledge afflicts professionals with deep and broad knowledge of a subject. When the curse of knowledge is in play, experts cannot imagine what it is like not to have their specialized knowledge.

Given their sophisticated knowledge, experts afflicted by the curse of knowledge assume that others will understand what they know in the same way they do. They present their knowledge using their abstract concepts and specialized terms of art. For example, a presenter talking to educators about the need to transform school systems to provide students with personalized learning experiences might say: "Instructional misalignment with the idiosyncratic learning needs of children creates academic failure." Why not say, "Instruction that is not designed to meet the personal learning needs of children will cause some children to fail"? The inability or unwillingness to describe ideas or beliefs in plain English using concrete and common terms is a significant communication error that results in a lack of support for new ideas.

Lever 5: Resources and Rewards—When trying to influence people's mind-sets about new ideas or mental models, there may be incentives that can be offered to stimulate people's interest in considering those new ways of doing things. The incentives, of course, must be ethical, legal, and appropriate.

Lever 6: Real-World Events—Sometimes there are powerful events that can shift mind-sets on a large scale. In the field of education, these kinds of powerful events are rare and often produce the opposite effect. For example, hegemonic federal legislation called No Child Left Behind was (and continues to be) a powerful legislative event, but the resultant changes being made in the field of education are producing unintended consequences (e.g., it has driven non-NCLB content out of instructional programs, and it has not resulted in substantial improvements to teaching and learning).

An example of a large-scale, real-world event that transformed education in a positive way was the arrival of the Industrial Age. It transformed education from the Agrarian Age paradigm for educating children to the Industrial Age paradigm for schooling that provided American society with an excellent and extraordinarily successful way to educate the working class and millions of new immigrants. However, education must now create and sustain four paradigm shifts that are aligned with the requirements of the Knowledge Age. Making these shifts, I believe, will also result in substantial benefit to our children, our communities, and our nation.

Other smaller scale real-world events that could influence educators' mind-sets about the required four paradigm shifts described earlier might be found in the success stories of educators, schools, and school systems that are implementing the mental models associated with the four paradigm shifts. These stories are examples of what Gardner calls "Lever 3—resonance." Sharing these success stories can increase the malleability of educators' mind-sets about those four paradigms and their related mental models.

Lever 7: Resistances—Dynamic equilibrium, as noted earlier, is a systems theory concept that in simple terms means stability. Individuals, groups, and organizations like stability. Sometimes stability is called the status quo, or, more colloquially, it's called "the way things are." Individuals, groups, and organizations tend to like the way things are and they naturally resist change.

BEHAVIORAL STRATEGIES AND OBSERVABLE BEHAVIORS

Behavioral Strategies

Given the four dominant paradigms in the field of education, their related mental models, and the mind-sets supporting the paradigm and mental models, individuals, groups, and entire school systems begin to devise strategies for how to behave within the dominant paradigms and about how to effectively implement their chosen mental models. These strategies are devised to help educators and their school systems succeed within the dominant paradigm by deciding about how they should work, when they should work, with whom they should collaborate to do the work, and so on. These strategies, when implemented, create observable behaviors.

Observable Behaviors

As individuals, groups, and entire school systems implement their behavioral strategies, observable behaviors are manifested. Ideally, these behaviors are clearly and unequivocally aligned with the dominant paradigm and mental models that govern the profession of education. These behaviors, when manifested effectively, move school systems toward their paradigm-driven visions.

Observable behaviors can be seen, heard, interpreted, and evaluated by others. If the observed behaviors are congruent with a school system's controlling paradigms and related mental models and mind-sets, then the people manifesting the observable behaviors are evaluated positively and rewarded. If their observed behaviors are not aligned with the controlling paradigm, mental models, and mind-sets, then these people are punished or ignored—sometimes subtly, as when an article is rejected for publication, and sometimes in embarrassingly obvious ways, like when a person is publicly denied an opportunity to serve on a powerful committee.

PARADIGM SHIFTING

As noted earlier, Kuhn (1962) used the term "paradigm" to characterize significant changes in the hard sciences of his time. He argued that scientific advancement is not evolutionary; rather, he believed scientific advancement is a relatively peaceful journey punctuated by aggressive intellectual revolutions that replace one world view with another (this view is also supported by Tushman, Newman, & Romanelli, 1986). In other words, a paradigm shift is a revolutionary change from one way of thinking (as embedded in paradigms and mental models), believing (as reflected in mind-sets), and doing (as reflected in behavioral strategies and observable behaviors) to another way. It is a revolution or disruptive transformation and does not just happen on its own; rather, for the field of education, it must be led by courageous, passionate, and visionary revolutionaries with a powerful and compelling vision for creating and sustaining an idealized future for America's school systems.[3]

Paradigm Shifting Strategy

As I have argued, creating a paradigm shift is no easy feat, and doing so is analogous to trying to convince an entire religious community to shift to a new religion. Let us say that we really want to create a true paradigm shift for the entire field of education. How would we do that? I believe that the initial target of paradigm-shifting efforts must be the mind-sets (or attitudes) of educators and stakeholders in the community. Our goal should be to motivate educators and stakeholders to open their minds to new possibilities, to increase the malleability of their mind-sets, and to introduce new ways of thinking, believing, and doing. A process that might help to do that is visually depicted in figure 5.4 and described below.

Phase 1: Prepare (the following activities must be completed before attempting to influence the mind-sets of educators)

1. Create simple, concrete, powerful, and compelling language to describe the four new paradigms (described earlier) and their mental models. Use Gardner's seven levers to create language that communicates to the heart and the head. Beware of the curse of knowledge, as described earlier.
2. Construct descriptions of the four new paradigms using language that satisfies the following communication principles (Heath & Heath, 2007):
   - *Principle 1: Simplicity*—language that is devoid of abstract terms and specialized jargon
   - *Principle 2: Unexpectedness*—examples that take people by surprise

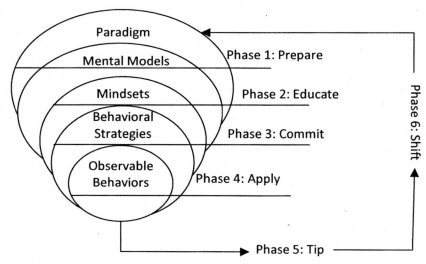

Figure 5.4.   A Paradigm Shifting Process

- *Principle 3: Concreteness*—examples and ideas that are down-to-earth and easy to understand
- *Principle 4: Credibility*—information that is backed by research or endorsed by those who have already implemented the ideas
- *Principle 5: Emotions*—information presented in ways that appeal to peoples' emotions and motivate them to care about the ideas
- *Principle 6: Stories*—information shaped into the form of stories about the successful use of the ideas
3. Design and test mental models that support the four new paradigms described earlier.
4. Design the new mental models so they are cost-effective, simple to use, and do not make educators' work lives harder.

Phase 2: Educate. Phase 1, above, focuses on preparing for phase 2. The ultimate outcome of phase 2 is to help educators open their minds to new possibilities by expanding their mind-sets. Expanding mind-sets is the absolute starting point for paradigm change because before shifting to a new paradigm, educators first need to be willing to consider the new paradigm and its supporting mental models. Willingness (or unwillingness) is consequence of a mind-set.

5. Provide educators with in-service opportunities to learn about the four new paradigms and their related mental models.
6. Demonstrate the effectiveness of the new mental models.

7. Provide access to other educators who are effectively using the new paradigms and their mental models.
8. Design and deliver educational activities that help educators learn about the philosophy, theories, concepts, principles, and research underpinning the four new paradigms and their mental models.

Phase 3: Commit

9. Influence carefully selected school systems with the capacity to engage in transformational change to commit to using the new paradigms and their mental models on a small scale (see Christensen, 2003; Christensen, Johnson, & Horn, 2008). Design the implementation of these small-scale initiatives so they do not compete head-on with the dominant paradigms (see Christensen, Johnson, & Horn, 2008, for an explanation of why this noncompetitive principle is important). Design these initiatives so they will be successful.

Phase 4: Expand

10. Gradually expand the successful initiatives created for phases 1 and 2 to include more programs within each participating school system, with the goal of achieving a tipping point for the initiatives launched in activity 9 so that they will displace the old paradigms and their mental models.

Phase 5: Tip

11. Replicate the above process (activities 1–10) in an increasing number of school systems. Use educators from transformed school districts as emissaries and advocates of the new paradigm and its mental models. This action employs Howard Gardner's (2004) resonance lever.

Phase 6: Shift

12. Always keep in mind that the paradigm-shifting goal is to reach a tipping point in the field of education (about 25 percent of all school systems) at which point a cascade of school systems shifting rapidly to the new paradigms could be triggered, which will be perceived as a sudden and dramatic revolution in thinking, believing, and doing.

CONCLUSION

The terms paradigm, mental models, and mind-sets are commonly used in the field of school improvement. The terms are often used as synonyms, but

I believe they are not synonymous. Although not synonymous, they are interconnected and they are mutually reinforced in ways that forge stiff resistance to new ways of thinking about teaching and learning, new ways of designing the internal social infrastructure of school systems, new ways of managing relationships with external stakeholders, and new ways of creating and sustaining change. This chapter described why I think these phenomena are distinct but interconnected; how they influence thinking, believing, and doing; and how to change them.

As described in this chapter, a paradigm is a set of theories, beliefs, assumptions, and so on that drive an entire profession. This seems to be the way that Thomas Kuhn (1962) first used the term to describe the phenomena that significantly influenced the hard sciences of which he was a part.

Mental models are created to support the four dominant paradigms. For example, the mental model of group-based, classroom-situated teaching and learning was created to support the Industrial Age paradigm for educating children. When mental models are used frequently and relatively successfully, they are reinforced, and educators develop hardened attitudes (mind-sets) about the value and effectiveness of the paradigms and mental models.

Mind-sets are attitudes hardened by a school system's internal social infrastructure (organization design, organization culture, the reward system, and so on). The mind-sets about the paradigms and mental models that control the design and performance of America's school systems influence educators' willingness to consider new ideas. If their existing mind-sets are hammered solidly into their hearts and minds, they will resist new ideas that challenge the controlling paradigms, mental models, and mind-sets. Therefore, any effort to create and sustain frame-breaking transformational change must first focus on opening the hearts and minds of educators so they become willing to consider new ways of teaching and learning, new ways of designing the internal social infrastructure of their school systems, new ways of interacting with external stakeholders, and new ways of creating and sustaining change.

The four controlling paradigms and their mental models influence mind-sets. The paradigms, mental models, and mind-sets, in turn, influence the design or selection of behavioral strategies that guide educators' performance in their systems. When implemented, the behavioral strategies create observable behavior.

When the behaviors are successful, and if they are clearly aligned with the dominant paradigms and mental models, educators are rewarded. The rewards stimulate motivation to continue thinking, believing, and doing things in ways that are aligned with the dominant paradigm and mental models. This creates an antichange immune system (Kegan & Lahey, 2001) within individuals, groups, and entire school districts.

The power of four dominant paradigms, their concomitant mental models, and associated mind-sets should not be underestimated. These phenomena are significant sources of resistance to simple, first-order change. They are turbocharged resisters when confronted with proposals for second-order transformational change.

NOTES

1. Douglas Doblar, a Ph.D. student in the Department of Instructional Systems Technology at Indiana University, Bloomington, introduced me to the concept of transformative learning in a research study he coauthored with Wylie Easterling and Charles Reigeluth titled "Formative Research on the School System Transformation Protocol: The Development of Transformational Leadership Capacity in a School District's Systemic Change Process" (unpublished).

2. Despite the restorative power of negentropy, all systems eventually reach the upper limits of their performance capacity, which becomes a "performance ceiling" (Handy, 1998; Branson, 1987, n.d.). As long as improvement efforts focus on making small adjustments to the current system by applying principles of continuous improvement, a school system will never break through its performance ceiling, and entropy will recur. The only way to create significant improvement, then, is to break through the performance ceiling to create a "brand new" system through transformation.

3. For example, the FutureMinds: Transforming American School Systems initiative sponsored by the Association for Educational Communications and Technology (www.futureminds.us).

6

Scanning the External Environment

OVERVIEW

One of the core premises of this book is that to lead transformational change effectively, change leaders need to be masters of awareness, masters of deliberate intention, and masters of methodology (the other core premise is that transformational change like that advocated in this book requires revolution—not evolution). Each set of competencies (awareness, deliberate intention, and methodology) has key knowledge, skills, and dispositions. This chapter is about one activity within the "mastery of awareness" competency set; that is, matching organization design to environmental characteristics.

THREE PATHS TO TRANSFORMATION

Earlier, I shared with you a three-path metaphor for creating and sustaining transformational change in school systems. Additional information about the three paths is presented later in this chapter. The three paths are:

- Path 1—transform core and support work processes
- Path 2—transform internal social infrastructure
- Path 3—transform environmental relationships

Unlike real-world paths, these change paths can be traversed simultaneously because they represent cognitive pathways. Each one is not a linear sequence of trail markers that are used to navigate the terrain of transformational change. Further, the pathways are serpentine with many switchback trails. Instead, thinking along the pathways unfolds something like this:

> If we want to introduce personalized learning into our school system (Path 1), what kind of organization design and reward system (Path 2) do we need to have in place? What level of political and financial support do we need from our external stakeholders (Path 3)? And if we want to get political and financial support, what kinds of changes do we need to make to our system (Paths 1 and 2)?

Making changes along only one path without considering what must change along the other two paths almost guarantees failed transformational change. Thinking along all three paths simultaneously is what system designers call "joint optimization" (e.g., see Cummings & Worley, 2001, p. 353).

"Mastery of Awareness" is an element of Path 3: transform environmental relationships. Path 3 is particularly important because stakeholders in the external environment have political influence, and they control the resources school systems need to operate. The external environment also contains multiple opportunities and significant threats that can affect the success of a school system's transformation. If a school system does not have the political support or the resources needed to engage effectively in transformational change, and if that system is blindsided by unanticipated threats or frustrated by missed opportunities, then efforts to transform that school system will certainly fail. Therefore, it is critically important to prepare for whole-system transformation by engaging in an environmental scan to become aware of key stakeholders, to assess their concerns and aspirations for the district, to determine which stakeholders' issues should be addressed, to evaluate their level of support for or resistance to transformational change, and to identify potential external threats and opportunities.

THREE PATHS TO SYSTEMIC TRANSFORMATIONAL CHANGE

We know a lot about how to transform entire systems (e.g., Ackoff, 1981; Banathy, 1996; King & Frick, 1999; Pasmore, 1988; Pava, 1983a, 1983b; Reigeluth, 1994). One of the core principles of whole-system transformation that emerges from this literature is that three sets of key organizational variables must be changed simultaneously (e.g., see Ackoff, 2001; Duffy, 2003; Duffy, Rogerson, & Blick, 2000; Pasmore, 1988). The principle of simultaneous change is called "joint optimization."

The three sets of key organizational variables referred to in the previous paragraph are characterized as change paths. The general terrain features of each change path are briefly described below.

Path 1: Transform a District's Core and Support Work Processes

Core work is the most important work of any organization. In school districts, core work is teaching and learning that is traditionally organized as a preK–12th grade instructional program (Duffy, 2002, 2003). Core work also includes what Adleman and Taylor (2010) call "learning supports." Adleman and Taylor argue that a comprehensive system of learning supports should be considered part of the core work process because these supports enable learning by addressing barriers to learning and teaching and by reengaging disconnected students. Learning supports are essential to ensuring that all students have an equal opportunity to succeed at school. Learning supports include the resources, strategies, and practices that provide physical, social, emotional, and intellectual supports to address barriers to learning and teaching and reengage disconnected students.

Core work is maintained and enriched by support work. In school districts there are two categories of support work: academic support work and nonacademic support work. Academic support work roles include instructional technologists, librarians, district-level and building-level administrators, supervisors, and other education specialists.

Nonacademic support work includes cafeteria workers, janitors, bus drivers, and others. Although these areas of a school system can be easily be overlooked or perceived as unimportant to the transformation of a school system, they should not be. The cleanliness of a building, the attractiveness of its grounds, the experience of riding on a school bus, and the quality and attractiveness of food served in the system's school-based cafeterias all have an effect on a child's learning experiences.

Although academic and nonacademic support work processes are important to the success of a school district, they are not the most important work. Teaching and learning are the most important work processes, and they must be elevated to that status if a school system wants to increase its overall effectiveness. Further, many believe that teaching and learning must shift from traditional classroom teaching to learner-centered education (see McCombs, 2008), which has some of the following characteristics:

- Personalized, self-directed learning
- Project- and problem-based activities
- Flexible blocks of study and activity times
- Multidisciplinary curricula with team teaching
- Teachers as mentors and facilitators
- Technologies used as essential resources for teaching and learning
- Performance-based assessment of student learning with mastery as the goal

While transforming student learning is the primary goal of Path 1: Transform core and support work processes, focusing only on improving student learning is a piecemeal approach to change. A teacher's knowledge and literacy is probably one of the more important factors influencing student learning (e.g., see Sanders & Rivers, 1996). So, taking steps to improve teacher learning must also be part of any school district's effort to transform its core work process.

While improving student and teacher learning are two important goals of improving core work in a school district, this is also a piecemeal approach to improving a school district, because a school system is a knowledge-creating organization and it is, or should be, a learning organization. Professional knowledge must be created and embedded in a school district's operational structures, and organizational learning must occur if a school district wants to develop and maintain the capacity to provide children with a quality education. So, school system learning (i.e., organizational learning) must also be part of a district's transformation strategy.

Path 2: Transform a District's Internal Social Infrastructure

Improving core and support work processes to improve learning for students, faculty and staff, and the whole school system is an important goal, but it is still a piecemeal approach to change. It is possible for a school district to have a fabulous learner-centered curriculum with extraordinarily effective instructional technology supporting it but still have an internal social infrastructure (which includes organization culture, organization design, communication patterns, power and political dynamics, reward systems, and so on) that is demotivating, dissatisfying, and demoralizing for teachers. Demotivated, dissatisfied, and demoralized teachers cannot and will not use a fabulous learner-centered curriculum in remarkable ways. Demotivated, dissatisfied, and demoralized support staff cannot and will not perform their duties in value-adding ways. So, in addition to improving how the work of a district is done, transformation efforts must focus simultaneously on improving a district's internal social infrastructure.

The social infrastructure of a school system needs to be redesigned at the same time the core and support work processes are redesigned because it is important to ensure that the new social infrastructure and the new work processes complement each other. The best way to ensure these complementarities is to make simultaneous improvements to both elements of a school system.

Path 3: Transform a District's Relationship with Its External Environment

A school district is an open system. An open system is one that interacts with its environment by exchanging a valued product or service in return for needed resources. If change leaders want their district to become a high-performing school system, they need to have a positive and supportive relationship with stakeholders in their external environment. But they cannot wait until they transform their district to start working on these relationships. They need positive and supportive relationships shortly before they begin making important changes within their district. So, they have to start improving their district's relationships with key external stakeholders as they prepare their school system to begin its transformation journey. This happens during phase 1 of the School System Transformation Protocol described later in chapter 12.

Hopefully this three-path metaphor makes sense, because the principle of simultaneous improvement along the three paths is absolutely essential for effective systemic transformational change (e.g., see F. E. Emery, 1977; Pasmore, 1988; Trist, Higgin, Murray, & Pollack, 1963). This systemic transformational approach to educational change, while considerably more difficult than piecemeal change, is possible and is indeed being carried out successfully in all kinds of organizations, including the Metropolitan School District of Decatur Township, Indiana.[1] Furthermore, many of us who advocate transformational change believe this is the only approach that can create and sustain breakthrough improvements in student learning in our twenty-first-century knowledge society.

SCHOOL DISTRICTS AS COMPLEX SYSTEMS

School districts are complex systems that are responsible for performing the extraordinarily complex task of educating children who come to school with a handbarrow full of diverse learning styles, needs, interests, and abilities. As an organization, a school system is also a collection of parts. We call those parts schools, programs, curricula, and so on. Each part performs an important function within the system, but no part by itself can do what the entire system does (see Russell Ackoff's systems characteristics in chapter 2). Further, the relationship between and among parts creates synergistic behavior that represents the overall performance of the system.

A common and popular approach to improving school systems is called school-based improvement, which is a subset of school-based management. This approach is extraordinarily resistant to the idea of whole-system change. Proponents argue that the only way to improve teaching and learning in a school district is to do that one school, one classroom at a time.

The science of complex systems (e.g., see Bar-Yam, 2004) suggests, however, that the school-based improvement approach alone cannot and never will succeed. Bar-Yam (2004) suggests that when parts of a system are independent, those parts are free to respond to independent demands from the environment. However, when the demands on one part of a system are linked to the demands on other parts, those parts will only perform well if they are connected to each other (p. 49). Since a child's education is more than what he or she learns in a particular grade or classroom, it is logical to argue on the basis of complex systems theory that all of the parts of a school system are and must be connected to each other. Schools, programs, and curricula must become increasingly interdependent rather than increasingly independent. But school-based improvement and school-based management increase independence and decrease interdependence—just the opposite of what's required for effective system performance.

Even though more interdependence is required to improve teaching and learning, that interdependence should not be so tight as to exclude some independent actions in classrooms and schools. There must be an artful balance between independence and interdependence. An analogy I use to illustrate this point is found in a child's toy called a "slinky." A slinky is a continuous coil of metal (or plastic). When set at the top of stair and nudged, it slinks its way down the steps. The lead segment of the coil falls first. Each subsequent coil segment follows on. The coil is flexible and adapts to the stair as it makes its way through its environment (the stair). The key to the success of the slinky is found both in its flexibility and in its integrity as a whole coil. In much the same way, a school system (the coil) must be designed with sufficient flexibility to allow individual schools and classrooms to experience some degree of independence while maintaining its integrity as a whole system.

PATH 3: TRANSFORMING ENVIRONMENTAL RELATIONSHIPS

All systems exist within a broader environment, and complex systems interact with and form relationships with elements of their external environments. As noted earlier, to be effective, the complexity of a system must match the complexity of its environment (Bar-Yam, 2004). This principle suggests that transforming a school system's relationship with its external environment is critical to the success of a school system's transformation journey and that the quality of that relationship will affect the future performance of the system.

The field of organization theory and design (e.g., Daft, 2006; Burton, 2006) offers abundant and time-tested concepts and principles for assessing a system's external environment and for matching a system's organization design to its environment. Examples of organization theory and design concepts and principles relevant to a school system's external environment are highlighted below.

General Environment versus Task Environment

General Environment. The general environment for all school systems is composed of the national society, a geographical region, the national economy, international events, and so on. Components of this broad environment can have a significant impact on a school system, but a single school system has no opportunity to exert any influence on its general external environment.

The relationship between a system and its general environment is unidirectional (from the outside-in), which means that the general environment affects the system but the system cannot affect the general environment. Even though a school system cannot influence its general environment (e.g., the national economy, societal change), change leaders need to conduct a scan of the general environment to anticipate threats and identify opportunities that may emerge from the general environment. With that knowledge, they can then devise strategies to deal effectively with the consequences of the threats or to seize the opportunities.

Task Environment. The task environment for a school system is a subset of its general environment. The task environment is composed of individuals, groups, and organizations that have a stake in the performance of a school system (thus, they are called stakeholders). The task environment also is composed of other variables, such as community demographics, availability of scarce resources, local property values, and so on. Further, the relationship between a system and its task environment is reciprocal, with multidirectional opportunities for mutual influence. Therefore, the quality of the relationship between a system and its task environment is very important, because that relationship will affect the system's performance and impact the availability of the technical, financial, and human resources that the system needs to "live."

The external environment for all organizations has ten sectors as illustrated in figure 6.1. That part of the environment that a system can influence is called its task environment or domain. In the figure, the boundary of a school system's domain is depicted as a dark, irregular band. Everything outside the system's domain is part of the general environment. School systems are unable to influence the general environment, but they can be significantly affected by it.

Examples of what can be found in a school district's general and task environments include:

1. Professional Field Sector: the profession of education and its controlling paradigms, mental models, and mind-sets
2. Suppliers Sector: suppliers of books, equipment, and so on
3. Human Resources Sector: labor market, employment agencies, and universities that prepare future teachers and administrators

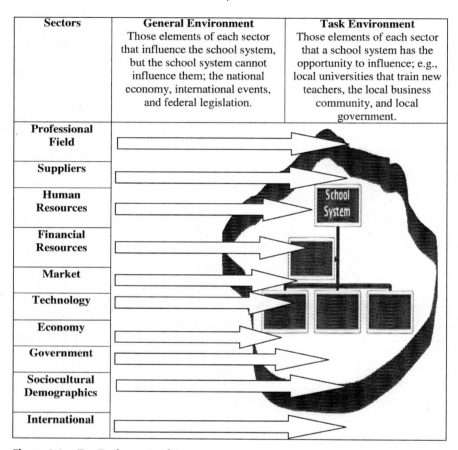

Sectors	**General Environment** Those elements of each sector that influence the school system, but the school system cannot influence them; the national economy, international events, and federal legislation.	**Task Environment** Those elements of each sector that a school system has the opportunity to influence; e.g., local universities that train new teachers, the local business community, and local government.
Professional Field		
Suppliers		
Human Resources		
Financial Resources		
Market		
Technology		
Economy		
Government		
Sociocultural Demographics		
International		

Figure 6.1.   Ten Environmental Sectors

4. Financial Resources Sector: availability of local, state, federal funds, and local property taxes that support education
5. Market Sector: the local community served by the district
6. Technology Sector: research on teaching and learning, computer technology, instructional management systems, and information management systems
7. Economic Conditions Sector: recession, unemployment rate, inflation rate, rate of return on investments, and local economic conditions
8. Government Sector: city, state, and federal laws and regulations, taxes, government services, and the state and federal departments of education
9. Sociocultural Sector: demographic data about the age, values, beliefs, education, religion, work ethic, and so on of the community served by the district

10. International Sector: student exchange programs and "sister" schools in foreign countries; politicians comparing the performance of American school systems with the performance of school systems in other countries

ASSESSING THE EXTERNAL ENVIRONMENT

As Bar-Yam (2004) pointed out, to be effective, the organization design of a system must match the complexity of its external environment. This principle compels change leaders in a school system to assess the characteristics of their system's general and task environments and then make choices about how to redesign the structural design of their systems to match the complexity of their external environments. To assess the complexity of the external environment, change leaders use a process called environmental scanning.

Environmental scanning methodologies and tools are easily accessible from the field of strategic planning. You apply these methodologies to identify issues, trends, threats, opportunities, and forces within each of the ten environmental sectors within your school system's general and task environments.

Identifying Key Stakeholders

After you assess what's happening in each of the ten sectors of your district's general and task environments, you then need to identify key external stakeholders in the task environment (there are also key stakeholders inside your school system, but these people and groups, by definition, are not part of your assessment of the external environment; however, you will need to assess their needs, interests, aspirations, and concerns in a separate transformation activity). A key stakeholder is any person or group with an interest in, or who will be significantly affected by, planned changes in your school system. Examples of external stakeholders in the task environment for school systems include:

- Parents
- Suppliers of books, supplies, equipment
- Critics
- State departments of education
- U.S. department of education
- Accrediting agencies
- College/university professional preparation programs for teachers and administrators
- Local government

- Local business leaders and groups
- Charter schools and private schools

A single change leader will have a difficult time identifying all of your district's key stakeholders, and he or she will surely be unable to assess all of their concerns, issues, dreams, aspirations, and so on. Identifying and assessing stakeholder concerns requires a team effort that is data-based rather than opinion-based (opinions are not to be excluded from an assessment, but they must follow, not precede, the collection and analysis of environmental scan data).

Stakeholder Mapping

An example of a tool that can be used by a team to identify key stakeholders is called "stakeholder mapping" (e.g., see Savitz & Weber, 2006). Stakeholder mapping is a process by which a school system learns about the perceptions, issues, dreams, aspirations, concerns, and expectations of its external stakeholders and then creates a "map" representing those data. These data are then used to communicate more effectively with the external stakeholders as the school system moves along the three change paths toward a transformed school district.

As you identify key external stakeholders and what they expect of your district, you can also assess and map the level of political support that each stakeholder provides to your district's transformation plans. This kind of political assessment (see Block, 1991) yields five groups of stakeholders based on their level of agreement with your transformation goals and the level of trust you have in each group (figure 6.2). Each stakeholder's relative amount of power (i.e., political influence) and the relative importance of their concerns are also assessed and mapped (figure 6.3).

After completing the stakeholder mapping process, change leaders then must decide what to do with those data. A matrix like the one shown in table 6.1 can be particularly helpful for making those kinds of decisions. Examples of how to use these assessment data to communicate during times of great change are presented below.

Priority 1: Powerful stakeholders with very important concerns. This group of stakeholders (that can include allies, bedfellows, opponents, adversaries, and fence-sitters) is extraordinarily important to the success of a transformation journey. They are influential people with important concerns. It makes political sense to engage these stakeholders in substantive conversations about their concerns and about how they can contribute to the success of the transformation.

In the case of powerful opponents with very important concerns (people who disagree with the transformation goals, but who are trusted), you may

High
Agreement
Low
Agreement
Bedfellows
Fence-Sitters
Allies
Adversaries
Opponents
Low Trust
High Trust

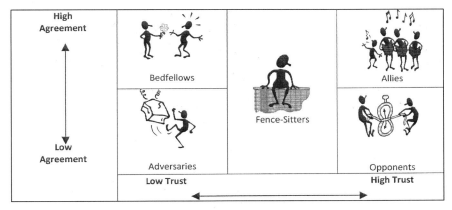

Figure 6.2. Political Assessment of Key Stakeholder Groups within the External Environment

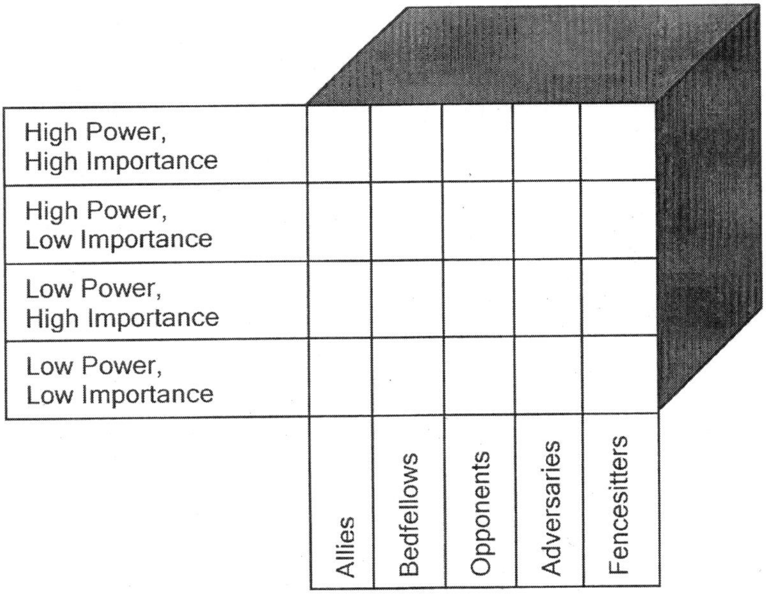

High Power,
High Importance
High Power,
Low Importance
Low Power,
High Importance
Low Power,
Low Importance
Allies
Bedfellows
Opponents
Adversaries
Fencesitters

Figure 6.3. Assessment of Stakeholder Power and the Importance of Their Issues

be able to convert them to allies if you listen carefully to their concerns and demonstrate a willingness to make adjustments to the transformation plans based on their input. With adversaries (people who disagree with the transformation and who are not trusted), you probably will not be able to con-

Table 6.1. Setting Priorities for Responding to Stakeholder Concerns

	Priority 1	Priority 2	Priority 3	Priority 4
Allies	High Power, High Importance	Low Power, High Importance	High Power, Low Importance	Low Power, Low Importance
Bedfellows	High Power, High Importance	Low Power, High Importance	High Power, Low Importance	Low Power, Low Importance
Opponents	High Power, High Importance	Low Power, High Importance	High Power, Low Importance	Low Power, Low Importance
Adversaries	High Power, High Importance	Low Power, High Importance	High Power, Low Importance	Low Power, Low Importance
Fence-sitters	High Power, High Importance	Low Power, High Importance	High Power, Low Importance	Low Power, Low Importance

vert them to allies or bedfellows; nevertheless, you should listen to their concerns and demonstrate to observers that you are treating them fairly and with civility.

Priority 2: Less powerful stakeholders with very important concerns. Often, low-influence people are simply ignored. They fade into the background and become invisible. Yet they have important concerns about the future of a school system that should be considered. So, the communication strategy for this group is to engage them in conversations about their concerns.

Priority 3: Powerful stakeholders with less important concerns. These people are highly influential, but their concerns are relatively unimportant. Nevertheless, because of their level of influence, it makes political sense to figure out a way to involve them in conversations about the transformation and to find ways for them to influence others to support the transformation. If nothing else, they can become champions for the transformation journey.

Priority 4: Less powerful stakeholders with less important concerns. This last group is probably the easiest one to ignore. Although members of this group are not very influential and although their concerns may be trivial, you do not want to alienate them, thereby converting them into adversaries. So, devising communication strategies that are built on civility and that express gratitude for their opinions will help preserve their support. If these people are opponents or adversaries, you may prevent their opposition from growing stronger by treating them with courtesy and gratitude for sharing their concerns.

Force Field Analysis

Kurt Lewin (1951) gave change leaders a tool for assessing the level of resistance to a proposal for change and the level of support for that change proposal. He characterized the resistance-support dynamics as "forces." As you identify and assess the relative strength of these forces, you are engaging in what Lewin called "force field analysis." This technique can be used to assess the relative degree of support for or resistance to change among a district's external stakeholders.

An example of how to map the forces for and against a proposal for change is displayed in figure 6.4.

COLLECTING ENVIRONMENTAL SCAN DATA

Environmental scanning requires data collection. Examples of data collection tools that are commonly used to scan the external environment are:

1. Surveys
2. Focus Groups/Interviews
3. Open Forums/Public Meetings
4. Observation/Site Visits
5. Media Monitoring
6. Anecdotes/Case Studies
7. Literature Reviews
8. Databases such as the U.S. Census database

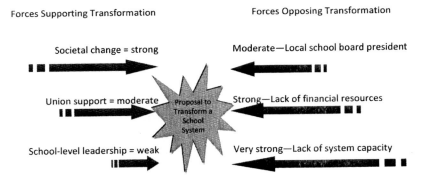

In this instance, the forces opposing transformation outweigh the forces supporting it. Therefore, while preparing the system to engage in transformation change leaders need to focus their attention on maintaining the supporting forces while devising strategies for reducing the strength of the oppositional forces. This principle of maintaining support while reducing opposition is tactically important because trying to increase supporting forces can backfire by causing a corresponding increase in resisting forces.

Figure 6.4. Force Field Analysis Map

Community Engagement Conferences

A large-group technique that is extraordinarily effective for bringing stakeholders from all five groups identified in table 6.1, above, into one room is the Community Engagement Conference (Duffy & Reigeluth, 2008). This conference is designed using principles of Owen's *Open Space Technology* (2008).

A Community Engagement Conference is a large-group event for external stakeholders who are carefully selected to participate in the conference. The event can accommodate thousands of people, but for most school systems the groups will probably only be in the hundreds.

Following the design principles of Owen's *Open Space Technology*, the event allows participants to self-organize into small discussion groups on topics of their choosing, all of which must be aligned with the main theme for the conference. As each small group engages in conversations about their "table topic," someone in the group records the main points and themes that emerge. At the end of each discussion period the scribe submits the notes to a staff person who converts the notes into an electronic format.

At the end of the conference, change leaders have a substantial amount of environmental data collected from carefully selected external stakeholders who participated in the event. Those data are then analyzed by the change leaders to identify patterns of concerns, opportunities, and threats.

SWOT Analysis

One of the important uses of the environmental scan data is to complete what strategic planners call a SWOT analysis. SWOT is an acronym for Strengths, Weaknesses, Opportunities, and Threats.

Given the environmental data collected up to this point, you now make a SWOT assessment of your school system. In other words, you ask, "Given what we now know about our environment, what are our district's strengths, weaknesses, opportunities, and threats?"

Strengths and weaknesses describe a school district's overall effectiveness as a system and reflect the internal operations of the system. Opportunities and threats are found in the external environment. A brief summary of possible diagnostic questions for each element of the SWOT analysis is provided below.

Strengths

Strengths represent a school system's resources and capabilities that contribute to the overall effectiveness of the system. Given the environmental scan data, you compare your district's performance to those data to identify your system's strengths. Your list of strengths should be able to answer questions like these:

- What are the school system's advantages within its external environment?
- What does the system do very well?
- Does the system have access to the human, financial, and technical resources it needs to engage effectively in transformational change?
- What do our external stakeholders think our strengths are?

Examples of strengths include the district's good reputation within the community, having timely access to needed resources, employing highly qualified faculty and staff, and producing superior student performance on state-mandated assessments.

Weaknesses

Weaknesses are weak points or deficiencies within a school system that inhibit the district's overall performance and that could become barriers to a school system successfully completing its transformation journey. Efforts should be made to identify these weaknesses honestly and accurately so they can be overcome as quickly as possible.

You can identify weaknesses by answering questions such as:

- What can be improved?
- What is done poorly?
- What should be avoided?
- What are we doing as a school system that could be done more effectively or efficiently?
- What is this school system *not* doing that it should be doing?
- If one thing could be changed that would trigger additional important changes, what would that be? (that "one thing" is called a "high-leverage change"—see Reigeluth, 2006b)

Examples of weaknesses include: wide gaps between high-performing schools and low-performing schools within the district, inability to meet state and federal standards for educating students, missing deadlines, frequent turnover in the superintendent's position, and significant complaints from many stakeholders.

Opportunities

Opportunities are favorable environmental conditions that exist today or that are likely to emerge in the near future. To identify opportunities you can answer questions like these:

- What are some changes in state or federal legislation that could benefit the district?
- What are some changes in the community's demographic profile that present an opportunity to create significant change in the district?
- What are some examples of new research about how school districts function as systems that can help us engage more effectively in transformational change?

Examples of opportunities in the external environment include the election of a new school board that is supportive of transformational change, changes in federal legislation that remove barriers to successful change, and the influx of much-needed financial resources from the state or federal governments.

Threats

Threats are external forces that present unfavorable possibilities that are potentially damaging now or in the near future. To identify threats you should be able to answer questions such as these:

- What obstacles do we face as we think about transforming our school system?
- What is our competition doing?
- Are the required state and federal standards changing in ways that will impact the district negatively?
- Is the knowledge-base about teaching and learning changing in ways that will impact the district negatively?
- Is the old paradigm of teaching and learning (the Industrial Age paradigm) hobbling the district's ability to educate children in more effective ways?
- Does the district have financial problems?

Examples of threats include significant shifts in the demographic profile of your community, withering political support for the school district's plans to engage in transformational change, the election of an adversarial school board, and increasing state and federal demands for improving teaching and learning that require significant increases in financial resources that you don't have.

ANALYZING ENVIRONMENTAL SCAN DATA

The environmental scanning process yields a significant amount of data. Those data need to be transformed into information and knowledge.

The transformation of the data proceeds through a process of careful analysis that:

1. identifies and assesses the broad characteristics of a school system's external environment;
2. identifies key stakeholders, assesses and maps their level of power and the importance of their concerns;
3. identifies SWOTs and predicts their impact; and
4. results in an accurate force field analysis.

Given these data, change leaders now determine how well the design and functioning of their school system matches the characteristics of its external environment.

MATCHING ORGANIZATION DESIGN
TO ENVIRONMENTAL CHARACTERISTICS

The field of organization theory and design tells change leaders clearly and consistently that the structural design of an organization must be aligned with the characteristics of its external environment if that organization wants to function effectively (e.g., Burns & Stalker, 1961; Daft, 2006; Lawrence & Lorsch, 1967). The structural design of an organization is an element of Path 2: Transform Internal Social Infrastructure. Determining the appropriate organization design is done by using data collected and analyzed in the assessment activities along Path 3: Transform Environmental Relationships.

Among the many features of the external general and task environments that influence the structural design of an organization, organization theorists attach particular importance to the level of environmental complexity (simple versus complex) and the rate of change (stable versus unstable).

Environmental Complexity

Environmental complexity is a function of stakeholder demands and expectations. If a school system has many stakeholders with many important demands and expectations, its external environment is complex. If the district has fewer stakeholders with fewer important demands and expectations, then its external environment is simple.

Environmental Change

The rate of environmental change is assessed by determining how much and how often change is happening in the external environment that has or will have a clear impact on a school system. If the level of change is substantial and rapid, the external environment is considered unstable. If the rate of change is less than substantial and slow paced, then the external environment is considered stable.

Mechanistic Organization Design versus Organic Organization Design

The intersection of environmental complexity (simple versus complex) and the rate of change (stable versus unstable) creates a two-by-two matrix as shown in figure 6.5.

Given a thorough assessment of the external environment, as suggested above, change leaders can make predictions about the nature of their school system's external environment and then identify the kind of organization design required by the characteristics of the environment. Specifically,

- A simple + stable environment requires a mechanistic organization design.
- A complex + stable environment requires an organization design that is mostly mechanistic.

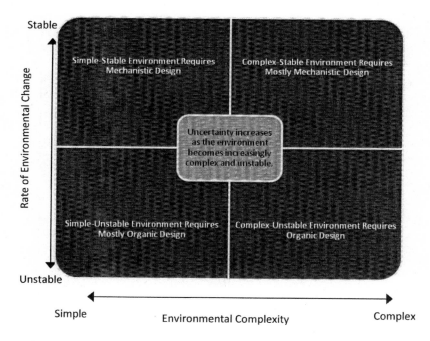

Figure 6.5.   Assessing Availability of Resources

- A simple + unstable environment requires an organization design that is mostly organic.
- A complex + unstable environment requires an organization design that is organic.
- Finally, as the environment becomes increasingly unstable and complex, the level of uncertainty about the future increases. As uncertainty increases, the need for an organic organization structure becomes increasingly important.

Assessing Availability of Resources

After determining the characteristics of the external environment and once the ideal organization design to match the environment is identified, then the next assessment activity determines the relative availability of needed resources to sustain the district's performance within the context of its new design. The assessment of resource availability will tell change leaders if the resources are either abundant or scarce. The assessment of the environment's complexity and stability in relation to the availability of resources is depicted in figure 6.6.

Given the results of the environmental scanning activities, change leaders then conceptualize a transformation journey for their school system that transforms their core and support work (Path 1), transforms their internal social infrastructure (Path 2), and transforms their system's relationship with its external environment (Path 3). The School System Transformation Protocol presented in chapter 12 is especially designed to create this kind of transformational change.

CONCLUSION

It is clear from the body of knowledge about organization theory and design that the environment within which a school district exists has a significant impact on the performance of that district. Further, school systems, like all other organizations, must know what their environment expects of them and then decide whether or not to meet those expectations and how to do that effectively. It is also clear from organization theory and design that school systems, like all other organizations, must be designed to match the complexity and stability of their systemic environments. Matching organization design to district-specific environmental characteristics is important because, as noted earlier, when the design of a system does not match the characteristics of its external environment, that system will move toward failure.

Finally, an assessment of the external environment for most contemporary school systems suggests that those environments are complex and unstable

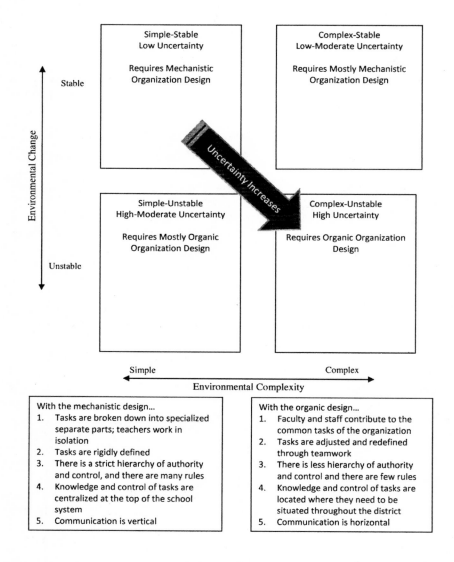

Figure 6.6. A School System's Structural Design Matched with Environmental Characteristics

and that resources are scarce. Organization theory tells us that when a system exists within that kind of environment those systems should be designed according to principles of organic design, which begs the questions, "Why are most school systems organized using a mechanistic, bureaucratic design?"

and "What can be done to change that situation?" The answer to the first question is that the dominant paradigm for designing and managing school systems is the Industrial Age mechanistic design, and it is stubbornly resistant to change. The answer to the second question is that school systems must be transformed to satisfy the requirements of an external environment that has already transformed to meet the requirements of the Knowledge Age. Making these kinds of changes requires a revolution!

NOTE

1. You may visit their website at www.indiana.edu/~syschang/decatur/the_change_effort.html. The transformation is being facilitated by Dr. Charles Reigeluth of Indiana University.

III

MASTERING DELIBERATE INTENTION

Mastering deliberate intention requires knowledge and skills for creating an idealized future for your school system. In chapter 7, you will read about two approaches to creating an idealized future.

Creating an idealized future for your system requires a good understanding of what it will take to create the future you desire for your system. Chapter 8 offers some advice and guidance for shaping the future of your school system.

The first paradigm that must change if a school system is to transform is the one that influences how teachers teach and how children learn. The new paradigm that is advocated in this book is called the Learner-Centered paradigm, and it would provide children with customized, personalized learning experiences. Sunkyung Lee Watson and Charles Reigeluth describe the Learner-Centered paradigm in-depth in chapter 9.

7

The Power of Deliberate Intention

OVERVIEW

This chapter provides an overview of the power of deliberate intention. Deliberate intention is created using principles of idealized design (Ackoff, 1981; Banathy, 1991) that yield a powerful, compelling, yet feasible vision for the future of a school system.

Deliberate Intention as a Reinforcing Loop

In the world of systems dynamics, there is a driving force called a reinforcing loop (Kim & Anderson, 1998). Reinforcing loops are neutral in their disposition toward the direction of change. Depending on the intentions of people or their disregard for establishing intentions, reinforcing loops can propel a system toward chaos and dissolution or toward order and high performance.

Deliberate intention can create a reinforcing loop that moves a system toward order and high performance. Attempting to transform a school system without a deliberate intention to create an idealized future for that system can create a reinforcing loop that drags a system's performance down, even to the point of having schools within the system seized by state departments of education.

What is your school district's deliberate intention? Is it driving all of you toward a transformed school district marked by high-quality teaching and learning, a motivating and satisfying work life for faculty and staff, and positive relationships with individuals and groups outside of your district?

Or, in the absence of a deliberate intention in the form of an idealized vision for the future of your system, are you experiencing desperation, futility, and failure? Further, transforming a school district doesn't happen automatically or without effort. It takes deliberate intention to do what's necessary. You must want to transform, decide to transform, make an effort to transform, and persist in transforming.

Flying on Autopilot

In many ways, your district's way of doing things (aka, the status quo) is like the autopilot on an airplane. Imagine that a plane you are piloting is stuck on autopilot and you want to change direction. You and your copilot can try to wrench the steering yoke toward the direction you want to go, but eventually you will both tire and release your grip. The autopilot will then retake control of the plane and move it back to its original flight path—the one that was programmed into the computer.

This is what happens when you try to transform your school district without reframing your district's deliberate intention—its idealized future. Your system's status quo is its autopilot. You can wrestle with change until you tire, and when you surrender to your fatigue, the district will move back to its original flight path—the one internally programmed into your district's culture.

There is a more effective way to transform a district: turn off your district's autopilot that is moving it forward (or backward) in undesirable directions. To start the process of exiting the autopilot function, you first imagine a substantially different future for your system, and then you engage your system in transformational change to move your system toward that future.

IDEALIZED DESIGN

Ackoff (1981) proposed a methodology for creating an idealized design for the future of organizations. Banathy (1991) built on the work of Ackoff, Checkland (1981), and Nadler (1981) to create a methodology for helping educators create an idealized design for school systems. In this section of the chapter, I provide highlights of both Ackoff's and Banathy's idealized design methodologies.

ACKOFF'S IDEALIZED DESIGN METHODOLOGY

Russell Ackoff (1999, 2001) astutely observed that corporate visions are frequently illusions or delusions. Effective visions, according to Ackoff, must be constructed to provide practitioners with an operational description of the organization design they would want if they could select from any organization design in the world; in other words, if you could create the school system of your dreams, without any constraints on your desires, what would it look like and how would it function? Ackoff (in Ackoff, Magidson, & Addison, 2006) also argues that this idealized vision must be created with input from all key stakeholders or their representatives.

Interactive Planning and Idealized Design

Interactive planning is at the core of Ackoff's idealized design process. Interactive planning has two parts—*idealization* and *realization*—and is subdivided into six interrelated phases: (1) formulating the mess, (2) ends planning, (3) means planning, (4) resource planning, (5) design of implementation, and (6) design of controls. The information about Ackoff's design principles presented below is adapted to fit school systems.

Part 1: Idealization

Phase 1: Formulating the mess (situational analysis). Every school system is confronted with a complex set of interacting threats and opportunities, a system of problems that Ackoff calls a *mess*. The outcome of this planning phase is to identify how a school system would eventually destroy itself if it continued performing as it currently is; that is, if the system did not adapt to its changing environment. Formulating the mess requires the following activities:

Activity 1: Complete a systems analysis. This analysis creates a detailed description of how the school system currently functions;

Activity 2: Complete an obstruction analysis. This analysis identifies obstacles that prevent the system from succeeding in a changing environment;

Activity 3: Create reference projections. These are projections of the school system's future based on (1) the assumption that there will be no change in how the system performs and (2) assumptions about the characteristics of the external environment that the school system expects in the near and distant future. Following the creation of these projections, planners then create a reference scenario, which is a description of how and why the school system might destroy itself if the assumptions were true.

Phase 2: Ends planning. This phase focuses on imagining an ideal design for the school system. The activities for this phase are:

Activity 1: Describe what the school system would ideally like to be *right now* if it could be whatever it wanted to be; and

Activity 2: Identify the gaps between this idealized vision and the school system that was projected earlier in the reference scenario (during phase 1, activity 3).

Part 2: Realization

Phase 3: Means planning. During this phase, system designers determine how to remove or reduce the gaps identified in ends planning (see above, part 1, phase 2, activity 2). Specifically, designers devise the means to pursue the idealized design that they envision for their school system. The identified performance gaps between the current system and the idealized system should be treated as if they were interconnected; that is, planners must avoid closing or removing individual performance gaps without considering how each gap affects and is affected by other gaps. Closing or narrowing gaps in this way is a systemic approach to change.

Phase 4: Resource planning. Given the means needed to achieve the idealized design for their school system, designers must now identify the resources needed to create and sustain the idealized design. Specifically, they determine:

1. What resources are needed?
2. How much of each type of resource will be required?
3. When, where, and how should resources be deployed to implement the means to achieve the idealized design?
4. How will resource shortages or excesses be identified and handled?

Phase 5: Design of implementation. This phase applies classic principles of transition management (e.g., Elzen, Geels, & Green, 2005). Specifically, designers develop a transition plan (i.e., a plan to move the school system from its current state toward its idealized state) by determining who does what, when, where, and how.

Phase 6: Design of controls. Activities during this phase focus on managing the transition period. Specifically, designers make decisions about:

1. how to monitor change-related task assignments and schedules;
2. how to adjust for failures to meet transition timelines; and
3. how to evaluate the change process and its outcomes and determine how to take corrective action if the change process and outcomes are not moving the school system in the direction of the idealized design.

Ackoff's six phases of interactive planning are most often implemented simultaneously and interactively because they are interconnected. Further, Ackoff argues that interactive planning is continuous; therefore, none of the six phases is ever totally completed, and results for each phase are produced throughout the entire process.

Ackoff's interactive planning methodology is an integral part of his principles of idealized design. These principles are summarized next.

Idealized Design Principles

Ackoff suggests that planners should assume that their school system was completely destroyed last night, but its external environment remains exactly as it was. Given that apocalyptic assumption, they then begin designing the new school system that would immediately replace the one that was "destroyed." The idealized design would only be subjected to two constraints (technological feasibility and operational viability) and one requirement (an ability to learn and adapt rapidly and effectively).

Technological feasibility. This constraint requires planners to create an idealized design that excludes features and functions that are currently known to be unfeasible. This does not preclude new uses of innovative ideas for change as long as they are feasible; rather, according to Ackoff, the constraint is intended to prevent the design from becoming a work of science fiction.

Operational viability. This constraint requires planners to create an idealized design that is fully capable of succeeding in the system's current external environment. However, there may be constraints in the current external environment that could delay the implementation of the idealized design (see chapter 6).

Learning and adaptation. This requirement focuses on creating a learning organization. To satisfy this requirement, the idealized school system should be designed to allow it to respond rapidly to changes in its external environment and to learn quickly from and adapt to its performance successes and failures. This requirement also suggests that the school system must remain open to ongoing periods of redesign.

Idealized Design versus an Ideal System

Ackoff makes an important distinction between idealized design and an ideal system. He argues that the product of idealized design is *not* an ideal system. An ideal school system is not created because the system is always subject to continuous improvement and it is neither perfect nor utopian. Instead, according to Ackoff, the new design for the school system should create an *ideal-seeking system*—the best system that designers can conceive of at this time.

Components of the Idealized Design Process

Ackoff's idealized design process has three parts: (1) formulating a mission statement, (2) specifying the features of the idealized school system; and (3) designing the envisioned school system.

Mission. A school system's mission statement is a concise description of its reasons for existence. It is most often constructed using a maximum of two or three sentences. It should not be confused with a vision statement, which is an elaboration of the mission statement that captures the system's core beliefs, values, and idealized future by using powerful metaphors and verbal images.

Specifying features. Specifications describe the features that planners want the idealized school system to have. Specifications are aspirations to achieve an idealized design for the school system.

Designing the system. The design describes how the specified features are to be obtained. In other words, the design is a set of instructions about how to achieve the idealized design.

Making Design Decisions

It is important to remember that Ackoff's idealized design methodology is based on a foundation of interactive planning. In practice, this requires the idealized design to be the product of participation and consensus. Participation means that designers should solicit and carefully consider the opinions and suggestions of colleagues throughout the school system. Consensus does not mean total agreement about what is the best thing to do, but it does require total agreement on what is worth doing.

Finalizing the Idealized Design

Once an idealized design is finalized, it should be shared with key stakeholders who have not been involved in the preparation of the design so that they can give comments, criticism, and suggestions. Wherever possible, their suggestions should be used to make adjustments to the design. When making adjustments based on suggestions is impossible or undesirable, then an explanation as to why the suggestions could not be incorporated in the design should be provided to those who offered the suggestions.

Finally, it must be remembered that implementing the idealized design requires *discontinuous* (aka, transformational) change. After implementing the idealized design, improvement of that design over time should be ongoing, using principles of continuous improvement.

BANATHY'S IDEALIZED SYSTEMS DESIGN METHODOLOGY

A second methodology for creating idealized designs specifically to transform school systems is Bela Banathy's (1991) *Idealized Systems Design* methodology. As noted earlier, Banathy's methodology builds on the work of Ackoff (1981), Checkland (1981), and Nadler (1981).

Banathy (1991) describes his methodology using a mapping metaphor. The first map he offers is one that charts the design journey in broad terms.

This map is illustrated in figure 7.1. His design methodology also uses the mapping metaphor. The methodology maps are depicted in figure 7.2. First, the broad features of his map of the design journey are described. Then, the key elements of the five maps that comprise his methodology will be summarized.

Mapping the Design Journey

Banathy's *Idealized Systems Design* methodology is portrayed as a "map of the design journey." That map is constructed using data, information, and knowledge derived from answers to eight diagnostic questions. The answers suggest key features of an idealized design for the system. The diagnostic questions and the key features to which they are connected are:

Feature 1: What have we learned from educational reform efforts?
Feature 2: What new thinking and what new approaches are needed?

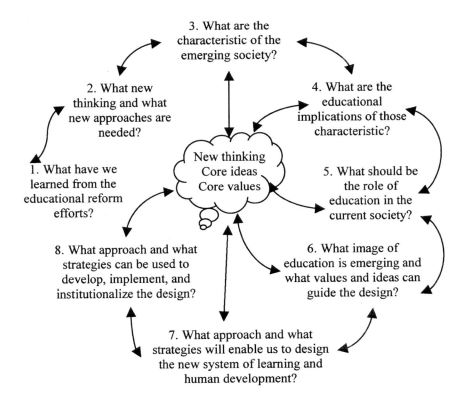

Figure 7.1. Banathy's Map of the Design Journey

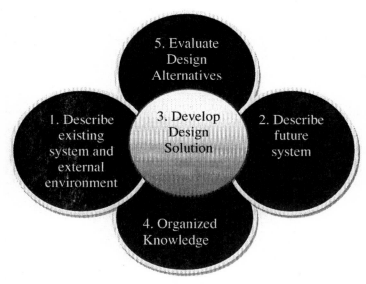

Figure 7.2.   Banathy's Idealized System Design "Maps"

Feature 3: What are the characteristics of the evolving society?

Feature 4: What are the educational implications of those characteristics?

Feature 5: What should be the role of education in the current society?

Feature 6: What image of education is emerging within society and what values and ideas can guide the design of our system?

Feature 7: What approach and what strategies will enable us to design our new system of learning and human development?

Feature 8: What approach and what strategies can be used to develop, implement, and institutionalize the design?

The answers to these eight questions create a map of the design journey. The answers also contain new mental models, new core ideas for change, and unambiguous descriptions of the system's core values.

Banathy's mapping metaphor continues by charting five maps of the terrain for his idealized design methodology. The maps are: (1) the terrain of departure, (2) the terrain of destination, (3) the design solution, (4) the knowledge base, and (5) evaluation alternatives. Each mapping activity is briefly summarized below.

Mapping the terrain of departure. This map is identified as map 1 in figure 7.2. It describes the current functioning of a school system with a focus on its strengths and weaknesses. The essential characteristics of the district's external environment are also assessed and described. Change leaders also prepare their system to engage in transformational change, which includes formulating ideas for what their system will look like and how it will function in the future.

Mapping the terrain of destination. This map is identified as map 2 in figure 7.2. Change leaders construct this map by engaging in visioning activities that create a model of the future system that they desire. They also assess environmental trends to predict threats and opportunities that could affect the design of their idealized system. Given the completion of the visioning and assessment activities, an implementation plan is devised.

Mapping the design solution space. This map is identified as map 3 in figure 7.2. It represents the most significant terrain for a transformation journey. The quality of this map is essential for the success of the transformation journey because most large-scale change efforts fail during the transition between the present and the desired future.

The first element of this map is the formulation of a definition of what the system's purpose is (its mission). This definition of mission must consider key societal functions assigned to school systems. Given the definition of the system's purpose, the next activities elaborate the core mission by asking questions such as "Who are our clients?" "What educational services should we be providing?" "How, when, and where should we be delivering those services?" The elaboration of the mission creates an idealized vision for the district.

The next component of this map is to identify key functions that will be required to achieve the system's core mission. These key functions include, for example, curriculum and instruction, administration, teaching, learning, learning supports, and so on. These key functions are then organized on paper in a coherent, interconnected map to illustrate the broad-brush features of the desired idealized school system.

Given the key functions needed to create the desired idealized design for the school system, the next element of map 3 is to create management subsystems; for example, management information systems, instructional management systems, record-keeping systems, and strategic communication systems.

Mapping the space of the knowledge base. To envision an idealized school system, educators need access to relevant data, information, and knowledge to inform their envisioning process. To create this map (shown as map 4 in figure 7.2), four knowledge domains are identified and charted. These are: (1) knowledge from the exploration of opportunities and threats in the school system's external environment and the implications of those opportunities and threats for the continuing existence of the school system (see chapter 6); (2) knowledge from the exploration of design options; (3) the school system's core values and ideals, its vision, and the dominant mental model(s) guiding the idealized design process; and (4) knowledge about the design process and how to manage it.

Mapping the design evaluation alternatives. Given several design options for an idealized school system, each option needs to be tested and evaluated (shown in figure 7.2 as map 5). A key element of the evaluation process is to make sure that the design alternatives being considered did not overlook important features that could affect the overall success of the new system. The outcome of this phase is the selection of the design option that is most likely to create the idealized school system about which educators are "dreaming."

CONCLUSION

The idealized design process is powerful. It relies heavily on engaging key stakeholders in the design process. It assumes that the current system must be replaced with a new system and, importantly, that the new system must be substantially different from the current one (if the new system is not substantially different, then transformation has not occurred).

While both Ackoff and Banathy have given us two different but related methodologies for creating idealized designs, Banathy's methodology was specifically created for school systems. The work of both men has significantly influenced the design of the School System Transformation Protocol described in chapter 12.

8

Shaping the Future
of Your School System

OVERVIEW

This chapter provides information that educators can use as part of their idealized design process described in chapter 7. The chapter begins with a review of the nature of the external environment for school systems. Next, information about what it takes to transform a school system is offered. The chapter concludes with specific recommendations for what it takes to shape an idealized future for school systems.

THE ENVIRONMENTAL CONTEXT
FOR TRANSFORMATIONAL CHANGE

The VUCA Environment

Not too long ago, the environment for school systems (see chapter 6) was rather simple and stable. Not anymore. Federal legislation such as No Child Left Behind and the triple societal engines of standards, assessments, and accountability have increased the instability and complexity of school districts' environments to extraordinary levels. Add to this frenetic mix our mobile society with its transient families who expect that their children's education in their next hometown will be at least as good as the education they receive in their current hometown, even if the new school district is three thousand miles away. This complexity and instability puts significant demands on educators in school systems with responsibility for envisioning an idealized future for their districts.

Many contemporary authors writing about organization transformation (e.g., Wheatley, 1999, 2001; Hock, 1995) rightly point out that those who manage organizations and try to improve them are locked inside an outdated and unhelpful Industrial Age mental model—a mental model often characterized as Newtonian or mechanistic. Yesterday's organizations were able to use and benefit from the mechanistic model because the environments they existed within were relatively stable and simple. Today's organizations, including school systems, find themselves in environments that are volatile, uncertain, complex and ambiguous (VUCA) (Murphy, 2002). An organization design best suited for unstable and complex VUCA environments is the organic design (Daft, 2001).

Some authors characterize a VUCA environment as chaotic. Dee Hock (1995) is one of these people. He coined the term *chaordic* (the combination of chaos and order) to describe this kind of environment. Change leadership within a chaordic, VUCA environment occurs within a strategic arena. The strategic arena for transforming school systems extends over at least three levels—local, state, and federal. Strategic leadership to transform a school system must focus on anticipating, identifying, and coordinating hopes, aspirations, policies, and legislation from all three levels. At the local level, strategic leadership focuses on a school district's community's hopes and aspirations for its youth. At the state level, strategic leadership to transform a school system focuses on the policies and requirements of state departments of education. At the federal level, strategic leadership to transform a school system focuses on interpreting and responding to the requirements of federal legislation affecting education (e.g., No Child Left Behind). In my opinion, if change leaders in school systems are blind to this three-level strategic arena, then they will fail to transform their school systems.

The turbulent environments within which many school districts exist also create metaphorical "white water" (Vaill, 1991). To navigate this white water, some change leaders in school systems and in the field of education are awakening to the need to transform school systems in fundamental ways by creating simultaneous changes along three change paths: Path 1—transform core and support work processes; Path 2—transform internal social infrastructure; and Path 3—transform relationships with the external environment (Duffy, 2003a; Duffy & Dale, 2001; Duffy, Rogerson, & Blick, 2000). These fundamental changes result in an examination and a redefinition of a district's basic purpose, its identity as an agency of its community, and its relationship with parents, community members, and other external stakeholders.

Revolutionary, transformational change is required to navigate the white water successfully. Incremental change, or, as it is sometimes called, continuous improvement, is grossly ineffective for school systems within a "white water" environment. It is ineffective because of the focus on tweaking the status quo to make the existing system incrementally better. There is, however, a role for continuous improvement in a transformation process: it must follow, not precede, transformation.

WHAT IT TAKES TO TRANSFORM SCHOOL SYSTEMS

School system transformation requires significant frame-breaking changes to a school system's core and support work processes (academic support and nonacademic support), its internal social infrastructure, and its relationships with its external environment. Deep and broad fundamental change also requires a new approach to organizing and managing school systems that leads to qualitatively different ways of perceiving, thinking, and behaving in those systems.

School system transformation also requires fundamental and radical changes in how educators perceive, think, and behave (i.e., changes in mental models, mind-sets, and behavioral strategies as discussed in chapter 5). Incremental change, like continuous improvement, *is not* a transformation strategy. Tweaking a school system and continuously improving the status quo won't work if you are trying to create fundamental, transformational change. To achieve transformation, you and your faculty and staff need to examine your collective assumptions, beliefs, and values about what your district stands for, how it functions, how it is designed, how it treats people, what its management philosophy is, and the numerous processes, procedures, policies, and so forth that shape people's behavior at the individual, team, and organizational levels.

The power of transformation is found in a compelling idea that is sown and grown inside the minds and hearts of your colleagues; that is, to transform your district, you and your colleagues must be liberated from the constraints of the past and present. Once liberated from these shackles, you and your colleagues will have the capacity and creativity to fashion an idealized design for your school system that significantly enhances student, faculty and staff, and whole-system learning.

For the promise of school district transformation to become powerful enough to unleash emotional and psychological energy and collective imagination, your change leadership must aim to: (1) crystallize the hopes and dreams of your people around an idealized vision that creates unity of purpose for your district while simultaneously giving your colleagues a degree of bounded autonomy to make decisions about how to best achieve the district's grand vision and (2) provide the means and resources to achieve that vision. Your people must see, understand, and embrace the vision with their heads and hearts and then believe that there are ways and resources to achieve it. People need to believe that the vision before them is within their grasp, not beyond their reach.

Establishing unity of purpose does not require uniformity of thought and action. You can have a shared idealized vision and still encourage and support divergent points of view about how to arrive there. In the field of organization development, encouraging divergent paths toward a single, unifying vision is called the "principle of equifinality" (Cummings & Worley, 2001).

APPROACHES TO FUNDAMENTAL (TRANSFORMATIONAL) CHANGE

All approaches to creating fundamental transformational change have five common features (Cummings & Worley, 2001, pp. 499–501). These features are described below. I added features 6 and 7 to this list. Transformation:

1. is triggered by disruptions in an organization's environment or within itself;
2. is systemic and revolutionary;
3. is driven by senior executives and line management;
4. requires continuous innovation and learning;
5. requires a new organizing paradigm;
6. requires a reshaping of organization culture;
7. requires courageous, passionate, and visionary leaders.

Let's take a closer look at each of these features.

Transformation is triggered by disruptions. Tushman, Newman, and Romanelli (1986) suggested that transformational change is stimulated by disruptions in an organization's external and internal environments. These discontinuities, interpreted for school systems, are summarized below.

1. *Industry discontinuities:* In education, these discontinuities are found in legal, political, economic, and technological conditions that affect how a district operates. The federal legislation called No Child Left Behind is an example of an "industry" discontinuity in the field of education.
2. *Product life cycle shifts:* In education, teachers are knowledge workers and school districts are knowledge-creating organizations (Duffy, 2002). One first-level outcome of their work—their "product"—is the information they learn, organize, and present to students. The second-level and primary outcomes of their work are educated students. Product "life cycle" discontinuities (e.g., new ways to teach and new ideas about how children learn) significantly affect their first-level outcomes—the information that is learned, organized, and presented to

students—and ultimately the second-level outcomes. Teachers are inundated with the latest "flavor of the month" teaching method, they are swarmed by the latest developments in how to tap into students' learning styles, and what they thought was state of the art suddenly becomes passé. If these discontinuities are perceived as valid and significant, they can trigger transformation.

3. *Internal company dynamics*: In education, these discontinuities include changes in a school system's culture, changing student demographics, changing teacher demographics, and superintendent turnover.

Disruptions like these can severely shake up a school district and push it to dramatically alter its grand strategy and, in turn, its mission, values, organization design, systems, and procedures. Of course, this is not always a bad thing. Sometimes these kinds of disruptions are required to break a system's inertia and start it moving toward transformation.

Transformation is systemic and revolutionary. Transformation requires fundamental and deep changes in a school district's core and support work processes, its internal social infrastructure (which includes organization design, mission, vision, information systems, human resource practices, and strategic direction), and in its relationship with its external environment. Changes of this kind and of this magnitude are often characterized as transformational or revolutionary.

Transformation requires tools and techniques that are quite different than those used for simpler forms of change (Burke, 2002). Transformation should also occur rapidly so that it doesn't get bogged down in organizational politics, individual resistance, or other forms of organizational inertia (Tushman, Newman, & Romanelli, 1986). In making the same point, Cummings and Worley (2001, p. 500) said, "The faster an organization can respond to disruptions, the quicker it can attain the benefits of operating in a new way."

Because school districts are systems, all of their features and components tend to connect to each other by complex cause-and-effect loops and tend to reinforce each other through a system phenomenon known as dynamic equilibrium (or status quo). These complex and mutually reinforcing system dynamics make it difficult to improve a system in a piecemeal manner (Cummings & Worley, 2001, p. 500). All of these dynamics fall into three broad categories, which I characterize as change paths: Path 1—core and support work processes; Path 2—internal social infrastructure; and Path 3—environmental relationships; and changes within these categories must be made simultaneously and in a coordinated fashion (Duffy, Rogerson, & Blick, 2000; Miller, Friesen, & Mintzberg, 1984; Pasmore, 1988).

Transformation is driven by senior and line managers. The literature and real-world experience is clear that senior executives and other line managers must drive transformation (Pettigrew, 1987; Waldersee, 1997). In school districts, the senior executives are the superintendent and his or her immediate assistants. The line managers are building principals. Without the unequivocal and highly visible leadership of these leaders, transformational change in school districts will fail.

Tushman, Newman, and Nadler (1988) described three key roles for executive leaders during times of transformational change:

1. *Envisioning*: articulating a clear and credible description of a new strategic orientation for the organization; setting new and challenging performance standards to move toward; appreciating the organization's past accomplishments
2. *Energizing*: demonstrating personal excitement for and unequivocal commitment to the new strategic direction and its related goals; communicating early success to build energy to support the transformation
3. *Enabling*: providing resources needed to complete the transformation; rewarding performance that supports the transformation; building a new management team to lead the transformed organization; developing management systems to support the transformation process

Transformation requires innovation and learning. Transforming a school system means that the way the district is designed and how it functions becomes significantly different than what it is now or has been in the past. To create this kind of transformation, substantial innovation and learning is required. Some of the most insidious obstacles blocking this kind of innovation and learning are personal and organizational mental models and their attendant mind-sets.

In organizations, there are generally two broad categories of mental models—personal and organizational (Duffy, 2003a; see chapter 5 for more on mental models and mind-sets). Revising and expanding personal mental models is greatly facilitated, I think, by using a knowledge-creation process (see Duffy, 2002). Knowledge-creation in school districts (see chapter 5) surfaces personal knowledge and mental models, makes that knowledge and those models explicit, and then converts the best of these into organization-wide knowledge and mental models while simultaneously helping people unlearn ineffective or inappropriate mental models.

Mind-sets are found in educators' attitudes toward their preferred mental models and the paradigm to which they are attached. To transform your district, educators in your district, including you, have to change the way you think and feel about it, because every human behavior in your district is shaped by its dominant mental models and mind-sets, and every key action taken is prompted by those models and mind-sets.

Another of the key changes in how people think about educating students in your district is for them to stop thinking thoughts that are self-centered. Everyone needs to start thinking about others. Administrators think about teachers, staff, and students. Teachers and staff think about students and administrators. When everyone starts thinking about others instead of about themselves, transformation can be facilitated.

Thoughts influence feelings and feelings influence behavior. This set of cause-and-effect loops is powered by choice. People choose to think a certain way, choose to feel a certain way, and choose to behave in a certain way. What people sometimes fail to realize, however, is that all choices have consequences. Many difficulties in transforming school systems occur because people base their choices on several frequently unreliable sources:

- Organization culture (everyone is doing it). Just because "everyone" (which usually isn't really everyone) is doing it is not the basis of a good choice.
- Tradition (we've always done it this way). Tradition is a manifestation of dynamic equilibrium, otherwise known as status quo. It often is expressed in the question, "What's the precedent for this?" If you want to transform your district in new and innovative ways, there is no precedent.
- Reason (it seemed like the logical thing to do). Human thinking processes are notoriously flawed. People often do not use well-structured reasoning processes and prefer to use mental heuristics (mental shortcuts) for making their decisions—heuristics that are frequently linked to emotion.
- Emotion (it just felt right). Some folks rely on how they "feel" about something when making decisions. These feelings are often rationalized as intuitive insights or common sense.

Instead of choices being made on the basis of the above sources, educators should create shared standards of organizational, team, and individual performance that are developed through a highly participative process that engages community members, faculty, and staff in structured interactions to create those standards (see chapter 12 to read about a methodology for doing this). Then choices are made against the standards of performance. Therefore, one of the most important steps you will take to transform your district is to settle the issue of what the standards of performance—organizational, team, and individual performance—will be.

To facilitate the unlearning and learning of mental models, educators in your district must have a positive attitude (i.e., a positive mind-set) toward unlearning and learning new mental models that allows them to:

1. receive new information;
2. read and understand that information;
3. remember what they learn;
4. reflect on what they learned; and
5. apply what is learned.

People fool themselves if they think that just because they learned new information, they have what it takes to transform their school systems. Quinn, Anderson, and Finkelstein (1998) argue that they must also convert their cognitive knowledge ("know what") it into three additional levels of knowledge:

• Advanced Skill—Know How
• Systems Understanding—Know Why
• Self Motivation—Care Why

And then, finally, they must apply that knowledge until they develop mastery.

Transformation requires four new organizing paradigms. Throughout this book I have referred to the four new paradigms that I believe are needed to transform America's school systems. The first new paradigm is one that transforms how teachers teach and how children learn. The second new paradigm transforms the organization design and work life for educators. The third new paradigm transforms a district's relationship with its external environment. The fourth new paradigm transforms the way in which school systems create and sustain change. The School System Transformation Protocol described in chapter 12 offers a methodology and a set of tools for creating and sustaining the above four paradigm shifts.

Transformation requires a reshaping of a school district's culture. Culture change focuses on the "people" part of a school system—the part called the internal social infrastructure. The internal social infrastructure supports (or constrains) people doing their work. It is composed of organization design, policies, power and political dynamics, procedures, job descriptions, and so forth, all of which are artifacts of a district's culture.

Internal social infrastructure also includes your school district's culture. Organization culture is what Duck (2001) calls "The Change Monster"—that collection of human forces that either facilitates or prevents transformation. Culture is most often reflected in the phrase "This is the way we do things around here." Culture is a complex, tightly woven, heavy fabric composed of people's assumptions, beliefs, values, mental models, and mindsets. A direct, head-on approach to changing culture will almost always meet with difficulty, resistance, and strong human emotion (Burke, 2002).

Culture change is one of the most important early outcomes of transformational change. In fact, I believe that if you cannot change your school district's culture (which is part of its internal social infrastructure), your transformation effort will fail—no culture change, no transformation. One of the reasons that organization culture is so powerful is that it is driven by your faculty and staff's collective mental models and mind-sets about the purpose of your district, the norms that govern behavior in the district, the values you all have for educating children, and how you treat the adults who work in the system. These basic mental models and mind-sets, when enacted individually and collectively, produce cultural artifacts. These artifacts include observable behavior, management systems, policies, procedures, organization design, and the physical design of your buildings.

School districts do their work within an increasingly complex and changing external environment. To adapt effectively to this complexity and rate of change, school districts need to redefine their strategic direction through organization transformation. However, implementing a new strategy aimed at transformation can meet serious resistance from a school district's existing culture. In this way, an organization culture that was once a source of strength for a district becomes a major liability. Reshaping a district's internal social infrastructure, which contains its culture, is therefore an important part of your school system's transformation journey.

Transformational change requires courageous, passionate, and visionary leaders. Courageous, passionate, and visionary leadership must begin at the highest level of a school system and then spread throughout a school district (Duffy, 2003a). Courage helps leaders stand their ground in the face of adversity. Passion gives them the emotional energy they need to persevere toward the goal of transformation. A vision marks a destination to move toward.

Courage, passion, and vision are useless in isolation. They must be simultaneously present in each change leader. A leader can have courage, but not have passion or vision. A passionate leader might lack the courage of his or her convictions and cave in to political pressure to give up the dream. A visionary leader without courage and passion is a person with a dream but without the strength of character or emotional energy to make that dream real. Courage, passion, and vision are powerful when they exist as an inseparable triad.

Courageous, passionate, and visionary leadership must also be transformational (see chapter 3). Burns (1978) distinguished between traditional managers (transactional leaders) and leaders who work to transform their organizations (transformational leaders). Tichy and Devanna (1986) expanded on Burns's ideas, asserting that managers engage in very little change, but manage what is present and leave things much as they found them when they depart; in other words, they become masters of the status quo. Transformational leadership, they observed, is marked by leadership for change and innovation, and that is provided in the spirit of entrepreneurship. These transformational leaders transform organizations by moving them toward a vision of a desirable future for the organization.

It is important to note, however, that transformational leaders do not abandon transactional management tasks. Instead, their leadership uses transactional skills as a foundation for providing transformational leadership. Their transactional management practices are required to complete daily routines (Leithwood, 1992, p. 9). Leithwood, however, maintains that these transactional practices "do not stimulate improvement . . . [rather] transformational leadership provides the incentive [for change]" (p. 9).

I believe that transformational leaders must exist first at the superintendent's level and then they must be distributed throughout a school district. If superintendents' courageous, passionate, and visionary leadership is conceived of as a leadership "tree," then in order to totally transform a district, a "forest" of courageous, passionate, and visionary leaders is needed. Therefore, transformational leadership must not be restricted to a single person. Anyone can deliver this kind of leadership. Leadership of this class can emerge from the ranks of building principals, teachers, cafeteria workers, bus drivers, janitors, central office staff, school board members, and students. Anyone who is proactive in the process of "translating intentions into reality" (Block, 1987, p. 98) can and should be identified and then developed into a transformational leader.

SHAPING THE FUTURE OF YOUR SCHOOL SYSTEM

Shaping your district's future must be guided by the knowledge that good school districts must move toward higher levels of performance. There are many good school systems in the United States. At the dawn of the twenty-first century, however, good is not good enough to bring our children to the knowledge they have a right to and with which they will bring us and themselves into the future. Not only is good not good enough, but as Collins (2001) says,

> Good is the enemy of great. And that is one of the reasons why we have so little that becomes great. We don't have great schools, principally because we have good schools. We don't have great government, principally because we have good government. Few people attain great lives, in large part because it is just so easy to settle for a good life. The vast majority of companies never become great, precisely because the vast majority become quite good—and that is their main problem. (p. 1)

Shaping your district's future entails identifying and exploring the controlling mental models and mind-sets that influence all aspects of life in your district. The controlling mental model is often reflected in your district's current vision statement and strategic plan. The dominant mind-sets are found in your colleagues' attitudes toward the controlling mental models and the paradigm of education that governs the profession of education. The mental models and mind-sets are always embedded in your district's internal social infrastructure—that collection of system features that supports (or inhibits) people at work and that includes organization design, organization culture, job descriptions, policies, procedures, communication patterns, and so on.

Shaping your district's future necessitates the direct and meaningful involvement of your district's customers (parents and students) and key external stakeholders (community groups, influential individuals in the community, and state department of education people, for example). Your district's faculty and staff must also be directly and meaningfully involved in shaping your district's future.

Shaping your district's future means you must know, understand, and apply effective approaches to strategic planning so you can create the idealized future you envision. When engaging your district in an idealized design process (see chapter 7), you must aim to create a district significantly different from the one you have now. If you don't, the planning will not be strategic (Cook, 2000), nor will it be transformational.

Shaping your district's future requires you and your colleagues to learn and become skillful at using an organization transformation methodology that is systemic, systematic, comprehensive, and organic; for example, the School System Transformation Protocol presented in chapter 12. The reason you need this kind of methodology is because organization transformation is complex and messy. A methodology with the aforementioned characteristics can help you sort out the complexity and work through the mess. A methodology especially designed to create and sustain systemic change should also be embedded in your district's organization design so that it becomes a permanent part of how your district operates. Even when your current superintendent leaves, the next superintendent, and all subsequent superintendents, should be required by school board policy to use that same methodology to create desirable and valued changes in your district.

Shaping your district's future takes you and your colleagues on a fascinating, exhilarating, and sometimes confusing and scary journey. Along the way you will be surprised by unplanned opportunities and unanticipated threats. You need to reshape your district's organization design to create flexibility and agility so your faculty and staff can anticipate and respond quickly and effectively to these surprises.

Shaping your district's future means you improve not only the academic side of your district but also the nonacademic support units. Children are in school to learn, but their experiences on the bus going to school, on the athletic playing fields, or in the cafeteria can either add value to their educational experience or they can make their lives in school miserable.

Shaping your district's future demands attention to aligning all parts of your school system to support a superordinate goal—the unifying goal, the big dream, the grand vision for your district. This alignment must be vertical up through your system and horizontal across teams, departments, schools, and clusters of schools.

Shaping your district's future compels you to counter the illusion of peak performance. In nature, successful organisms adapt to their environments by evolving to peaks of success. Successful school districts are like this too because they have evolved to their current performance peaks. For school districts, however, there are multiple peaks that evoke images of the Rocky Mountains, where some peaks are lower than others. What if the peak your district sits atop is low compared to others, but folks inside the district don't realize it? Wouldn't this lack of perspective create a false sense of success?

Shaping your district's future requires a new paradigm for creating and sustaining change. The new paradigm transports you and your colleagues from the world of "change" to the world of "flux" (Kelly, 1998; Morgan, 1986). While simple change focuses on creating differences, flux is about managing creative and controlled destruction followed by nascence. Flux breaks down the status quo while creating a temporary foundation for innovative puzzle-solving and rebirth. Innovation destroys the status quo by introducing creative innovations to a system. The quest for innovation is amaranthine. Robust innovation sustains itself at the edge of chaos.

Shaping your district's future requires all people in your district to take deliberate actions to sustain the changes you create. Sustaining innovation is particularly tricky since innovation requires a system to be in a state of creative and managed disequilibrium. Thus, a school district wanting to sustain innovative thinking and puzzle-solving must create for itself a state of controlled disequilibrium whereby it remains suspended in an almost falling state—inclined to fall, but continually catching itself and never quite toppling. To be innovative, to move to the next higher peak of performance, a school system cannot anchor itself to its past or current performance peak.

Shaping your district's future requires you to give up trying to solve problems and focus instead on seeking opportunities. The power of compounded results (e.g., compounded interest) is one of the most potent physical forces on earth. Each opportunity seized in a school district can be compounded if it becomes a platform for launching yet other innovations. Like a chain reaction, one well-placed innovation can trigger dozens of innovation progeny. New opportunities are created in a combinatorial fashion just as people combine and recombine the same twenty-six letters of the alphabet to create words that are used to write an infinite number of books.

Shaping your district's future demands strategic alignment (Duffy, 2004). Strategic alignment has two dimensions: vertical and horizontal. Vertical alignment assures that the work of individuals supports the goals of their teams, the work of the teams supports the goals of their schools (or supports work units), the work of the schools supports the goals of their clusters, and the work of the clusters supports the grand vision and strategic direction of the district. Horizontal alignment connects individuals, teams, schools, and clusters with your district's customers and external stakeholders.

CONCLUSION

You and your colleagues can create an idealized future of your school district by engaging in transformational change. Your district's future, however, is not sitting out there in time and space waiting for your arrival. You must be proactive in shaping that future by influencing events, making strategic decisions, and taking strategic action that moves you ever closer to the idealized future you and your colleagues envision for your school district. Along the way, your district has to be flexible and agile enough to respond quickly to unanticipated opportunities and threats. Responding to these opportunities and threats will then reshape the future that you envisioned for your district. This reshaping is normal and should be expected because organizations of all kinds never perfectly achieve the future they envision for themselves.

9

The Learner-Centered Paradigm of Education

Sunkyung Lee Watson and Charles M. Reigeluth

OVERVIEW

One of the themes running through this book is that there is a pressing need to replace four dominant Industrial Age paradigms that control the design and performance of school systems: Paradigm 1: the paradigm of teaching and learning; Paradigm 2: the paradigm for the design of the internal social infrastructure of school systems; Paradigm 3: the reactive, crisis-oriented paradigm guiding how school systems interact with their external environments; and Paradigm 4: the piecemeal, nonsystemic paradigm for creating and sustaining change in school systems. In this chapter, Watson and Reigeluth present a cogent argument for replacing Paradigm 1 with the Learner-Centered paradigm of education. Also, please refer to appendix D to see Reigeluth's specifications for using technology to implement the new paradigm.

The dissatisfaction with and loss of trust in schools that we are experiencing these days are a clear hallmark of the need for change in our school systems. The strong push for a learner-centered paradigm of instruction in today's schools reflects our society's changing educational needs. We educators must help our schools to move into the new Learner-Centered paradigm of instruction that better meets the needs of individual learners, of their workplaces and communities, and of society in general. It is also important that we educators help the transformation occur as effectively and

An earlier version of this chapter first appeared as the third in a series of four articles on paradigm change in education as Watson, S. L., & Reigeluth, C. M. (2008). The learner-centered paradigm of education. *Educational Technology*, 48(5), 42–48. Used with permission.

painlessly as possible. This article begins by addressing the need for transforming our educational systems to the Learner-Centered paradigm. Then it describes the nature of the Learner-Centered paradigm.

THE NEED FOR CHANGE AND THE (CRITICAL) SYSTEMS APPROACH TO EDUCATIONAL CHANGE: INFORMATION AGE VERSUS INDUSTRIAL AGE EDUCATION

Whereas society has shifted from the Industrial Age into what many call the Information Age (Reigeluth, 1994; Senge et al., 2000; Toffler, 1984), current schools were established to fit the needs of an Industrial Age society (see table 9.1). This factory-model, Industrial Age school system has highly compartmentalized learning into subject areas, and students are expected to learn the same content in the same amount of time (Reigeluth, 1994). The current school system strives for standardization and was not designed to meet individual learners' needs. Rather, it was designed to sort students into laborers and managers (see table 9.2), and students are forced to move on with the rest of the class regardless of whether or not they have learned the material. Thus, many students accumulate learning deficits and eventually drop out.

The (Critical) Systems Approach to Educational Change

Systemic educational transformation strives to change the school system to a learner-centered paradigm that will meet all learners' educational needs. It is concerned with the creation of a completely new system, rather than a mere retooling of the current system. It entails a paradigm shift as opposed to piecemeal change. Repeated calls for massive reform of current educa-

Table 9.1.   Key Markers of Industrial Age versus Information Age Education

Industrial Age Bureaucratic Organization	Information Age Team Organization
• Autocratic leadership	• Shared leadership
• Centralized control	• Autonomy, accountability
• Adversarial relationships	• Cooperative relationships
• Standardization (mass production, mass marketing, mass communications, etc.)	• Customization (customized production, customized marketing, customized communications, etc.)
• Compliance	• Initiative
• Conformity	• Diversity
• One-way communications	• Networking
• Compartmentalization (division of labor)	• Holism (integration of tasks)

Source: Reigeluth, 1994.

Table 9.2.   Key Features of Information Age Education

Sorting-Based Paradigm of Education	Learning-Based Paradigm of Education
• Time-based • Group-based • Teacher-based • Norm-based assessment	• Attainment-based • Person-based • Resource-based • Criterion-based assessment

tional and training practices have consistently been published over the last several decades. This has resulted in an increasing recognition of the need for systemic transformation in education, as numerous piecemeal approaches to education reform have been implemented and have failed to significantly improve the state of education. Systemic transformation seeks to shift from a paradigm in which time is held constant, thereby forcing achievement to vary, to one designed specifically to meet the needs of Information Age learners and their communities by allowing students the time that each needs to reach proficiency.

Systemic educational change draws heavily from the work on critical systems theory (CST) (Flood & Jackson, 1991; Jackson, 1991a, 1991b; Watson, Watson, & Reigeluth, 2008). CST has its roots in systems theory, which was established in the mid-twentieth century by a multidisciplinary group of researchers who shared the view that science had become increasingly reductionist and the various disciplines isolated. While the term *system* has been defined in a variety of ways by different systems scholars, the central notion of systems theory is the importance of relationships among elements comprising a whole.

CST draws heavily on the philosophy of Habermas (1973, 1984, 1987). The critical systems approach to social systems is of particular importance when considering systems wherein inequality of power exists in relation to opportunity, authority, and control. In the 1980s, CST came to the forefront (Jackson, 1985; Ulrich, 1983), influencing systems theory into the 1990s (Flood & Jackson, 1991; Jackson, 1991a, 1991b). Liberating Systems Theory uses a postpositivist approach to analyze social conditions in order to liberate the oppressed, while also seeking to liberate systems theory from tendencies such as self-imposed insularity, cases of internal localized subjugations in discourse, and liberation of system concepts from the inadequacies of objectivist and subjectivist approaches (Flood, 1990). Jackson (1991b) explains that CST embraces five key commitments:

- Critical awareness of examining values entering into actual systems design
- Social awareness of recognition in pressures leading to popularization of certain systems theories and methodologies

- Dedication to human emancipation for full development of all human potential
- Informed use of systems methodologies
- Informed development of all alternative positions and different theoretical systems approaches

Banathy (1991) and Senge and associates (2000) apply systems theory to the design of educational systems. Banathy (1992a, 1992b) suggests examining systems through three lenses: a "still picture lens" to appreciate the components comprising the system and their relationships; a "motion picture lens" to recognize the processes and dynamics of the system; and a "bird's-eye view lens" to be aware of the relationships between the system and its peers and suprasystems. Senge (1990) applies systems theory specifically to organizational learning, stating that the organization can learn to work as an interrelated, holistic learning community, rather than functioning as isolated departments.

Current Progress of Systemic Change in Education

While systemic educational transformation is a relatively new movement in school change, there are currently various attempts to advance knowledge about it. Examples include: The Guidance System for Transforming Education (Jenlink, Reigeluth, Carr, & Nelson, 1996, 1998), Duffy's *Step-Up-To-Excellence* (2002), Schlechty's guidelines for leadership in school reform (1997, 2002), Hammer and Champy's Process Reengineering (1993, 2003), and Ackoff's Idealized Systems Design (1981).

There are also stories of school districts making fundamental changes in schools based on the application of systemic change ideas. One of the best practices of systemic transformation is in the Chugach School District (CSD). The two hundred students in CSD are scattered throughout 22,000 square miles of remote area in south-central Alaska. The district was in crisis twelve years ago due to low student reading ability, and the school district committed to a systemic transformation effort. Battino and Clem (2006) explain how the CSD's use of individual learning plans, student assessment binders, student learning profiles, and student life-skills portfolios supports and documents progress toward mastery in all standards for each learner. The students are given the flexibility to achieve levels at their own pace, not having to wait for the rest of the class or being pushed into learning beyond their developmental level. Graduation requirements exceed state requirements, as students are allowed extra time to achieve that level if necessary, but must meet the high rigor of the graduation level. Student accomplishment in academic performance skyrocketed as a result of these systemic changes (Battino & Clem, 2006).

Caine (2006) also found strong positive changes through systemic educational change in their extensive engagement on a project called "Learning to Learn" in Adelaide, South Australia, an initiative of the South Australian government that covered a network of over 170 educational sites. From preschool to twelfth grade, brain-based, learner-centered learning environments were combined with a larger set of systemic changes, leading to both better student achievement and significant changes in the culture and operation of the system itself.

IMAGINING LEARNER-CENTERED SCHOOLS

Given the need for paradigm change in school systems, what should our schools look like in the future? The changes in society as a whole reflect a need for education to focus on learning rather than sorting students (McCombs & Whisler, 1997; Reigeluth, 1997a; Senge et al., 2000; Toffler, 1984). A large amount of research has been conducted to advance our understanding of learning and how the educational system can be changed to better support it. There is solid research about brain-based learning, learner-centered instruction, and the psychological principles of learners that provides educators with a valuable framework for the Information Age paradigm of education (Alexander & Murphy, 1993; Bonk & Cunningham, 1998; Brush & Saye, 2000; Bransford, Brown, & Cocking, 1999; Lambert & McCombs, 1998; McCombs & Whisler, 1997).

APA learner-centered psychological principles. With significant research showing that instruction should be learner-centered to meet all students' needs, there have been several efforts to synthesize the knowledge on learner-centered instruction. First, the American Psychological Association conducted wide-ranging research to identify learner-centered psychological principles based on educational research (American Psychological Association Presidential Task Force on Psychology in Education, 1993; Lambert & McCombs, 1998). The report presents twelve principles and provides the research evidence that supports each principle. It categorizes the psychological principles into four areas: (1) cognitive and metacognitive, (2) motivational affective, (3) developmental and social, and (4) individual difference factors that influence learners and learning (see table 9.3).

National Research Council's How People Learn. Another important line of research was carried out by the National Research Council to synthesize knowledge about how people learn (Bransford, Brown, & Cocking, 1999). A two-year study was conducted to develop a synthesis of new approaches to instruction that "make it possible for the majority of individuals to develop a deep understanding of important subject matter" (p. 6). Their analysis of a wide range of research on learning emphasizes the importance

Table 9.3.   Learner-Centered Psychological Principles

APA Learner-Centered Psychological Principles	
Cognitive and Metacognitive Factors	• *Nature of the learning process.* The learning of complex subject matter is most effective when it is an intentional process of constructing meaning from information and experience. • *Goals of the learning process.* The successful learner, over time and with support and instructional guidance, can create meaningful, coherent representations of knowledge. • *Construction of knowledge.* The successful learner can link new information with existing knowledge in meaningful ways. • *Strategic thinking.* The successful learner can create and use a repertoire of thinking and reasoning strategies to achieve complex learning goals. • *Thinking about thinking.* Higher-order strategies for selecting and monitoring mental operations facilitate creative and critical thinking. • *Context of learning.* Learning is influenced by environmental factors, including culture, technology, and instructional practices.
Motivational and Affective Factors	• *Motivational and emotional influences on learning.* What and how much is learned is influenced by the learner's motivation. Motivation to learn, in turn, is influenced by the individual's emotional states, beliefs, interests and goals, and habits of thinking. • *Intrinsic motivation to learn.* The learner's creativity, higher-order thinking, and natural curiosity all contribute to motivation to learn. Intrinsic motivation is stimulated by tasks of optimal novelty and difficulty, relevant to personal interests, and providing for personal choice and control. • *Effects of motivation on effort.* Acquisition of complex knowledge and skills requires extended learner effort and guided practice. Without learners' motivation to learn, the willingness to exert this effort is unlikely without coercion.

Developmental and Social Factors	• *Developmental influences on learning.* As individuals develop, there are different opportunities and constraints for learning. Learning is most effective when differential development within and across physical, intellectual, emotional, and social domains is taken into account.
	• *Social influences on learning.* Learning is influenced by social interactions, interpersonal relations, and communication with others.
Individual Differences Factors	• *Individual differences in learning.* Learners have different strategies, approaches, and capabilities for learning that are a function of prior experience and heredity.
	• *Learning and diversity.* Learning is most effective when differences in learners' linguistic, cultural, and social backgrounds are taken into account.
	• *Standards and assessment.* Setting appropriately high and challenging standards and assessing the learner as well as learning progress— including diagnostic, process, and outcome assessment— are integral parts of the learning process.

Source: American Psychological Association's Board of Educational Affairs, Center for Psychology in Schools and Education, 1997.

of customization and personalization in instruction for each individual learner, self-regulated learners taking more control of their own learning, and facilitating deep understanding of the subject matter. They describe the crucial need for, and characteristics of, learning environments that are learner centered and learning-community centered.

Learner-centered schools and classrooms. McCombs and colleagues (Baker, 1973; Lambert & McCombs, 1998; McCombs & Whisler, 1997) also address these new needs and ideas for instruction that supports all students. They identify two important features of learner-centered instruction:

a focus on individual learners (their heredity, experiences, perspectives, backgrounds, talents, interests, capacities, and needs) [and] a focus on learning (the best available knowledge about learning, how it occurs and what teaching practices are most effective in promoting the highest levels of motivation, learning, and achievement for all learners). (McCombs & Whisler, 1997, p. 11)

This twofold focus on learners and learning informs and drives educational decision making processes. In learner-centered instruction, learners are included in these educational decision making processes, the diverse perspectives of individuals are respected, and learners are treated as cocreators of the learning process (McCombs & Whisler, 1997).

Personalized Learning. Personalized Learning is part of the learner-centered approach to instruction, dedicated to helping each child to engage in the learning process in the most productive and meaningful way to optimize each child's learning and success. Personalized Learning was cultivated in the 1970s by the National Association of Secondary School Principals (NASSP) and Learning Environments Consortium (LEC) International, and was adopted by the special education movement. It is based upon a solid foundation of the NASSP's educational research findings and reports as to how students learn most successfully (Keefe, 2007; Keefe & Jenkins, 2002), including a strong emphasis on parental involvement, more teacher and student interaction, attention to differences in personal learning styles, smaller class sizes, choices in personal goals and instructional methods, student ownership in setting goals and designing the learning process, and technology use (Clarke, 2003). Leaders in other fields, such as businessman Wayne Hodgins (in Duval, Hodgins, Rehak, & Robson, 2004), have presented the idea that learning will soon become personalized, where the learner both activates and controls her or his own learning environment.

Differentiated Instruction. The recent movement in differentiated instruction is also a response to the need for a learning-focused (as opposed to a sorting-focused) approach to instruction and education in schools. Differentiated instruction is an approach that enables teachers to plan strategically to meet the needs of every student. It is deeply grounded in the principle that there is diversity within any group of learners and that teachers should adjust students' learning experiences accordingly (Tomlinson, 1999a, 1999b, 2003). This draws from the work of Vygotsky (1986), especially his "zone of proximal development" (ZPD), and from classroom researchers. Researchers found that with differentiated instruction, students learned more and felt better about themselves and the subject area being studied (Tomlinson, 2003). Evidence further indicates that students are more successful and motivated in schools if they learn in ways that are responsive to their readiness levels (Vygotsky, 1986), personal interests, and learning profiles (Csikszentmihalyi, 1990; Sternberg, Torff, & Grigorenko, 1998). The goal of differentiated instruction is to address these three characteristics for each student (Tomlinson, 2003).

Brain research and brain-based instruction. Another area of study that gives us an understanding of how people learn is the work on brain research that describes how the brain functions. Caine and Caine (1997) and Caine, Caine, McClintic, and Klimek (2005) provide a useful summary of work on how the brain functions in the process of learning through the twelve principles of brain-based learning. Brain-based learning begins when learners are encouraged to actively immerse themselves in their world and their learning experiences. In a school or classroom where brain-based learning is being practiced, the significance of diverse individual learning styles is taken for granted by teachers and administrators (Caine & Caine, 1997). In these classrooms and schools, learning is facilitated for each individual student's purposes and meaning, and the concept of learning is approached in a completely different way from the current classrooms that are set up for sorting and standardization.

An Illustration of the New Vision

What might a learner-centered school look like? An illustration or synthesis of the new vision may prove helpful.

Imagine that there are no grade levels for this school. Instead, each of the students strives to master and check off their attainments in a personal "inventory of attainments" (Reigeluth, 1994) that details the individual student's progress through the district's required and optional learning standards, kind of like merit badges in the Boy Scouts. Each student has different levels of progress in every attainment, according to his or her interests, talents, and pace. The student moves to the next topic as soon as she or he masters the current one. While each student must reach mastery level before moving on, students also do not need to wait for others who are not yet at that level of learning. In essence, now, the schools hold time constant and student learning is thereby forced to vary. In this new paradigm of the learner-centered school, it is the pace (learning time) that varies rather than student learning. All students work at their own maximum pace to reach mastery in each attainment. This individualized, customized, and self-paced learning process allows the school district to realize high standards for its students.

The teacher takes on a drastically different role in the learning process. She or he is a guide or facilitator who works with the student for at least four years, building a long-term, caring relationship (Reigeluth, 1994). The teacher's role is to help the student and parents to decide upon appropriate learning goals and to help identify and facilitate the best way for the student to achieve those goals—and for the parents to support their student. Therefore, each student has a personal learning plan in the form of a contract that is jointly developed every two months by the student, parents, and teacher.

This system enhances motivation by placing greater responsibility and ownership on the students, and by offering truly engaging, often collaborative work for students (Schlechty, 2002). Teachers help students to direct their own learning through the contract development process and through facilitating real-world independent or small-group projects that focus on developing the contracted attainments. Students learn to set and meet deadlines. The older the students get, the more leadership and assisting of younger students they assume.

The community also works closely with schools, as the inventory of attainments includes standards in service learning, career development, character development, interpersonal skills, emotional development, technology skills, cultural awareness, and much more. Tasks that are vehicles for such learning are authentic tasks, often in real community environments that are rich for learning (Reigeluth, 1994). Most learning is interdisciplinary, drawing from both specific and general knowledge and interpersonal and decision-making skills. Much of the focus is on developing deep understandings and higher-order thinking skills.

Teachers assess students' learning progress through various methods, such as computer-based assessment embedded in simulations, observation of student performances, and analysis of student products of various kinds. Instead of grades, students receive ratings of "emerging," "developing," "proficient" (the minimum required to pass), or "expert."

Each teacher has a cadre of students with whom she or he works for several years—a developmental stage of their lives. The teacher works with three to ten other teachers in a small learning community (SLC) in which the learners are multiaged and get to know each other well. Students get to choose which teacher they want (stating their first, second, and third choice), and teacher bonuses are based on the amount of demand for them. Each SLC has its own budget, based mainly on the number of students it has, and makes all its own decisions about hiring and firing of its staff, including its principal (or lead teacher). Each SLC also has a school board made up of teachers and parents who are elected by their peers.

While this illustration of a learner-centered school is based on the various learner-centered approaches to instruction reviewed earlier, and the latest educational research, this is just one of many possible visions, and these ideas need revision, as some are likely to vary from one community to another, and most need further elaboration on details. Nonetheless, this picture of a learner-centered paradigm of schooling could help us to prevail over the Industrial Age paradigm of learning and schools so that we can create a better place for our children to learn.

CONCLUSION

Our society needs learner-centered schools that focus on learning rather than on sorting (McCombs & Whisler, 1997; Reigeluth, 1997a; Senge et al., 2000; Toffler, 1984). New approaches to instruction and education have increasingly been advocated to meet the needs of all learners, and a large amount of research has been conducted to advance our understanding of learning and how the educational system can be changed to better support it (Alexander & Murphy, 1993; McCombs & Whisler, 1997; Reigeluth, 1997a; Senge et al., 2000). Nevertheless, transforming school culture and structure is not an easy task.

Isolated reforms, typically at the classroom and school levels, have been attempted over the past several decades, and their impact on the school system has been negligible. It has become clear that transforming the paradigm of schools is not a simple job. Teachers, administrators, parents, policymakers, students and all other stakeholder groups must work together, as they cannot change such a complex culture and system alone. In order to transform our schools to be truly learner-centered, a critical systems approach to transformation is essential.

The first article in this series (Reigeluth & Duffy, 2008) described the FutureMinds approach for state education departments to support this kind of change in their school districts. The second article (Duffy & Reigeluth, 2008) described the School System Transformation (SST) Protocol, a synthesis of the current knowledge about how to help school districts use a critical systems approach to transform themselves to the Learner-Centered paradigm of education. Hopefully, with state leadership through Future-Minds, the critical systems approach to educational change in the SST Protocol, and the new knowledge about learner-centered instruction, we will be able to create a better place for our children to learn and grow. However, this task will not be easy. One essential ingredient for it to succeed is the availability of powerful tools to help teachers and students in the Learner-Centered paradigm. The fourth article in this series will address this need.

IV

MASTERING METHODOLOGY

Even if you master awareness and deliberate intent, having competencies in these areas will not serve you well if you do not know how to create and sustain transformational change. Knowing how to create and sustain this kind of change requires you to master a methodology and set of tools that you can use.

In chapter 10, Kurt Richter and Charles Reigeluth compare and contrast several contemporary change methodologies that could be used to transform a school system. To provide children with a customized, personalized learning experience, school systems will need to use a Learning Management System. Knowing about this kind of technology and how to use it is an important part of your skill set for creating and sustaining transformational change. In chapter 11, Charles Reigeluth and several of his current and past graduate students discuss in detail the essential characteristics of several Learning Management Systems.

In chapter 12, you will be introduced to a methodology and set of tools especially designed to transform school systems. The methodology is called the School System Transformation Protocol. The protocol is research based and field-tested. Finally, in chapter 13, you will be introduced to seven key objections to transformational change. Learning to anticipate and respond to these objections before they become serious obstacles to change is an important part of your methodology skill set.

10

Systemic Transformation in Public School Systems

Kurt B. Richter and Charles M. Reigeluth

OVERVIEW

This chapter is based on the literature review for Kurt Richter's doctoral dissertation at Indiana University. His study examined selected elements of a whole-system transformation journey for the Metropolitan School District of Decatur Township, Indiana, where he served (and continues to serve) as part of a team of facilitators from Indiana University led by Dr. Charles Reigeluth to facilitate the transformation of that school district. The district's transformation journey was originally guided by Dr. Reigeluth's *Guidance System for Transforming Education (GSTE)*. Currently, the district is using a hybrid transformation methodology created by blending Dr. Reigeluth's GSTE method with Duffy's *Step-Up-To-Excellence* method. This new hybrid methodology is called the *School System Transformation (SST) Protocol* and it is described in chapter 12.

Dr. Richter's study sought to improve some of the process guidelines described in the GSTE by using a qualitative research methodology described as formative research (Reigeluth & Frick, 1999). This methodology asked

This chapter is based on Dr. Richter's review of the literature for his doctoral dissertation titled "Integration of a decision-making process and a learning process in a newly formed leadership team for systemic transformation of a school district." The chapter first appeared as Richter, K. B., & Reigeluth, C. M. (2007). Systemic transformation in public school systems. *The F. M. Duffy Reports, 12*(4),1–21. Questions about the dissertation research should be directed to Dr. Richter at kurichte@indiana.edu. Questions about the transformation of the Decatur Township school district should be directed to Dr. Reigeluth at reigelut@indiana.edu. Used with permission.

what worked well, what did not work as well as it could have, and what could be done to improve the process.

Specifically, Richter examined the application of the GSTE in the middle stages of the systemic transformation process with a leadership team of twenty to twenty-five stakeholders in the transforming school district. That district has 5,954 students in a semiurban, Midwestern setting. Richter, working as a cofacilitator in the systemic transformation process, studied the processes of team learning and of decision making while creating a *framework of vision, mission, and beliefs* to guide the school district's transformation effort. His dissertation reported the results of that qualitative research.

SYSTEMIC TRANSFORMATION IN PUBLIC SCHOOL SYSTEMS

There is a strong need for systemic change in public school systems in the United States. This article discusses why such a strong need exists, what alternative approaches can be used to foster systemic change, and what models currently exist to guide the most promising approach to systemic change.

Changes in Society Make the Current System Obsolete

As the United States evolves deeper into the Information Age, our society's needs and problems are changing dramatically. During the Industrial Age, most jobs were manual labor. Now, the majority of jobs require knowledge work. During the Industrial Age, a comfortable middle-class life was possible without much education, whereas in this age of global competition and digital technologies, considerably higher levels of education are needed to have a comfortable life. Workplace skills required to do entry-level jobs, identified by the U.S. Department of Labor's Secretary's Commission on Achieving Necessary Skills (SCANS), include the following skills that fall into three domains:

- "Basic skills: reading, writing, speaking, listening, and knowing arithmetic and mathematical concepts;
- Thinking skills: reasoning, making decisions, thinking creatively, solving problems, seeing things in the mind's eye, and knowing how to learn; and
- Personal qualities: responsibility, self-esteem, sociability, self-management, integrity, and honesty" (Whetzel, 1992, p. 1).

As we evolve deeper into the Information Age, societal systems, jobs, and even personal lives are becoming more complex. The Information Age is developing increasingly powerful computer-based tools for dealing with such complexity, but according to Spiro (2006), these "post-Gutenberg" technologies require the development of a different style of thinking, through "prefigurative schemas" (schemas for the development of schemas), which requires dramatic changes in both the goals and means of education.

The typical response in school districts to this growing educational crisis is piecemeal, "fix-the-broken-part" approach to change. A reading program does not work well, so remediation is offered. Falling test scores are evident, so yearly statewide testing for everyone is introduced. Rising rates of obesity result in the removal of soda machines from schools. These changes are made by schools to adjust to immediate challenges that arise during the normal course of schooling.

What is seldom recognized is that dramatic changes in educational needs require changes in the fundamental structure and organization of school systems. Reigeluth talks persuasively about the need to rethink what Schlechty calls "rules, roles, and relationships" for the ways we use "time, talent, and technology" (Reigeluth, 1997a, p. 205) in school districts. For example, regarding time, it is known that different students learn at different rates (Mayer, 1999), yet we require all students to learn the same amount of content in the same amount of time. By holding time constant, we force achievement to vary. Our current educational system was designed for sorting students more than for learning, which was appropriate in the Industrial Age, because we did not need to, and could not afford to, educate large numbers of students to high levels. But the Information Age, with its predominance of knowledge work and global competition, has dramatically changed that, making learning a much higher priority than sorting.

In the Information Age paradigm, it is no longer satisfactory to promote learners to the next level simply because they have spent a year in the previous level. It is no longer acceptable to emulate the factory model and to teach all children at the same rate. In the Information Age paradigm we need to educate more children to their potential. Faster learners must no longer be forced to waste time until the class is ready to move on, and slow learners must no longer be forced to move on before they have mastered the content, condemning them to accumulate learning deficits that make it even more difficult to learn material that builds on that content.

Time must become flexible and customized to each learner's needs. Imagine schools without class periods and grade levels. This change in the use of time would require fundamental changes in the use of talent (teachers and students) and technology (Schlechty, 2002). It would require fundamental changes from standardization to customization, from control to empowerment, from compliance to initiative, and from uniformity to diversity (Reigeluth, 1999).

KEY MARKERS OF INDUSTRIAL AGE
AND INFORMATION AGE COMPARED

Coevolution is a system evolving in harmony with its environment. Modern-day society has evolved from the Agrarian Age, in which agricultural activities formed the backbone of society, to the Industrial Age, in which the assembly line and mass production created products and goods for consumption by the public, and most recently, to the Information Age, in which knowledge work has replaced manual labor as the predominant form of work. Key markers of the Industrial Age compared to the Information Age are listed in table 10.1.

As can be seen in table 10.1, the key markers of the Information Age are descriptors of a paradigm that puts emphasis on the team over the bureaucracy, on autonomy over control and command, and on initiative over compliance. At every level of the educational system, the needs of society now require different criteria for success, criteria that correspond closely with the Information Age key markers. To be relevant and meet the needs of society and its members, education must seek to evolve in ways that express the fulfillment of Information Age needs and expectations.

What Is Systemic Change?

In the evolving discipline of systemic change in educational transformation, there is little agreement as to the meaning and concept of the term "systemic change." It often seems as though the term systemic change is used to describe "almost any large scale project" (Carr-Chellman, 1999, p. 369). If one examines the programs making up the reform efforts included in the New

Table 10.1. Key Markers of the Industrial Age and the Information Age

Industrial Age	Information Age
Standardization	Customization
Bureaucratic organization	Team-based organization
Centralized control	Autonomy with accountability
Adversarial relationships	Cooperative relationships
Autocratic decision making	Shared decision making
Compliance	Initiative
Conformity	Diversity
One-way communications	Networking
Compartmentalization	Holism
Parts oriented	Process oriented
Planned obsolescence	Total quality
CEO or boss as "king"	Customer as "king"

Source: Reigeluth, 1999, p. 17. Used with permission.

American Schools Development Corporation (Stringfield, Ross, & Smith, 1996), this is often the case. Here, programs as diverse as "The Modern Red Schoolhouse," "Roots and Wings: Universal Excellence in Elementary Education," and "Los Angeles Learning Centers: An Initiative of Los Angeles Unified School District, United Teachers Los Angeles" are all described by Stringfield and colleagues (1996) as systemic efforts. Upon closer inspection, these programs are actually adopted by clients for the purpose of initiating school-based improvement without transformational paradigm change. The programs provide a structure which can be adopted and implemented, to which teachers and students must adapt without substantial alteration of the existing paradigm. They all share the quality of being systematic, but they demonstrate widely varying definitions of systemic change.

To clarify and focus the definition of systemic change, we first describe what systemic change is not, followed by a working definition of what it is. Systemic change is not piecemeal change. If only one element in a system is changed, no matter where in that system the element resides, it is still piecemeal change. The key indicator of systemic change is paradigm change (Reigeluth, 1999), which means that a significant change in one part of the system is accompanied by significant changes in practically all other parts, due to interrelationships and interdependence among parts.

Banathy (1991) addresses piecemeal change in school districts when he describes how the Carnegie Corporation "labeled the existing system an outdated assembly line and made fifty-eight specific nonintegrated proposals to 'radically transform' schools" (p. 11). He describes most of the improvement techniques that have been used as ineffective because they fail to

> recognize the complexity of current issues surrounding education and [they] have not grappled with the essential nature of education as a societal system; a system interacting with other societal systems, a system which is embedded in the rapidly and dynamically changing larger society. (p. 12)

Systemic change must encompass a broad scope and be large in scale within the system of interest. A fundamental change in curriculum would not constitute systemic change in a school district. Such a change could affect individual classrooms in all schools in the district, but because other elements in the system's structure have not changed, the effect on the greater system would not be systemic, but piecemeal. To become a systemic change, there would have to be changes throughout all aspects of the system related to the new curriculum. Piecemeal changes can "produce the appearance of change but not much real improvement in outcomes" (Harman, 1984, p. 3).

Squire and Reigeluth (2000) discuss four types of systemic change, which they refer to as statewide, district-wide, schoolwide, and ecological systemic change. They have found that a user's conception of systemic change depends on their experience and the type of system with which he or she is familiar. Ecological systemic change matches the definition for systemic change used in this article.

Ecological systemic change is an approach that requires an understanding of a school district as a system. This approach encompasses and contains the relationships among all stakeholders: community members, parents, school and district staff, students, teachers, principals, administrators, and state-level education personnel. These multiple stakeholders are included and embraced at the earliest stages of the transformation effort and are involved in democratic participation in the change process. Experts may be brought into the process as support, but their main job is to act as support in the process and "not to shape the product of design" (Squire & Reigeluth, 2000, p. 6).

Changes in mind-sets, which are "mental positions or outlooks from which people approach problems" (La Piana Associates, 2006), are critical to systemic change. Such mind-set change is brought about through dialogue, or the process by which a group "becomes open to the flow of a larger intelligence" (Senge, 1990, p. 239) and self-examination. Mind-set change is absolutely required for creating and sustaining transformational change.

The definition of systemic change used in this article—one that is compatible with the concept of ecological systemic change—is described by Jenlink, Reigeluth, Carr, and Nelson (1998). They define systemic change as an approach that:

- recognizes the interrelationships and interdependencies among the parts of the educational system, with the consequence that desired changes in one part of the system must be accompanied by changes in other parts that are necessary to support those desired changes; and
- recognizes the interrelationships and interdependencies between the educational system and its community, including parents, employers, social service agencies, religious organizations and much more, with the consequence that all those stakeholders are given active ownership over the change effort (p. 219).

APPROACHES TO SYSTEMIC CHANGE

External Design versus Internal Design

There are two approaches available to school districts that decide to engage in systemic change: (1) implement a standard design that was invented elsewhere, or (2) engage in a process that helps their stakeholders design their own new system. The first approach—standard designs that are invented elsewhere—is typified by efforts such as the school designs of the New American Schools Development Corporation. These kinds of efforts are not truly systemic, but are combinations of piecemeal changes that have been applied in a systematic manner. Such shortsighted efforts have led to minimal educational returns in places like Washington, DC, and Memphis, Tennessee (Mirel, 2001; Pogrow, 2000a, 2000b, 2002). Chief complaints about externally designed efforts include teacher and union resistance, a general feeling of dissatisfaction, and isolation.

Other examples of the expert design are found in such programs as Roots and Wings (Slavin, Madden, & Wasik, 1996), The Modern Red Schoolhouse (Heady & Kilgore, 1996), Success for All (Hurley, Chamberlain, Slavin, & Madden, 2001; Pogrow, 2000a, 2000b, 2002), the Expeditionary Learning Outward Bound Design (Goldberg, Richards, & BBN Corporation, 1996), and others.

The expert design strategy fails to address specific needs of most school districts. Experience tells us that this externally designed approach to change is ineffective and, over time, often detrimental.

In the internal design approach, the focus is on a process that helps participants learn and work together and stimulate each other to evolve their individual and collective mind-sets about education. From the consensus-building process, values that govern the change process emerge and drive the process forward. From these process values, approaches to instruction and education emerge that are used to guide the design of the new paradigm of education. As long as stakeholders develop ownership of the process and are willing to engage in mind-set change, the internal process is far more likely to yield a positive and long-lasting change in the fundamental structure of schooling in a district.

Instead of selecting an externally designed product for implementation, schools can choose to engage in an internal design process. The internal design approach relies heavily on the user-designer model. For a successful user-design to emerge, many people from all stakeholder groups must become a part of the process. As they engage in the process, stakeholders come to consensus on values, the mission of education, and beliefs that support the culture of education. Through the design process, stakeholders come to understand the real needs of the school system and learn how to work together to address those needs. Well-facilitated engagement in the process by all users will eventually result in a user-designed plan for systemic change.

The internal design process is done neither quickly nor easily. First, it requires that representatives from every stakeholder group served by the school district meet in a leadership team over an extended period of time. Members on the leadership team must include district and school administrators, the teachers' union(s), district and school staff, and parents meeting in an atmosphere of equality and consensus building.

Second, because of the need to find common ground in an Information Age environment, all stakeholders must be open to evolving their thinking (mind-set change) about education, often considered to be one of the most difficult tasks that they will face.

Third, the traditional model of top-down leadership must be abandoned in favor of a developmental leadership model that shares responsibility and develops leadership among all stakeholders.

Finally, systemic change occurs most realistically and effectively when approached as a process of engagement that entails a long-term commitment for improving the system of interest. With these elements in place, stakeholders are ready to engage in the internal design process approach to systemic change.

Given these general characteristics, the following is a review of the current knowledge about the internal design process.

OVERVIEW OF INTERNAL DESIGN MODELS

Step-Up-To-Excellence

Step-Up-To-Excellence (SUTE) (Duffy, 2006, p. 3) was developed as a response to the needs of change leaders as they attempt to seek ways in which entire school systems can be transformed. It is described as a "whole-system transformation protocol especially constructed to help educators navigate the three paths toward whole-district transformation" (Duffy, 2006, p. 3). In this summary of SUTE, we first summarize the three paths that occur at each of the levels. We discuss the personnel and groups who are charged with initiating, implementing, and maintaining change. We then discuss the conferences that occur among each group participating in each step of the process. We conclude with a description of each of the steps in the SUTE Change Protocol.

There are three sets of organizational variables that require concurrent improvement if a whole school system is to be transformed. Within the context of SUTE these sets are called change paths, and they recur at every level of a school system throughout SUTE.

Path 1: Transform a district's core and support work processes. The core work of contemporary school districts is accomplished within a "sequenced instructional program conjoined with classroom teaching and learning" (Duffy, 2006, p. 3). Core work is supported by two kinds of support work: Academic support that includes those in administrative, supervisory, and curriculum development positions and nonacademic support that includes transportation, cafeteria, and janitorial positions, as well as others in similar positions. All work processes must be improved for systemic transformation to be successful.

369

Path 2: Transform a district's internal social infrastructure. Variables along this path include "organization culture, organization design, communication patterns, power and political dynamics, reward systems, and so on" (Duffy, 2006, p. 4).

Path 3: Transform a district's relationship with its external environment. Change leaders must ensure that relationships between key external stakeholders in the community and the school system are strong before engaging in a systemic transformation, and then these relationships must be maintained throughout the transformation journey.

Change Leadership within SUTE

The individual responsible for initiating transformational change in a school district is a superintendent in collaboration with a small team of colleagues. The superintendent forms a prelaunch team to prepare the system for transformation. Later in the process, a Strategic Leadership Team is formed that includes educators from each level of the school system. A change navigation coordinator is also appointed or hired to provide tactical leadership for the transformation. Various change leadership teams are also formed—one for each cluster of schools in the district, one for the central administration office, and one for a cluster of nonacademic supporting work units (e.g., cafeteria services, transportation services, and building and grounds maintenance services). As the SUTE process continues, Site Improvement Teams are also formed for each school building and nonacademic supporting work unit. All of these teams make up a change management structure for the district.

The Structure of SUTE

SUTE is organized using a prelaunch preparation phase and three steps. Each one is briefly described below.

Prelaunch Preparation. Prior to launching a transformation journey, the readiness of the district to participate in transformational change is assessed by the superintendent of schools and the small prelaunch team. During this phase, an abbreviated environmental scan is conducted to identify threats that face the district and opportunities that can be seized if they engage in transformational change. Additional internal assessments are made to determine the district's readiness to participate in transformational change.

Additional considerations that determine readiness to proceed are described by Sirkin, Keenan, and Jackson (in Duffy, 2006, p. 10) as the "hard factors of change" (Duffy, 2006, p. 10):

- Duration: the amount of time needed to complete the transformation initiative

- Integrity: the ability of the change leadership teams to complete the transformation activities as planned and on time; which is directly affected by the team members' knowledge and skills for leading a transformation journey
- Commitment: the level of unequivocal support for the transformation demonstrated by senior leadership as well as by employees
- Effort: the amount of effort above and beyond normal work activities that is needed to complete the transformation (p. 10)

At some point early in the prelaunch phase of SUTE, the prelaunch team will make a "launch/don't launch" decision. If the decision is to launch a transformation journey for the district, then a new leadership team is formed and trained. That team is called a Strategic Leadership Team. This team is composed of the superintendent, one or two of his or her immediate subordinates, and school-based administrators and teachers from each level of schooling in a district. It might also include a school board member, a teacher union representative, parents, and students.

The school-based members of this team are not selected by the superintendent; instead, they are appointed to the team by their peers in the schools. This appointment process prevents the impression that the Strategic Leadership Team was handpicked by the superintendent.

Transformational change requires leadership from all quarters of a school district. Distributed leadership will only be as effective as the people who provide this leadership. Leadership for transformational change should also be in the hands of people who are allies in the change process. Allies are trusted colleagues who are in high agreement with the transformation goals.

One individual is chosen to coordinate the efforts of the Strategic Leadership Team, and that individual is known as the change navigation coordinator (Duffy, 2006, p. 9). Ideally, this coordinator should be an assistant or associate superintendent. This person will probably need training to become a master of transformational change. In large districts, the coordinator may form a change leadership team that will collaborate with him or her to lead their district's transformation journey.

The Strategic Leadership Team oversees the work of the change navigation coordinator and his or her change leadership team. The coordinator starts to create a change management structure to support the transformation journey. This structure requires that the district be organized into academic clusters, a central administration cluster, and a nonacademic support work cluster.

The academic clusters contain individual school buildings and classrooms. To conform to principles of systemic change, the academic clusters must contain the entire instructional program of the district; for example, in a district that is organized P–12th grade, the academic clusters will contain a high school and all the middle and elementary schools that feed into it. This is very important because of a systemic change principle called "upstream errors flow downstream." This means that errors made early in the teaching and learning process, if they are not identified and corrected, will flow downstream and cause significant problems downstream in the instructional program; for example, if students accumulate early learning deficits as they progress through their district's instructional program, their "downstream" learning will become progressively more difficult, and ultimately they will experience increasing levels of academic failure.

Another principle of systemic change is that the central administration office must be transformed into a central service center that serves educators and support staff working in the district. To facilitate this transformation, the central administration office is conceived of as a cluster that will undergo transformational change.

Nonacademic support work includes cafeteria services, transportation services, and building and grounds maintenance services. These support services must be transformed, too; for example, the New York City school system transformed its cafeteria services by hiring an executive chef from the private sector who created brand new food selections for all the schools in the system.

Another element of the change management structure that is created to implement SUTE is the formation of "scouting parties." These small groups of educators from the district will start looking for really great ideas that might be used to transform their district; for example, they might seek out school systems that provide customized, personalized education to students.

Also, the change navigation coordinator and his or her team start looking for sources of money to fund their transformation journey. They don't request the money right now, because they have no idea how much they will need, but they need to identify where they can submit their requests later on in the SUTE process.

Near the end of the prelaunch phase, two important conferences are organized and conducted. The first is called a Community Engagement Conference. This one-to-three day conference is designed to invite hundreds of community members into one room, where they will then self-organize into discussion groups to talk about their dreams, expectations, and concerns for their school district. Notes are taken at each discussion table and submitted to secretarial staff who enter them into a word processing program. These data from external stakeholders are used later to plan the district's transformation.

The next conference that is conducted is for the faculty and staff working in the district. It is called a System Engagement Conference. The System Engagement Conference is designed using principles of Future Search as described in Schweitz, Martens, and Aronson (2005), or principles of search conferencing as described by Merrelyn Emery (2006). Either set of design principles will work for this conference.

One of the key principles for designing this conference is that the whole system must be in the room. What this means is that at least one person from every school and every support work unit must be invited to participate. The purpose of this one-to-three day event is to create a new "fuzzy" vision for the district, as well as a new strategic framework that reflects the district and community's core beliefs and values. Data from the Community Engagement Conference are carefully considered during this conference.

One outcome of the System Engagement Conference is a strategic framework for the district that includes new mission and vision statements and a strategic framework for guiding the transformation of the school system. Following the System Engagement Conference, the Strategic Leadership Team and change navigation coordinator organize the district into clusters: academic, central office, and nonacademic support work units. Each cluster is led by a Cluster Design Team that engages in training designed to develop and enhance their knowledge and skills for leading transformational change.

The conclusion of the System Engagement Conference marks the beginning of a design process that will lead to proposals to transform the district's academic clusters, central administration office, and support work units. The design work happens in Step 1: Redesign the Entire School District.

Step 1: Redesign the entire school district. During the prelaunch phase, the district was organized into three kinds of clusters: academic, central office, and nonacademic support work units. Step 1 begins with one of the academic clusters.

The first academic cluster creates a Cluster Improvement Team to guide their cluster's transformation journey. The change navigation coordinator works closely with this team. The Cluster Improvement Team then creates school-based improvement teams for each school in the cluster. These teams are called Site Improvement Teams.

The Cluster Improvement Team, with help from the change navigation coordinator, plans and conducts a Cluster Engagement Conference. All educators from all the schools in the cluster are invited to participate in this conference. Parents and other community members may also be invited to this conference. The purpose of this conference is to determine how the cluster and the schools can be designed to support the district's new vision and strategic framework.

Following the Cluster Engagement Conference, Site Improvement Teams are formed for each school in the cluster. Each Site Improvement Team then engages in highly structured Redesign Workshops that will lead them through a process to identify how they can transform their individual schools to align with their cluster's improvement goals and with the district's vision and strategic framework. The redesign workshops ask educators to create ideas to (1) improve their relationship with the external environment, (2) improve their core work processes, and (3) improve their internal social infrastructure. It is the responsibility of the members of the Site Improvement Teams to work on making progress along the three change paths mentioned above. The primary outcome of the redesign workshops are proposals "for transforming each cluster and every school within each cluster" (Duffy, 2006, p. 10).

As plans are made and support requirements begin to change, the responsibility for engaging in the redesign process moves to the central office and nonacademic supporting work units. They, too, engage in a Cluster Engagement Conference and Redesign Workshops to transform their environmental relationships, work processes, and internal social infrastructure.

During phase 1, as the change proposals are developed and organized into a master proposal to transform the entire district, the Strategic Leadership Team and change navigation coordinator are charged with the task of finding money to support the proposed changes. Initially, the effort can seek money from grants by public or private entities and foundations, but in the long run, it is necessary to reallocate district money to support the ongoing redesign efforts.

As the change proposals are implemented, On-Track Seminars enable participants to engage in formative evaluation to ensure that the transformation work continues to adhere to district vision and goals. The seminars also:

- facilitate individual, team, and district-wide learning;
- educate and train faculty and staff to use inquiry skills;
- create opportunities to model collaboration, cooperation, and participation behaviors;
- establish linkages between learning and performance;
- facilitate the search for ways to create greater understanding of what affects the district's success and failure; and
- rely on diverse perspectives to develop understanding of the district's performance (Duffy, 2006, p. 12).

Step 2: Create strategic alignment. In step 2, individuals work to align their work with the goals of teams, the work of teams with the goals of schools, the work of schools with the goals of their clusters, and the work of the clusters with the new mission, vision, and strategic framework of the district.

Step 3: Evaluate whole-district performance. In previous steps, formative evaluation is conducted to keep the transformation journey on course toward desirable vision for the district. In this step, summative evaluation is conducted to "measure the success of everyone's efforts to educate children with the framework of the newly transformed school system" (Duffy, 2006, p. 13).

Though step 3 measures success, it is not the end of the cycle, because the district must recycle the change process to the prelaunch preparation phase. This is an essential characteristic of SUTE because it is built on the philosophy that transformation is not an event—it is a journey that spirals a district continuously upwards toward higher and higher levels of performance. Achieving high performance is a lifelong journey for a school district.

Schlechty's Process

Phillip Schlechty has written extensively on school reform since the late 1960s. Many of his ideas are summarized in *Schools for the 21st Century: Leadership Imperatives for Educational Reform* (Schlechty, 1990). He discusses qualities that schools must have if they are to be prepared for the increasing expectations in the new century. The work of the school is knowledge work, defined as "putting to use ideas and symbols to produce some purposeful result" (Schlechty, 1990, p. 35), and it emphasizes mental effort. Schools engage in knowledge work and must engage in reform if they are to remain relevant as an institution (Schlechty, 1997).

Schlechty (2002) discusses the importance of the kind of work that is provided to students in the course of instruction. In contrast to manual work, which involves the completion of physical tasks, knowledge work emphasizes "management and control of symbols, propositions, and other forms of knowledge; and the use of these intellectual products in the achievement of goals" (Schlechty, 2002, p. xv). Schoolwork should consist of knowledge work that promotes the intellectual and moral development of the student. This supportive framework is called "Working on the Work" (WOW). The main features of Schlechty's WOW framework (Schlechty, 2002, p. xviii) are:

1. One of the most important responsibilities for teachers is to provide students with information to learn. Schlechty calls that information "work."
2. A second responsibility of teachers is help students succeed in learning what they need to learn.
3. Therefore, Schlechty concludes that teachers are leaders and inventors and students are volunteers who volunteer their attention and commitment.
4. Differences in student commitment and attention produce differences in the degree to which a student is engaged in learning what must be learned.
5. Differences in the level and type of engagement affect the amount of effort a student expends on learning-related tasks.
6. The level of effort applied to learning tasks affects learning outcomes at least as much as intellectual ability.

7. According to Schlechty, the level and type of student engagement will vary depending on how teachers design and deliver learning activities and information.
8. Therefore, Schlechty reaches the conclusion that teachers can directly affect student learning by designing learning activities that have those qualities that are most engaging to students.

Schlechty's WOW framework addresses the types of work that must be done to "improve student performance in school" (Schlechty, 2002, p. xiv), but this most recent work is part of a larger body of work that provides process knowledge about how schools should proceed to enact systemic change. Also discussed by Schlechty (1997) are the powerful values and assumptions that should be used in any redesign or systemic change effort. Schlechty's work explores the importance of leadership and clear vision by saying that "ideas begin with individual women and men: they do not begin with groups" (Schlechty, 1990, p. 60).

Effective leaders begin by working with educators and educational personnel at every level in the schools to create a clear vision that extends to all members of the system through "participatory leadership" (Schlechty, 1990, p. 60). Once that vision has been created, it must be marketed to those who will be affected by it. A distinction is made between a sales approach, in which those who offer the product (change) try to overcome resistance to the product, and the market approach, in which the "needs and values of those whose support is essential" (Schlechty, 1990, p. 64) are met.

For implementation of changes, Schlechty lists five functions that require fulfillment: (1) Intellectual leaders must emerge and be able to conceptualize the idea and the structure of the change effort; (2) Those who will be involved in the change must be recruited and informed of the nature of plans for change; (3) Feedback about the change must be solicited from those who will be called upon to support the change; (4) Implementation activities must be implemented; and (5) Ongoing support and training must be made available to all concerned. Schlechty (1990) refers to these functions "as the conceptualizing function, the marketing function, the developmental function, the implementation function, and the service and support function" (p. 98), respectively.

Systemic change requires strong transformational leadership as a guiding force. Schlechty describes such a leader in the superintendent. Qualities of the superintendent include being a nonauthoritarian leader who believes in participatory leadership. The superintendent is seen not as a democratic leader but as one who is "strong enough to trust others with his or her fate, just as he or she expects their trust in return (Reigeluth & Frick, 1999).

THE GUIDANCE SYSTEM FOR
TRANSFORMING EDUCATION (GSTE)

The GSTE is a set of guidelines for facilitating systemic change in school districts (Jenlink, Reigeluth, Carr, & Nelson, 1998). The guidelines offered by the GSTE outline an internal-design process approach to systemic educational change that relies upon the premise that real systemic change can only occur if the demand for change is supported by all who are affected by the change. Because of the increased involvement of community stakeholders, the GSTE appears to have greater potential for successful implementation than most other models. The GSTE provides flexible and detailed process guidelines to a facilitator who chooses to engage in a district-wide systemic change effort. The following description of the GSTE is based upon *Guidelines for Facilitating Systemic Change in School Districts* (Jenlink, Reigeluth, Carr, & Nelson, 1998).

The GSTE is divided into three parts: guiding beliefs, discrete events, and continuous events. Jenlink et al. describe twenty-two guiding beliefs and values that are proposed as being important to a successful systemic change effort. These beliefs guide the actions of the facilitator and stakeholders, for the values should be incorporated in each of the discrete and continuous events that will occur in the course of the change process as noted in table 10.2.

The discrete events of the Guidance System for Transforming Education (GSTE) are organized into five phases, each of which contains specific activities and steps.

Phase I: Assess readiness and negotiate an agreement. During this phase, the outside facilitator(s) first assess their readiness and interest in becoming a facilitator of a systemic change effort. Next, the facilitators must either contact a school district or engage in discussions about the parameters of such a change effort. Then the facilitators engage with the district to determine the

Table 10.2. Guiding Beliefs and Implied Values in the Guidance System for Transforming Education

Caring for children and their future	Systemic thinking
Inclusivity	Stakeholder ownership
Coevolution	Facilitator
Process orientation	Context
Time	Space
Participant commitment	Respect
Responsibility	Readiness
Collaboration	Community
Vision	Wholeness
Language	Conversation
Democracy	Culture

Source: Jenlink, Reigeluth, Carr, & Nelson, 1998. Adapted with permission.

readiness for change. This phase culminates in a formal agreement that is signed between the governing body (the school board) and the change team that specifies the nature of the change process. Finally, in this stage the facilitators must assess the district's ability, or "capacity for change" (Jenlink, Reigeluth, Carr, & Nelson, 1998, p. 225). The four distinct events in this phase are shown in table 10.3.

Phase II: Prepare a core team for the change process. A small core team of five to seven individuals is created and charged with the responsibility to explore and evaluate the current system with respect to systemic change. The newly formed team must generate a team culture and dynamic in which systemic change is carried out. The facilitators must help the core team to develop skills and understandings in systems design and group process. In event eight of this phase, the core team utilizes their knowledge of systems design to redesign and customize the next three events and to tailor them to meet the specific needs of the district. Event nine asks the core team to identify any other change events that might compete for time or resources. In event ten, they evaluate the openness to change within the district and community. In event eleven, the "existing beliefs, assumptions, and mindsets about educational change" (Jenlink, Reigeluth, Carr, & Nelson, 1998, p. 226) are evaluated. This phase ends with event twelve, in which the core team redesigns the process in events ten through fifteen as they prepare to expand into a Decisioning Team and a Design Support Team. The eight distinct events in this phase are shown in table 10.4.

Phase III: Prepare expanded teams for the process. The core team is responsible for preparing to expand into the Decisioning Team and the Design Support Team. These two groups work interactively. In event thirteen, the core team expands into a team of approximately twenty members, including representative members from every stakeholder group. Event fourteen can be done either before or after event fifteen and consists of building

Table 10.3.   Distinct Events in Phase I: Assess Readiness and Capacity

1. Assess and enhance your readiness to be a facilitator. Prepare the facilitator for facilitating the change effort through self-assessment.
2. Establish or redefine your relationship with a school district and then make site visits to determine whether or not to proceed on the basis of the district's readiness for change. This step helps to identify a school district with which to work.
3. Assess the district's readiness for change and negotiate a formal agreement. This event involves assessing the district's readiness for systemic change by looking at documents and interviewing key people. A decision is made whether or not to enter into a formal relationship at this stage.
4. Assess the district's capacity for change. Facilitator meets with stakeholders within the district and identifies existing and lacking capacities for systemic change.

Source: Jenlink, Reigeluth, Carr, & Nelson, 1998.

Table 10.4.   Distinct Events in Phase II: Prepare the Initial Core Team

5. Select the participants for the core team. Key district leaders should assist you in selecting the types of people who should be included on the core team. This selection is announced publicly and should help to create public awareness of the event.

6. Create the core team dynamic. The core team attends a two-day retreat. They work together to develop a team culture, teaming skills and group knowledge. This becomes an experience base to design team-building experiences for newly developed teams later in the process.

7. Train the initial core team in systems design. Included in this training is systems theory, practice, and systems design. Emphasis is on deep understanding and appreciation for user-designer approach to systems design.

8. Design events 9–11. Events 9–11 are just-in-time activities requiring core team selection and redesign.

9. Identify competing change efforts. The core team identifies change efforts in the district that are currently under way that may compete for time or resources

10. Evaluate openness to change. In addition to evaluating the district's openness to change, the core team must also identify why the district is open or closed to change.

11. Evaluate the existing culture for change. The core team must evaluate the existing beliefs, assumptions, and mind-sets about educational change. This involves fostering an understanding of what a culture of change is along with understanding the language of change.

12. Redesign events ten through fifteen. This consists of designing the steps that will be used to expand the core team into a Decisioning Team (twenty to twenty-five people) and a Design Team (eight to twelve people) whose jobs include making the decisions that will affect the changed system or to design the new educational system. The order in which these two events occur determines whether event thirteen or fourteen will come next.

Source: Jenlink, Reigeluth, Carr, & Nelson, 1998.

the Design Support Team, a group that includes five members from the original Decisioning Team and an additional five members. Event fifteen provides for training the Design Support Team "with respect to applications of the systems theory, systems practice, and various model of systems design" (Jenlink, Reigeluth, Carr, & Nelson, 1998, p. 228). As in phase II, event sixteen asks the participants to redesign events seventeen through twenty-four in preparation for the next phase. The four distinct events in this phase are shown in table 10.5.

Phase IV: Engage in design of the new educational system. With the groundwork for change laid, the community is now engaged in the design process. Event seventeen asks participants to identify their own mind-set and to understand "how mind-sets contribute to our perceptions of education (Jenlink, Reigeluth, Carr, & Nelson, 1998, p. 229). Event eighteen asks participants to explore idealized beliefs and assumptions about education to help participants create a foundation for expectations about coming steps in the design process. Event nineteen gives the Design Support Team guidance in imple-

Table 10.5. Distinct Events in Phase III: Prepare the Expanded Teams

13. Expand and build the Decisioning Team. The core team expands to approximately twenty members broadly representing all stakeholder groups. This event includes a two-day retreat similar to that used to build the core team, with the responsibility of identifying personality profiles and identifying common beliefs (event 6).
14. Select and build the Design Support Team. If done after event 10, five members of the Decisioning Team spin off to serve on the Design Team as well. These five form the nucleus of approximately ten people. They must foster understanding of the role of the Design Team in the systemic change effort. They must plan a two-day retreat similar to that described in event 10, with similar expectations for planning the mode of operation.
15. Train and enculturate the Design Support Team. Facilitation of additional training for the Design Team with respect to applications of systems theory and practice, and various models of systems design are learned in event 14 (see event 7). Explore alternative views and approaches to the change process.
16. Redesign the change process. The Design Support Team redesigns its own design process using what was learned in event 15 and what is provided in the guidebook for events 17–24. Foster understanding of evaluation as an important part of learning within the systemic change effort.

Source: Jenlink, Reigeluth, Carr, & Nelson, 1998.

menting the "self-selection of small design teams based on individuals' beliefs within the framework of the district-wide beliefs" (Jenlink, Reigeluth, Carr, & Nelson, 1998, p. 229). In event twenty, the facilitator works with Design Support Team members "in the process of reaching consensus on the particular beliefs about learning and education that they would like their school to reflect with the framework of the district-wide beliefs" (Jenlink, Reigeluth, Carr, & Nelson, 1998, p. 229).

In event twenty-one, Design Support Team members develop a system for evaluating the results of the change process. In event twenty-two, the Design Support Team designs a system of functions to enable it to attain its vision of a new educational system. In event twenty-three, the components for accomplishing the functions identified in event twenty-two are designed. Finally, in event twenty-four, all design teams join together to design both sitewide and district-wide "administrative and governance systems" (Jenlink, Reigeluth, Carr, & Nelson, 1998, p. 230). These eight distinct events in this phase are shown in table 10.6.

Phase V: Implement and evolve the new system. Ideal designs having been generated and approved, the community develops and uses an implementation process to transition into the new system in event twenty-five. In event twenty-six, the process is implemented, evaluated, and revised while implemented, along with implementation, evaluation, and revision of the new system as it evolves. The two distinct events in this phase are shown in table 10.7.

Table 10.6.   Distinct Events in Phase IV: Design a New System

17. Evolve mind-sets about education. The facilitator must foster an understanding of what mind-sets are and how they contribute to our perceptions of education. You must help the Design and Decisioning Teams clarify the basis of their mind-sets and to move beyond their current mind-sets.

18. Explore ideal beliefs and assumptions about education. The facilitator must assist the Design and Decisioning Teams to develop a core set of ideal beliefs and assumptions about education that they want to see throughout the new system. This new system must incorporate an understanding of and appreciation for ideal design.

19. Select and build multiple design teams. The facilitator assists the Design Team to plan and implement the self-selection of small design teams based on individuals' beliefs within the framework of districtwide beliefs. Each new team engages in a two-day retreat at which they work on team building and development of appropriate skills and knowledge (see event 14). Results of prior evaluations are shared with the teams and they determine their own mode of operations and communication with the districtwide Design Team.

20. Explore ideal visions based on the common beliefs. The facilitator assists and cofacilitates the districtwide Design Team members to facilitate each design team in the process of reaching consensus on learning and education. This consensus, along with an ideal vision based on common beliefs and assumptions, will be incorporated into the new "school" design that they will create. Further, this vision shall incorporate an instructional system to support these kinds of learning experiences. The importance of ideal visions and the place they play in bringing about systemic change through stakeholder participation is key to creating commitment to the ideal vision.

21. Develop a system for evaluating the results of the change process. The facilitator will assist the districtwide Design Team members to help each Design Team to develop an evaluation system for its design. This evaluation system will reflect the development of an understanding of the role of critical examination, reflection, positive feedback systems, and self-renewal in the evaluation process. All stakeholders must have clear agreement as to that which is important to evaluate and what is not important to evaluate.

22. Design a system of functions for each ideal vision. Each design team now identifies and designs a set of functions that will enable it to attain its vision of a new educational system. The districtwide Design Team members facilitate an understanding of a function, and guide the design team members into increasingly specific and detailed levels of subfunctions.

23. Design the components for accomplishing each function. Every design team designs each necessary component to accomplish each function of the new system. The progression of vision to functions to components is a gradual process in which greater detail is continually developed.

24. Evolve, evaluate, and revise the new system. The process is implemented while engaging in evaluation and revision of the new system as it evolves. The system designed in event 21 can be used for this purpose. Explore new possibilities and problems of the design as it evolves.

Source: Jenlink, Reigeluth, Carr, & Nelson, 1998.

Table 10.7.   Distinct Events in Phase V: Implement and Evolve the New System

25. Develop a process for evolving to the new system. Because it is likely many aspects of the ideal system will not be immediately attainable, each design team should determine how to evolve ever closer to the ideal over time. They should attempt to minimize incompatibilities between the early elements of the new system and the remaining elements of the old system.
26. Evolve, evaluate, and revise the new system. Through a constant process of evaluation and revision in the course of implementation, it is possible to evolve the new system even as it is being implemented. The object is to evolve closer to the idealized vision.

Source: Jenlink, Reigeluth, Carr, & Nelson, 1998.

Continuous Events

Finally, the GSTE outlines a series of eighteen continuous events that require attention throughout the course of the change effort. These address such things as sustaining the motivation of the various groups involved in the effort, building and maintaining trust within and among the different groups, and monitoring and dealing with various elements occurring in the environment that can affect the change effort. Attention to these issues is equal in importance to the other elements, but they must be constantly monitored and addressed throughout the change process. The eighteen continuous events are listed in table 10.8.

Since January 2001, the GSTE has been undergoing testing, refinement, and elaboration through field trial in the Indianapolis Metropolitan School District, and I was able to join the reform effort as a cofacilitator in 2003. In that field trial, it has become apparent that the development and activities of the Decisioning Team (which they called the Leadership Team) in phase III are particularly difficult yet crucial to the success of the systemic change effort.

A Decisioning Team is asked to engage in mind-set change that may challenge their notions of culture, education, and the purpose of schools. This kind of change is especially difficult since it may run contrary to the professional training and experience the individuals have received.

They are asked to engage in idealized design, explore ideal visions, and evaluate the results of the change process in which they are engaged. Finally, they are asked to implement these new visions and beliefs in a new educational system that will affect the lives of all who are so engaged. The Decisioning Team's actions and decisions, especially in the early stages of their formation, will greatly affect the remaining course of the change effort, and it is important both to describe these actions as well as their consequences, and to explore alternatives that might be offered in future implementations of the GSTE. Since the Decisioning Team needs to become effective in the shortest amount of time possible, there is a strong need for

Table 10.8. Continuous Events of the GSTE

1. Evaluate and improve the change process
2. Build and maintain political support
3. Sustain motivation
4. Develop and sustain appropriate leadership
5. Build and maintain trust
6. Evolve mind-set and culture
7. Periodically secure necessary resources
8. Develop skills in systems thinking
9. Periodically and appropriately allocate necessary resources
10. Develop group-process and team-building skills
11. Build team spirit
12. Engage in self-disclosure
13. Engage in reflection
14. Develop design skills
15. Communicate with stakeholders (two-way)
16. Build and evolve community
17. Foster organizational learning
18. Build an organizational memory

Source: Jenlink, Reigeluth, Carr, & Nelson, 1998.

improving the guidance for events twelve and eighteen by integrating the team's learning activities with their decision-making activities in such a way that the team is able to begin making important decisions sooner. The purpose of this article is to address this need.

CONCLUSION

This chapter discussed the challenge of transforming schooling in American school districts and compared different approaches to meeting this challenge. Improving schooling has been traditionally addressed using what is commonly called piecemeal change. Piecemeal change, unfortunately, has not lived up to its promises to improve teaching and learning for America's school-aged children.

In the shadow of piecemeal change, which often goes by the name "school-based improvement," another change paradigm lurks—the paradigm of systemic transformational change. As educators have observed and been frustrated by the failures of school-based reform, the systemic transformational change paradigm has begun to emerge from the shadows. Different approaches to systemic transformational change were analyzed in this article.

Creating and sustaining systemic transformational change in school districts requires four paradigm shifts (Duffy, 2007). Duffy identifies these shifts as:

- Paradigm Shift 1: Shift from a reactive stance in response to the environment to a proactive stance.
- Paradigm Shift 2: Shift from the Industrial Age paradigm of schooling to an Information Age paradigm, and include the supporting work processes in a school system within this shift.
- Paradigm Shift 3: Shift from a command and control organization design to a participatory organization design.
- Paradigm Shift 4: Shift from a piecemeal approach to change to a systemic transformational change approach.

Given these four required paradigm shifts, it is clear that systemic transformational change is complex. But complex does not mean impossible—it means there is a lot to think about and a lot to do. Fortunately, there are methodologies available for creating and sustaining systemic transformational change. One of the most promising methodologies is a hybrid created by blending Duffy's *Step-Up-To-Excellence* methodology with Reigeluth's *Guidance System for Transforming Education* methodology. This hybrid methodology is called the School System Transformation Protocol (which is presented in chapter 12).

Even with the availability of methodologies for creating and sustaining transformational change in school districts, supplanting the entrenched school-based improvement philosophy will not be easy. It will be difficult because

> when the rise of a new theory suggests a change of direction in scholarship, history attests to a common pattern of reaction among the established intellectual community. There is often flat dismissal or at best vehement attack in order to kill and bury the theory, especially if it signals an imminent as well as immanent possibility of shaking the secure and comfortable foundation upon which the existing paradigm of thinking rests. (Nagatomo & Hull in Yasuo, 1993, pp. ix–x)

Resistance to the idea of systemic transformational change is seen, for example, in how advocates of school-based improvement have adopted the language of systemic change to argue for the validity of their approach. A popular example of this adopted language is found in the phrase "a system of schools," which is then contrasted with disdain to the term "school system" (as in "a system of schools versus a school system"). The implication is that a "system of schools" focuses on improving individual school buildings, and the unstated assumption is that improving these pieces will ultimately improve the entire school system. However, we all know the old adage about "the whole is greater than the sum of its parts." A system is more than its individual parts. It seems that the "system of schools" advocates believe that "the whole is EQUAL to the sum of its parts."

Almost every aspect of our society has moved steadfastly into the Information Age. School districts need to make that journey too. And making that journey will require them to engage in systemic transformational change that helps them make four paradigmatic shifts, as noted above. Failure to make these shifts will result in school districts that are increasingly irrelevant in our society.

11

Learning Management Systems

Charles M. Reigeluth, William R. Watson, Sunkyung Lee Watson,
Pratima Dutta, Zengguan Chen, and Nathan D. P. Powell

OVERVIEW

This chapter presents a detailed description of the powerful and necessary role which technology can play in the Information Age paradigm of education. This chapter calls for a learning management system (LMS), a comprehensive and integrated application of technology to the learning process, that will provide four primary roles for student learning: record-keeping, planning, instruction, and assessment. Each of these four major roles is described in terms of the functions it needs in order to support student learning. Finally, secondary roles such as communication and general data administration are described in order to illustrate the systemic nature of LMS technology necessary to fully support the learner-centered approach needed in the Information Age paradigm of education.

PARADIGM CHANGE IN PUBLIC EDUCATION

Sunkyung Lee Watson and Charles Reigeluth (2008) discussed the need for changing the paradigm of education from the sorting-focused, Industrial Age factory model of schools to the learning-focused, Information Age, customized paradigm. They also presented one possible vision of this new

An earlier version of this chapter appeared as the third article in a series of four articles on systemic transformational change by the authors with the title "Roles for technology in the Information Age paradigm of education: Learning management systems," in *Educational Technology*, 48(6), 32–39. Used with permission.

paradigm, based on several important bodies of research. They closed by saying that powerful technological tools would be necessary for this new paradigm to succeed in providing a quantum improvement in student learning. This article offers suggestions for some of the main roles or functions that such tools might need to fulfill.

We currently see four major roles and four secondary roles, all of which should be seamlessly integrated into a single system. While the term "learning management system" (LMS) has been used with several different meanings, it comes closest to capturing the meaning of such a comprehensive, integrated tool for the Information Age paradigm of education (Watson, Lee, & Reigeluth, 2007). The major roles for such an LMS include record-keeping for student learning, planning for student learning, instruction for student learning, and assessment for (and of) student learning. The secondary roles include communication, general student data, school personnel information, and LMS administration. Each of these is discussed next.

MAJOR ROLES FOR INFORMATION AGE LEARNING MANAGEMENT SYSTEMS

Role 1: Record-Keeping for Student Learning. The new paradigm of education requires the student, teacher, and parents to be informed of what the student has actually learned at any point in time, to assure that progress is continuous and personalized, and to make good decisions about what to learn next. The record-keeping tool of an Information Age LMS will replace the current report card. The report card, in general use, serves to compare one student with another and tells you little to nothing about what a student has actually learned. In contrast, this tool will provide systematic and comprehensive information about what each student has learned. We imagine that this tool will have three components: (1) a general record of what can be learned, including required educational standards set at national, state, and local levels, and optional educational standards; (2) a personal record of what has been learned by each student; and (3) a personal record of student characteristics that influence learning for each student. Each of these is discussed next.

1.1 Standards inventory. The purpose of this general record is to inform the planning process (see role #2 below) by providing information about the required standards set at national, state, and local levels, and information about additional standards that cultivate the student's particular interests and talents. This information will provide the student, teacher, and parents with a vision as to what should be and could be achieved. Furthermore, the standards will be organized into maps for each domain of learning based on Domain Theory (Bunderson, Wiley, & McBride, 2009). Each domain map will include (a) major attainments, with boundaries showing the easiest and hardest version of each attainment, (b) categories of attainments, where each category represents a pathway for learning, and (c) a difficulty-based sequence of attainments along each pathway. For each attainment in the map, there will be an indication as to whether or not it is a required standard, and if so, what level of difficulty is required. In essence, the standards inventory will present a list of things that should or can be learned, along with levels, standards, and/or criteria at which they should or could be learned.

1.2 Personal attainments inventory. The purpose of this personal record is also to inform the planning process (role #2), only it will do so by keeping track of each student's progress in meeting the required and optional standards, and therefore what is within reach for the student to learn next. It will serve as a customized mastery progress report to the student, teacher, and parents. In this tool, attainments will be checked off as they are reached, and if any are not listed in the standards inventory, they can be added to the personal attainments inventory. Each attainment will be documented and reported by date attained, and the record will identify any required standards (in the standards inventory) that are overdue and which ones are due next in each domain. Each attainment will also be linked to evidence of its accomplishment, ranging from original artifacts with a formal evaluation to summary data from a simulation-based performance test. Given this information, the student will be able to easily generate different kinds of portfolios for different purposes by pulling out selected attainments and artifacts. All the information recorded, including the attainments and evidence, will have flexibly controlled access to protect the learner's privacy.

1.3 Personal characteristics inventory. This personal record is intended to inform both the planning process (role #2) and the instructional process (role #3). It will keep track of each student's characteristics that influence learning, such as learning styles, profile of multiple intelligences, student interests, major life events, and so forth. These data will be convenient to refer to when major decisions about learning objectives and goals are to be made for the student and will be especially useful for teachers who are not familiar with the student. They will help teachers to customize each student's learning plan to best suit his or her interests, learning styles, life experiences, and educational background. But the personal characteristics inventory will also be an effective tool to customize the instruction itself. The student data will be fed into computer-based tutorials, simulations, and other computer-based learning tools to automatically tailor appropriate parameters of the instruction for each student. And the teachers will refer to these data to improve the way they coach and advise the student during projects and other instructional events.

Clearly, a customized paradigm of education requires keeping a lot of records. Technology can tremendously alleviate the time, drudgery, and expense of maintaining and accessing those records. The record-keeping tool will provide systematic and comprehensive information for customizing the learning process, including an inventory of what is to be learned, an inventory of what the student has learned, and an inventory of the student's characteristics that influence instruction. It will facilitate collaborative efforts among students, parents, teachers, the community, the state, and the nation to assure that appropriate standards are being met while customized attainments are achieved by each student. And it will facilitate customizing the instruction to each student's individual needs.

Role 2: Planning for Student Learning. Sunkyung Lee Watson and Charles Reigeluth (2008) described a contract for a personal learning plan (PLP) as an important feature of the new paradigm of education. Assisting with development of that contract is the second major role for an Information Age LMS. This planning will usually be done in a face-to-face meeting between the student, his or her mentor-teacher, and the student's parent(s) or guardian(s), while using the planning tool.

This planning tool will have many functions. It will help the student, parents, and teacher to (1) decide on long-term goals; (2) identify the full range of attainments (current options) that are presently within reach for the student that could help meet those long-term goals; (3) select from those options the attainments that they want to pursue now (short-term goals), based on requirements, long-term goals, interests, opportunities, and so on; (4) identify projects (or other means) for attaining the short-term goals; (5) identify other students (teams) who are interested in doing the same projects (if desired); (6) specify the roles that the teacher, parent, and any others might play in supporting the student in learning from the project; and (7) develop contracts that specify goals, projects, teams, roles, deadlines, and milestones. Each of these is discussed next.

2.1 Long-term goals. Many students graduate from college not knowing what they want to do with their lives. We propose that students should be encouraged to think about life goals (not just career goals) from an early age and be encouraged to be constantly on the lookout for better goals. A study by Harackiewicz, Barron, Tauer, Carter, and Elliot (2000) found that setting achievement goals has a positive effect on how "students approach, experience, and perform in class." Setting of goals—a means to building self-efficacy—proves to be a highly effective method for encouraging self-regulated learning (Schunk, 1990, 1991; B. J. Zimmerman, 1990). Long-term goals can help students pick motivating topics to study and give instrumental value for much of what they study. Therefore, the planning tool will help a student, teacher, and parents to develop and revise, in a collaborative fashion, the student's long-term goals. It will include access to motivating, informational, interactive multimedia programs about different careers and ways of life.

2.2 Current options. Another important function in educational planning is to know what attainments are within reach, given what the student has already learned. The planning tool, therefore, will access the student's personal attainment inventory and compare it to the general standards inventory to automatically identify the full range of attainments that are current options for the student. This will be the student's world of possibilities for her or his next PLP.

2.3 Short-term goals. The student's PLP will specify what learning goals the student will accomplish during the next contract period (variable, but typically about two months, shorter for younger students). Thus, the planning tool will help the student, teacher, and parents to select from the current options the attainments to pursue now, based on requirements, long-term goals, interests, opportunities, and so forth. These goals typically will come from many different competency or subject areas. This is a crucial function of the planning tool because it will set the goals for the next learning contract, or PLP.

2.4 Projects. Having identified the ends for the PLP, the next step will be to identify the means, so this is another function for the planning tool. Typically, projects will be used as the means, but other options will sometimes be available (e.g., readings with discussions, or tutorials). The tool will help the student, teacher, and parents to identify projects or other means available in the school or community or online that will enable the student to attain the short-term goals. This tool will identify, say, a dozen projects rank ordered by the number of short-term goals (attainments) that each addresses. The student will then select the projects that are most related to their interests and long-term goals and cover all the short-term goals. Depending on the scope of each project, a student will undertake from one to about five projects during a single contract period. Finally, this tool will also have a feature that allows teachers and community people—and students—to post projects that they have developed or are sponsoring.

2.5 Teams. "The unfolding of the self always grows out of interaction with each other" (Ranson, Martin, Nixon, & McKeown, 1996, p. 14). Collaborative learning is a powerful form of learning (Gokhale, 1995). Thus, in most cases, students will work together in small teams on their projects. This means that another important function for the planning tool is to identify other students who are interested in working on the same project at the same time. Friends will sometimes choose projects so that they can work together, but teachers will only allow so much of that and will also require their students to work with students they don't know, seeking to create teams that are highly diverse (age, race, gender, socioeconomic status). The planning tool will also use personality inventories (e.g., Myers-Briggs) to help students understand why their teammates may behave quite differently and how to deal with that.

2.6 Roles. In addition to collaborating with peers, students will receive support from their teacher, their parents, and perhaps various others (like community members or task experts). Therefore, another function for the planning tool is to help the teacher and the parents to define what they will do to support the student's learning on each project. Roles of the students and others who are not present in the planning meeting between the student, teacher, and parents will be determined with help from the contract-planning tool.

2.7 Contracts. The final step of the planning process will be to create the contract that contains the PLP. Reigeluth and Garfinkle (1994a) identify learning contracts as a written agreement that "will serve a planning and monitoring function" (p. 64). A learning contract will essentially be an agreement between a student, teacher, and parents that specifies the goals that the student wishes to achieve, the means (primarily projects) that will be used to achieve them, the teacher's and parents' roles in supporting the student, and the deadline for completing each project (negotiated with the teammates for each project). Parents, teachers, and students, as Reigeluth and Garfinkle note, will meet once every two months or so, to review the results of the previous contract and plan a new contract for the next period. Typically there will be a separate contract for each project during the period.

Clearly, the planning tool will be crucial to the instructional process in an Information Age educational system. It would likely be impossible to customize the learning experience for each student without it. It will specify what the student, teacher, and parents will do, and it will be instrumental for monitoring the student's progress. In addition, Reigeluth and Garfinkle (1994) point out that "only through this kind of collaborative teaching approach will we overcome many obstacles to learning in some home environments" (p. 64), as this activity will force reluctant parents to partake in the educational development of their children.

Role 3: Instruction for Student Learning. Once a contract has been developed and signed, the projects need to be conducted. This is when instruction, broadly defined as "anything that is done purposely to facilitate learning" (Reigeluth & Carr-Chellman, 2009), takes place. To implement the kind of learner-centered instruction described by Sunkyung Lee Watson and Charles Reigeluth (2008), the teacher will not be able to do all the teaching. The teacher's role will change to selecting or designing instructional tools for students to use and coaching students during their use of those tools. So what functions need to be performed in this third major role for an Information Age LMS? We see four major functions: (1) project initiation, (2) instruction, (3) project support, and (4) instructional development. Combined, these four functions will ensure that an LMS truly supports learner-centered instruction in the Information Age paradigm of education.

3.1 Project initiation. The project initiation tool will help the teacher and students to get started on each project. Depending on the age of the students, this tool will be used by the student, teacher, or both. The primary functions it serves will be to introduce the students to the project or problem to be solved (its goals and initial conditions), and help them get organized. They will already know a little about the project from the planning tool, and they will have already set a deadline for completing the project with their teammates. This project initiation tool will provide access to more information about the project (or problem) and will help the teammates identify tasks to perform, how they will work together on each task (collaboratively on the same tasks, or cooperatively on different tasks), the resources they will need, and milestones for different tasks during the project (time management). This information about the project will often be provided in a multimedia simulation, such as Bransford's STAR LEGACY (see Schwartz, Lin, Brophy, & Bransford, 1999).

3.2 Instruction. Once the students get organized for a project, they will begin working on it. As they work on it, they will encounter (identify) attainments they need in order to be successful. These will include such attainments or components of an attainment as: information that needs to be memorized, understandings that need to be acquired, skills that need to be developed, and various kinds of affective development. Some of these attainments and components will be developed by leaving the "project space" (which often occurs in a computer-based simulation) and entering the "instructional space," comprised of customizable learning objects of various kinds (Gibbons, Nelson, & Richards, 2002; Hodgins, 2002; Wiley, 2002), including minisimulations, tutorials, WebQuests, and drill-and-practice (some in the form of educational games), that allow full development of an individual attainment or component, complete with its "automatization" (Anderson, 1983; Salisbury, 1990), if appropriate for mastery of it. Some attainments and components will also be acquired by using research (information-access) tools on the LMS. But not all such attainments and components will be developed in the LMS. Others will be developed by using offline resources, doing offline activities, and/or working with other people in the school or community (including teachers and parents), but those resources will be located primarily through the LMS. Once those attainments and/or components have been mastered, the student will reenter the project space and continue work on the project, cooperating or collaborating with teammates as appropriate. Debriefing and reflection on the project activities at the end of the project—and periodically during the project—will also be important to the learning process and will be facilitated by the instructional tool.

3.3 Project support. This function of the instructional tool has two purposes: helping the students to manage the project and helping the teacher and parents to monitor and support the students' work on the project. Students will review project planning materials and check off project milestones and goals as they are completed. The system will alert teachers and parents to student progress on the project, such as notifying teachers of the submission of project deliverables or the completion of project milestones, in order to encourage and guide the student's progress, make recommendations, and facilitate the completion of the project. The teacher will also suggest resources or provide comments on submitted project deliverables to guide the student while he or she continues to work on the project.

3.4 Instructional development. The final function for the instructional tool is to support teachers, staff, parents, and even students in the development of new instruction—projects, learning objects, and other instructional tools. The LMS will contain a large repository of instructional tools that provide varied approaches to instruction. However, it seems that there will never be enough powerful instruction for all learners in all contexts. Therefore, an important feature for an LMS will be to support the development of new instructional tools, which will often serve as learning objects and will then be added to the repository and evaluated for effectiveness (see next section), ensuring that instruction continually improves. A powerful authoring system will support the creation of these new instructional tools by providing instructional guidance and even automatic development and programming of the instruction, similar to Merrill's (Merrill & ID2 Research Group, 1998) ID Expert. User-created content is an everyday reality in today's Information Age, with popular video games including toolkits to allow players to create their own versions of games, and Internet users developing their own content in the form of wikis and blogs, as well as videos and podcasts that they upload to share with others and continue the cycle of development and modification (Brown & Adler, 2008). This instructional development tool will provide similar support in customizing and creating customized instruction and projects. Furthermore, the easy and efficient application of learning object standards to created instruction will be a necessity in order to better share learning objects and evaluate their suitability and interoperability for different platforms (Connolly, 2001).

This section has highlighted the instructional functions that an LMS should provide. These include (a) introducing the project to a learner (or small team), (b) providing instructional tools (simulations, tutorials, drill-and-practice, WebQuests, research tools, communication tools, and learning objects) to support learning during the project, (c) providing tools for monitoring and supporting student progress on the project, and (d) providing tools to help teachers and others develop new projects and instructional tools. The next section will discuss features that support the fourth major role of an Information Age LMS: assessment for (and of) student learning.

Role 4: Assessment for (and of) Student Learning. The assessment tool will be integrated with the instructional tool so that teaching and testing will be fully integrated (Mitchell, 1992; Wiggins, 1998). To accomplish this, we envision the assessment tool fulfilling six functions: (1) presenting authentic tasks for student assessment, (2) evaluating student performances on those tasks, (3) providing immediate feedback to the student on the performances, (4) assessing whether or not an attainment has been reached (certification), (5) developing student assessments, and (6) improving instruction and assessment.

4.1 Presenting authentic tasks. The same authentic tasks that are used during instruction will be used for student assessment. The project itself will be an authentic task. And so will the instances (or cases) used in the "instructional space," where much of the learning occurs. Those instances, however, will not be restricted to the project that motivates the learner to master the attainments. To truly master an attainment, the learner must be able to use it in the full variety of situations for which it is appropriate. Those authentic situations will be used as the instances for the demonstrations (or examples) and applications (practice) of the attainment. There will be a large pool of authentic instances to draw from that will include all the types of instances. And the learner will continue to do the applications until an established criterion is met across all the desired types of instances. In this manner, the applications will serve a dual role of instruction and assessment (both formative and summative). Simulations will often be used to enhance authenticity. Authenticity of applications will enhance transfer to real situations in which the attainments are needed. Authenticity will also help students understand why they are learning a particular attainment and how it could be useful to them. This will help students become or stay motivated to learn (Frederickson & Collins, 1989).

4.2 Evaluating student performances. Whether in a simulation or a tutorial or a drill-and-practice, the assessment tool will be designed to evaluate whether or not the criterion was met on each performance of the authentic task on the LMS. If the performance is not done on the LMS, then a teacher or other trained observer (who could even be a more advanced student) will have a handheld computer with a rubric for evaluating success on each criterion, and that information will be uploaded into the LMS.

4.3 Providing immediate feedback. Research has shown that frequency of formative assessments is positively related to student achievement (see, e.g., Marzano, 2006). Thus, based on the evaluation of student performance, the learner will be provided immediate feedback of either a confirmatory or corrective nature. This immediate feedback will often even be given during the performance for the greatest effect on learning, in which case it will be similar to coaching, scaffolding, or guiding the learner's performance, or it could be given at the end of the performance.

4.4 Certification. When the criterion for successful performance has been met on x out of the last y unassisted performances, the summative assessment will be complete and the corresponding attainment will be automatically checked off in the student's personal inventory of attainments, and a link will be provided to the evidence for that attainment (e.g., in the form of test results or artifacts produced). However, in cases where feedback is given during a performance, successful performance will not count toward the criterion. To count, the student's performance must be unassisted.

4.5 Developing student assessments. The assessment tool will also serve the function of supporting teachers and others in the development of formative and summative assessments for new instruction. Due to the integration of instruction and assessment in the LMS, the test development tools will also be integrated with the instructional development tools, which will deal with feedback. For certification, the major function will be to help the developer identify the criterion for attainment and develop any necessary rubrics, so the tool will tap into information in the standards inventory described earlier and will help the test developer link them to the standards.

4.6 Improving instruction and assessment. The final function of the assessment tool will be to formatively assess the instruction and assessments in the LMS. It will do so by automatically identifying areas in which students are having difficulties, and it will even have diagnostic tools that offer a menu of suggestions for overcoming those problems. Those diagnostic tools will include proven principles of instruction, such as those represented by "First Principles of Instruction" (Merrill, 2009).

Integration of the Four Roles. Note that these four roles will be seamlessly integrated. The record-keeping tool will provide information automatically for the planning tool. The planning tool will identify instructional tools that are available. The assessment tool will be integrated into the instructional tool. And the assessment tool will feed information automatically into the record-keeping tool. Also, there will be other roles or functions for an Information Age LMS. These secondary roles are described next.

Role 5: Secondary Roles. The final set of roles necessary for an ideal learning management system will encompass secondary roles, or functions, which are not necessarily directly related to student learning, although some, such as communication functions, can be used for learning. These functions are organized into the following four kinds: (1) communication, (2) general student data, (3) school personnel information, and (4) LMS administration. While these functions will not always deal directly with student learning, they will nevertheless be necessary functions for the LMS to be truly systemic in nature and provide the functionality needed to manage the entire learning process for a school or school district.

5.1 Communication. Communication functions are essential in supporting a learner-centered environment, as they allow teachers to communicate and collaborate with other teachers and staff, with their students, with their students' parents, and with members of the community and other stakeholders in the learning process. Students will communicate and collaborate with each other and will contact their teachers for help outside of the classroom, and parents will check on their children's progress and be more involved in their learning. Being able to communicate remotely via Internet technologies will allow education to extend beyond the walls of the classroom. Therefore, an Information Age LMS will support Web communication technologies such as these. Furthermore, Web 2.0 technologies that allow for user-created content have become increasingly popular, and the web has become a participatory social space to such a degree that *Time* magazine named their person of the year for 2007 as "You" (Grossman, 2006). Furthermore, these Web 2.0 technologies, such as wikis, blogs, and podcasts, and video-sharing sites such as YouTube have helped to increase the participatory nature of learning (Brown & Adler, 2008). Additionally, LMS support for such additional Internet technologies as webpage creation, discussion boards, and whiteboards will provide valuable tools for collaboration and communication. The inclusion of RSS feed support (Duffy & Bruns, 2006), which allows users to subscribe to favorite websites and be notified of updated content, will put further power for communicating and organizing information into the hands of all users and stakeholders. While the use of these Web technologies will not always be applied directly to the learning process, more and more researchers are discussing the application of wikis (Augar, Raiman, & Zhou, 2004; Duffy & Bruns, 2006; Lamb, 2004), blogs (Duffy & Bruns, 2006; Williams & Jacobs, 2004), podcasts (Lum, 2006), and video-sharing sites such as YouTube (Bonk, 2008) to education, so these Web 2.0 technologies will certainly be powerful tools for instruction as well as communication.

5.2 General student data. One type of data the LMS will be responsible for handling is student data. These data will include the student's name, address, birthdate, parent information, health information, attendance, and so forth. However, in supporting the Learner-Centered paradigm of education, the LMS will also handle student information necessary for supporting Information Age schools, which have moved beyond the current constraints of grade levels, class periods, and so forth. Therefore, the LMS will also manage such student data as who the student's mentor-teacher is, records of major life events, what school or learning community the student belongs to, the student's homeroom, and community organizations he or she is involved with. It will also keep track of the physical location of the student by radio-frequency identification (RFID) or by the student swiping his or her student identification card when entering or leaving a school room or building, as most students will not be restricted to set rooms at set times. In sum, the management of student data will be a key function of an Information Age LMS. The LMS will gather, secure, and allow easy management of data such as those described above in order to effectively support the truly learner-centered environment necessary to meet the needs of today's communities and their learners.

5.3 School personnel information. The third secondary function is the management of school personnel information. As an LMS is systemic in nature (Watson, Lee, & Reigeluth, 2007; Watson & Watson, 2007) and responsible for managing the entire learning process of a learning organization (Szabo & Flesher, 2002), it needs to be capable of managing all of the data related to learning, including that of the school personnel. These data will include general information, such as name and address, but also data related to learner-centered instruction, such as assigned students, certifications and awards received, professional development plan and progress, and the teachers' physical locations (again managed through RFID or card swipes). These data will also serve the teacher in providing evidence of excellence by identifying awards and recognitions received by students and storing samples of exemplary student work and evidence of learning. Additional information will be tied directly to the teacher's instructional activities and will include learning objects, other instructional components, and assessments developed by the teacher, as well as records of student evaluations performed by the teacher. Proper management of this information by the LMS will support the new role of teachers as facilitators, coaches, and mentors that is required in a learner-centered environment (McCombs & Whisler, 1997).

5.4 LMS administration. Another secondary function focuses on administration of the LMS itself. As software that manages the entire learning process, the LMS will necessarily gather and store a great deal of data, including some that is sensitive. An important feature of the LMS will therefore be supporting the administration of these data and providing and restricting access to them. While it will be extremely important that data such as medical records and Social Security numbers be kept secure by the LMS, it will also be important that proper access to data and the reporting features of the LMS be handled in a consistent and efficient manner. The ability to input, retrieve, and update data will be managed by user role. Therefore, some teachers will have access to some of a student's personal information, such as attendance records, parents' names and contact information, and so forth; and some support personnel, such as a school nurse and a guidance counselor, will have access to other personal information, such as physical and mental health records. Furthermore, data will be kept not only on students, but also on teachers and staff. It is therefore very important that the LMS offer strict security while still providing appropriate access to data in order to effectively support the information needs of the school or school district personnel.

This section has highlighted some secondary functions that an Information Age LMS will provide. These include functions related to communication, general student information, school personnel information, and LMS administration, and there are certainly others that we have not mentioned here. However, it is not appropriate for an LMS to address purely administrative functions, such as budgeting, payroll, and purchasing.

CONCLUSION

It should be apparent that technology will play a crucial role in the success of the Information Age paradigm of education. It will enable a quantum improvement in student learning, and likely at a lower cost per student per year than in the current Industrial Age paradigm. Just as the electronic spreadsheet made the accountant's job quicker, easier, and less expensive, the kind of LMS described here will make the teacher's job quicker, easier, and less expensive.

LMS fills a primary necessity for truly learner-centered instruction by freeing teachers to take on their new roles in a learner-centered environment: facilitators, counselors, and coaches, rather than being the main source of instructional content (McCombs & Whisler, 1997). In order to support this, an LMS will provide a variety of instructional features that allow teachers to truly customize learning for each learner, and to facilitate choice and control for the learners as they work toward mastery of required attainments and deep knowledge of all standard subjects and skills. Furthermore, an LMS will support students directly in their new roles as active agents of their own learning (Schlechty, 2002).

However, such dramatic changes in the roles of teachers, students, parents, and technology are not easy to navigate. They require dramatic changes in mind-sets about education for all those involved, and this requires a systemic transformation process that is carefully conceived and executed. The School System Transformation (SST) Protocol (Duffy & Reigeluth, 2008) is a well-developed and field-tested guidance system for helping school districts to engage in such transformational change. The problem is that paradigm change is a time-intensive and therefore expensive process that requires considerable resources as well as expertise in the transformation process. The SST Protocol is not enough. It is our sincere hope that the FutureMinds Initiative (Reigeluth & Duffy, 2008) will help state departments of education to build the capacity to provide both the resources and the expertise needed for successful paradigm change.

12

The School System Transformation Protocol

Francis M. Duffy and Charles M. Reigeluth

OVERVIEW

This chapter provides a broad overview of a methodology especially designed to create and sustain systemic transformation in school systems. The
methodology is called the *School System Transformation (SST) Protocol*. Prior
to describing the methodology, the context for the design, development,
and implementation of the methodology is described. The description of
the context reiterates and reinforces concepts and principles of systemic
transformational change that have been discussed throughout this book.

THE CONTEXT FOR THE SST PROTOCOL

The environmental context for the SST Protocol is important because it
provides a rationale for the design, development, and implementation of
the SST Protocol. The description of the context revisits several of the main
themes discussed earlier in the book; specifically, the context (1) describes
the confusion about the definition of systemic change, (2) clarifies how
school districts function as complex systems, (3) identifies four complementary paradigm changes that must occur to transform a school system,
and (4) provides a rationale for why a school district is the preferred unit

An earlier version of this chapter was originally published as Duffy, F. M., & Reigeluth, C. M.
(2008). The school system transformation (SST) protocol. *Educational Technology*, 48(4), 41–
49. Used with permission.

of change. Additionally, the description of the context characterizes transformational change as a "wicked problem" and outlines knowledge and
skill sets that I believe are required for effective change leadership.

Systemic Change

There is a resurgence of interest in systemic change, including proposed
federal legislation that recognizes the importance of systemic change for
helping school districts create twenty-first-century learning environments
(i.e., the Achievement Through Technology And Innovation [ATTAIN] Act).
The resurgence of interest notwithstanding, there is still a significant lack of
understanding about the meaning of systemic change, and there is robust
pushback against that approach from advocates of the dominant paradigm
for improving schooling—the school-based improvement paradigm. Because of this lack of understanding, we start by revisiting the multiple
meanings of systemic change that were presented in chapter 2.

There is widespread confusion about the meaning of systemic change in
school districts. Several different definitions of the term used in the school
improvement literature comprise the main source of this confusion. The
following definitions were identified by Squire and Reigeluth (2000):

1. *Statewide policy systemic change*: creating statewide changes in tests, curricular guidelines, teacher certification requirements, textbook adoptions, funding policies, and so forth that are coordinated to support
   one another. This meaning is how policymakers typically think of
   systemic change.
2. *District-wide systemic change*: producing changes in curriculum or programs throughout a school district. This meaning is how P–12 educators typically think of systemic change.
3. *Schoolwide systemic change*: creating change inside individual school
   buildings. This is the definition used by school-based improvement
   advocates.
4. *Ecological systemic change*: making changes based on upon a clear understanding of interrelationships and interdependencies within a
   system and between the system and its external environment. Change
   leaders subscribing to this view recognize that significant change in
   one part of their system requires changes in other parts of that system.
   This is the definition accepted by "systems thinkers" such as Peter
   Senge, Russell Ackoff, and Bela Banathy.

The first three definitions apply some principles of systemic change, but
they do not create systemic change. The fourth definition is an example of
true systemic change, but it does not always create transformational para-

digm change. Thus, the one definition of systemic change missing from Squire and Reigeluth's original compendium of definitions is the one for systemic transformational change.

Systemic transformational change. Eckel, Hill, and Green (1998) define this special form of systemic change as one that:

1. alters the culture of the institution by changing select underlying assumptions and institutional behaviors, processes, and products;
2. is deep and pervasive, affecting the whole institution;
3. is intentional; and
4. occurs over time.

Duffy added the following two requirements to the above definition:

1. creates a school system that continuously seeks an idealized future for itself (see chapter 7); and
2. creates a future system that is substantially different than the current school system; that is, the system must be transformed to perform within a different paradigm.

We use the term *transformational change* or *paradigm change* to refer to this kind of systemic change. The SST Protocol focuses on this kind of systemic change because we believe *there is no other way* to recreate school systems for success in the twenty-first-century Knowledge Age.

SCHOOL DISTRICTS ARE COMPLEX SYSTEMS

There is a stunning lack of understanding about how school districts function as complex, organic, and adaptive systems. This lack of understanding produces change efforts that are unable to create and sustain deep and broad whole-system change in school districts. This lack of understanding also underpins the dominant approach to improving schooling; that is, the piecemeal, one-school-at-a-time approach.

All complex systems are composed of parts, or subsystems. The parts have parts, too. A classroom is part of a school, a school is part of a cluster of schools, a cluster is part of a school system, a school system is part of a community, which is part of a state, which is part of a region, which is part of our country, which is part of our planet, which is part of the universe.[1] But trying to improve a system that complex is beyond human capacity. Instead, Merrelyn Emery says that we need to target the "system of interest" for the purpose of managing the transformation process. To identify the system of interest, Emery (in Emery & Purser, 1996) says we need to draw a circle around all of the departments, programs, and so on, that must collaborate daily and closely to deliver a product or service to a customer. For the purpose of improving teaching and learning, the circle goes around what we traditionally call a school system. Everything outside that circle is the school system's external environment.

Another phenomenon that influences the performance of school systems is synergy. Synergy happens when parts of a system interact to create an effect greater than the parts can create in isolation. People commonly describe this phenomenon as "the whole is greater than the sum of its parts." Many contemporary approaches to improving education in school districts, however, seem to distort this principle to become "the whole is equal to the sum of its parts." This distortion is implied by how school-based improvement advocates ignore the whole system and focus only on the "parts"; that is, they focus exclusively on improving education within individual schools and classrooms and ignore how those schools, classrooms, and academic and nonacademic support functions are and must be interconnected to educate children. The unstated assumption seems to be that if only enough parts are fixed, then the performance of the whole school system will improve. Furthermore, the implied operating principle of school-based improvement seems to be that the schools and classrooms are and should be relatively independent of the whole system (sometimes the term "loosely coupled" is used to characterize this assumed independence). However, complexity theory (see chapter 4) tells us that when one part of a system is linked to other parts, a significant change in one part will succeed only if there are significant complementary changes in the connected parts. Failure to grasp the significance of this systems principle explains why school-based improvement has not yielded significant improvements in the overall performance of school systems.

Changes made in individual schools and programs are and must be linked to corresponding changes made to other schools and programs in a school system. This is an important principle because a child's education is more than what he or she learns in a particular grade or level of schooling. His or her learning is the cumulative effect of P–12 learning (in a P–12 district), even if a child moves from one district to another. Furthermore, the quality of education that a child receives in any particular grade or level of schooling has a direct effect on his or her future learning. For example, studies (e.g., Sanders & Rivers, 1996b) suggest that when children have two or three bad teachers in a row, those children continue to learn, but they never catch up to their peers who had better teachers. These learning deficits are a reflection of a systems principle called "upstream errors flow downstream." In other words, mistakes that are made early in a work process (in teaching and learning at the elementary education level), if not identified and corrected, will flow downstream and create even greater problems later on in the work process (in teaching and learning at the middle and second-ary education levels). In systems, upstream errors always flow downstream and learning deficits always accumulate if not corrected.

So, it can be argued that if schools and classrooms in a school district are treated as if they are loosely coupled or relatively independent of each other, they should not be. Schools and classrooms should not be loosely coupled because a child's education requires interdependence among vari-ous parts of a school system. Since the education of a child requires inter-dependence among various parts of a school system, the school-based im-provement strategy is insufficient, because it reinforces and sustains the disconnections between and among a school system's parts; that is, it cre-ates a lack of synergy (if not downright incompatibility) among schools and programs within the system. This fact explains why the promised improve-ments offered by school-based improvement advocates often have failed to improve teaching and learning throughout entire school systems, and where school-based improvement has created improvements, those changes created temporary pockets of excellence (in the schools that improved) while leaving pockets of mediocrity (in the schools that maintained average performance) and pockets of despair (in the schools that continued to fail) all within the same system.

Finally, another characteristic of complex systems is that if changes are made to a few parts of a system and not to others, the changed parts become incompatible with the remaining parts of the system. In response to this incompatibility, the unchanged parts apply significant pressure on the changed parts and force those changed parts to revert to their prechange status, thereby enacting that famous French adage, "the more things change, the more they stay the same." An example of this phenomenon is frequently observed in contemporary approaches to school-based improvement; for example, many wonderful school-based changes such as the *Saturn School of Tomorrow* (Bennett & King, 1991) became incompatible with the rest of the school system, and they were ultimately forced to change back to their prechange state.

FOUR PARADIGM SHIFTS ARE REQUIRED FOR TRANSFORMATION

The literature on systemic change in organizations (e.g., Ackoff, 1974; Nevis, Lancourt, & Vassallo, 1996; Pasmore, 1988; Pava, 1983b; Trist & Murray, 1993) suggests that change leaders need to simultaneously con-sider four interconnected paradigm shifts to create and sustain transforma-tional change. The first three paradigm shifts are created simultaneously as educators think along three "change paths" (Duffy, 2002, 2003a). The fourth paradigm shift is created as educators use the principles of systemic transformational change that are designed into the SST Protocol. The four paradigm shifts are:

- *Paradigm Shift 1*: The core work processes—teaching and learning— must be transformed to a paradigm that is customized to learners' individual needs and is focused on attainment of proficiencies (Reigeluth, 1994), and the support work processes must be transformed to best support the primary work processes. This shift happens along *Path 1—transform the system's core and support work processes.*
- *Paradigm Shift 2*: The school system's social infrastructure (e.g., organization culture, communication practices, job descriptions, reward systems, and so forth) must be transformed from a command-and-control organization design to a participatory organization design. This shift happens along *Path 2—transform the system's internal social infrastructure.*
- *Paradigm Shift 3*: The relationship between the school system and its systemic environment must be transformed from an isolative, crisis-oriented, and reactive stance by the school system to a collaborative, opportunity-seeking, and proactive stance. This shift happens along *Path 3—transform the system's relationship with its external environment.*
- *Paradigm Shift 4*: To transform school systems there must be a shift from the piecemeal, one-school-at-a-time paradigm for change to the paradigm of systemic transformational change. This shift happens as educators use the SST Protocol.

Although the four paradigm shifts must be made simultaneously, given the interdependencies among parts of a school system, changes in the teaching-learning process (the core work process that is part of paradigm shift 1) should drive the nature of the changes created for paradigm shifts 2 and 3 (especially for paradigm shift 2). Complementary changes for paradigm shifts 1 and 2 are important because if changes are only made to the work processes and not to the social infrastructure, this strategic error can create situations where school systems have the most powerful teaching and learning model in the world, but their teachers are demotivated, dissatisfied, and unskilled, and teachers experiencing these conditions will not and cannot use that powerful new model in remarkable ways.

Changes for paradigm shift 3 are required for gaining and maintaining external political support for a district's transformation journey. Without this political support, change leaders will not be able to get the human, technical, and financial resources they need to launch and sustain their district's transformation. Further, the literature on organization effectiveness (e.g., Daft, 2006) tells us that to be effective, an organization must have a positive, proactive relationship with its environment. Creating this kind of positive, proactive relationship is one of the goals of paradigm shift 3.

Finally, the fourth paradigm shift is required to move a school system away from the piecemeal approach to change to a whole-system transformation approach. The systemic transformation approach is nonnegotiable if the first three paradigm shifts are desired and sought.

THE SCHOOL DISTRICT AS THE PREFERRED UNIT OF CHANGE

Since the ultimate goal of transformational change is to transform an entire school system to align with the requirements of four new paradigms appropriate for the twenty-first century, individual schools and classrooms are the inappropriate unit of change for achieving this goal. The appropriate unit of change for transformation is the whole school system.

Although a whole school district is the unit of change, I recognize that changing a whole system all at once is probably an impossible task. So transformational change has to start somewhere inside the district and then spread throughout the entire system. Finding that ideal starting point for transformational change requires the application of a systems change principle called "leveraged emergent design" (Reigeluth, 2006a; and see chapter 4). This principle requires change leaders to start their district's transformation journey by changing a part or parts of the system that can exert powerful leverage on unchanged parts of the system and thereby countervail the forces within the system that want to stop the change process and return the system to its prechange state.

Starting with a few high-leverage changes can make the whole systemic change process considerably quicker and easier. An example of an ideal high-leverage starting point is an academic cluster (a set of interconnected schools) that contains the district's entire instructional program. In larger districts with multiple high schools, there would be one academic cluster for each high school. In districts without a P–12 instructional program (e.g., in elementary districts), each cluster would still contain the district's entire instructional program and all the age levels it spans.

A support work cluster also needs to be formed for the central administration office functions, and another support cluster for nonacademic services such as cafeteria services, transportation services, and building and grounds maintenance services. These clusters also engage in transformation activities, because improving support work is a critical part of the transformation journey (as part of Paradigm Shift 1: Transform core and support work processes, described above).

School System Transformation as a "Wicked Problem"

Because school districts are complex systems that must engage successfully in four paradigm shifts (described earlier) to create and sustain transformational change, transforming school systems is an example of what Rittel and Webber (1973) called a "wicked problem." A wicked problem has incomplete, contradictory, and changing requirements. Solutions to them are often difficult to create because of the complex interdependencies that created the problems in the first place; for example, while trying to solve a wicked problem, the solution may reveal or create other, even more complex problems.

Ackoff (1974) described wicked problems as "messes." He said, "Every problem interacts with other problems and is therefore part of a set of interrelated problems, a system of problems. . . . I choose to call such a system a mess" (pp. 20–21). Pava (1986) also commented on these kinds of problems. He said:

> Ill-defined, complex problems often require systematic change in behavior and values. However, the uncertainty of such issues polarizes different stakeholders and impedes collaborative solutions. Traditional approaches to managing change are unable to deal with these situations, where both complexity and conflict are intensified. (online document)

Bar-Yam (2004) tells us that there is no one way to solve wicked problems, and there are no "best practices" that apply to all situations. Any workable solution, Bar-Yam says, has to be related to the specific characteristics of the problem (p. 15). Yet many contemporary school reform "best practice" models are heralded as "one-size-fits-all-and-all-you-have-to-do-is-replicate-it" approaches. Almost without exception, the replication of the "best approach" fails; for example, of the twenty-two school systems that received training from the Re-Inventing Schools Coalition (RISC) on how to replicate Alaska's Chugach School District's successful transformation, which won that district one of the first Baldrige quality awards in education, only three were able to succeed in replicating Chugach's success. Why? Because each school district has a unique set of characteristics and problem-sets, and replication of some other district's successful change effort predictably fails because it does not "fit" the system that tries to adopt and replicate the "best practice."

Instead of trying to replicate some other district's successful change effort, a school system needs to invent its own unique solutions to its unique characteristics and problem-sets. Instead of trying to find and replicate a school reform model, they need to use a methodology that will help them identify *their* unique characteristics, explore *their* unique problem-sets, create an idealized vision for *their* future, and engage in a process of invention and design that will lead them to *their* idealized future.

KNOWLEDGE AND SKILL SETS FOR
EFFECTIVE CHANGE LEADERSHIP

Given the complexity of school system transformation, change leaders need special knowledge and skill sets to lead this kind of change. These knowledge and skill sets are found in:

- a change vehicle (a specially designed methodology and set of tools for creating and sustaining transformational change);
- a map and compass (knowledge of systems theory, systems dynamics, complexity and chaos theory, and knowledge of what needs to change); and
- superior change navigation skills that include:
  - *Mastery of Awareness*—becoming skillful in collecting, analyzing, interpreting, and reporting need data (that push people toward change) and opportunity data (that draw people toward change);
  - *Mastery of Intention*—becoming skillful in creating and communicating a compelling and emotionally powerful vision of an idealized future for a school system; and
  - *Mastery of Methodology*—becoming skillful in using a methodology especially designed to create and sustain transformational change, and the tools that are part of that methodology.

Given the confusion about the meaning of the term "systemic change," the characteristics of school districts as complex systems, the four complementary paradigm shifts that must be made to create and sustain transformational change, the whole-school system as the preferred unit of change, the nature of transformational change as a "wicked problem," and the knowledge and skill sets required for effective change leadership, change leaders who want to transform their school systems need a new methodology especially designed in response to this complexity so they can create and sustain transformational paradigm change. This new methodology is the *School System Transformation (SST) Protocol*.

THE SCHOOL SYSTEM TRANSFORMATION (SST) PROTOCOL

Working without knowledge of the other's work, the authors each designed and constructed a methodology to create and sustain transformational change in school districts. Both of us drew the concepts and principles that formed the framework of our methodologies from the literature on systems thinking, systemic change, complexity and chaos theory, organization theory and design, organization development, and learning organizations.

Reigeluth's (Jenlink, Reigeluth, Carr, & Nelson, 1996; Reigeluth, 2006b) methodology was called the *Guidance System for Transforming Education* (GSTE), and Duffy's methodology (2002) was called *Step-Up-To-Excellence* (SUTE) (originally called *Knowledge Work Supervision* in Duffy, Rogerson, & Blick, 2000).

Once we learned of each other's work, we noticed the similarities and differences, and we decided that we should blend our methodologies to design a new hybrid methodology. That hybrid methodology is the *School System Transformation (SST) Protocol*, and it is currently being used to facilitate the transformation of the Metropolitan School District of Decatur Township, Indiana. The *Transformational Dialogue for Public Education* and the *KnowledgeWorks Foundation* are also considering using the SST Protocol to transform education in Ohio. The SST Protocol is also part of the nationwide FutureMinds: Transforming American School Systems initiative launched by the Association for Educational Communications and Technology (see chapter 14).

The SST Protocol Framework

The SST Protocol was designed to create and sustain transformational change in school districts. Figure 12.1 illustrates the protocol.

The logic used to design the SST Protocol is built on the following premises:

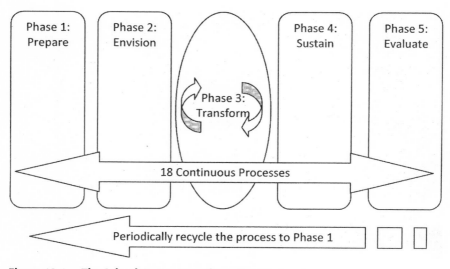

Figure 12.1.   The School System Transformation Protocol

- Premise 1: Paradigm change begins with mind-set change (see chapter 5), which requires broad stakeholder ownership, participatory leadership, and consensus-based decision making.
- Premise 2: Paradigm change also requires invention, which requires idealized design, systems thinking, continual learning, and an emergent design process that starts with high-leverage changes.
- Premise 3: Paradigm change requires changing all parts of the system, including the district's core and support work processes (instructional system, assessment system, record-keeping system, central office functions, transportation services, cafeteria services, and so on), its internal social infrastructure (e.g., rules, roles, and relationships; organization culture; organization design; reward system, and so forth); and its relationships with its external environment.
- Premise 4: Paradigm change also requires using a substantially different approach to creating and sustaining change.

The SST Protocol has some sequential elements and some elements that need to be addressed continuously throughout the transformation process. The sequential elements fall into five phases. Each phase has several steps, and each step has multiple tasks and activities. Flowing continuously throughout the protocol is an important collection of eighteen "continuous processes" (from Jenlink, Reigeluth, Carr, & Nelson, 1996), represented in figure 12.1 by the large arrow that transects the five phases. The eighteen continuous processes are displayed in table 12.1.

Table 12.1. Eighteen Continuous Processes in the SST Protocol

1. Evaluate and improve the change process
2. Build and maintain political support
3. Sustain motivation
4. Develop and sustain appropriate leadership
5. Build and maintain trust
6. Evolve mind-set and culture
7. Periodically secure necessary resources
8. Develop skills in systems thinking
9. Periodically and appropriately allocate necessary resources
10. Develop group-process and team-building skills
11. Build team spirit
12. Engage in self-disclosure
13. Engage in reflection
14. Develop design skills
15. Communicate with stakeholders (two-way)
16. Build and evolve community
17. Foster organizational learning
18. Build an organizational memory

Source: Jenlink, Reigeluth, Carr, & Nelson, 1998.

The SST Protocol also uses a wide range of effective tools for helping mind-sets to evolve, building consensus, engaging external stakeholders, developing internal commitment to change, visioning, and so on.

The five phases in the protocol should not be thought of as a lockstep sequence. Instead, they should be perceived as a set of flowing activities that converge, diverge, and backflow from time to time, and do so repeatedly until the entire system is transformed. Further, transformational change is not a one-time event. It should be a cyclical, lifelong journey with periods of continuous improvement between periods of transformational change. The cyclical nature of transformational change is built into the SST Protocol and is portrayed as the arrow in figure 12.1 with the words "Recycle to Phase 1." This level of complexity was deliberately built into the design of the protocol because we wanted the protocol to align with the complexity of school systems and their external environments (a principle that is derived from complexity theory; see chapter 4).

The Five Phases

Phase 1: Prepare. Preparing a system for transformational change is absolutely critical to the success of a transformation journey. Kotter (1996) identified eight reasons for failed transformational change. Six of those eight reasons are linked to inadequate or short-circuited preparation of the system.

Preparation activities include developing a district's capacity to engage in transformational change. Capacity includes the existence or confirmed emergence of specific conditions prior to launching a systemic transformation journey. Some of the criteria for evaluating capacity apply to an entire school system (table 12.2, Reigeluth & Duffy, 2009), while others apply to change leaders and their followers (table 12.3, Duffy, 2008).

Preparation activities also focus on developing internal and external political support for transformational change, identifying sources of funding to support transformational change, and creating change management structures and processes (e.g., organizing the district into clusters of schools, and chartering and training change leadership teams).

The length of time required to complete phase 1 will vary from district to district and will be influenced by a district's prior experience with change, the size of the district, and the demographic complexity of the district's external environment.

Phase 2: Envision. In this phase, change leaders design and implement a collection of transformation activities to help educators in the system envision an idealized future for *their* school district (see chapter 7). A critically important early task in this phase is to engage educators in activities especially designed to help them evolve their mind-sets about the nature of teaching and learning in the twenty-first-century Knowledge Age. The re-

Table 12.2. Criteria for Gauging System Capacity for Engaging in Transformational Change

Criterion 1: Leadership style
- To what extent is the superintendent a transformational (or developmental) leader?
- To what extent are other formal leaders transformational leaders?
- To what extent does the school board avoid micromanagement?
- Stakeholder empowerment requires a different paradigm of leadership from the traditional, top-down, command-and-control paradigm of leadership.

Criterion 2: Commitment to systemic change (Assess separately for each stakeholder group)
- Do they recognize the need for systemic change? If so:
  ○ Why do they think they need systemic change?
  ○ What are the strengths and weaknesses of their reasons?
  ○ Are there any factors that make them hesitant to engage in systemic change?
- How much time are the board and superintendent willing to commit to the systemic change effort?
- Are the board and administration willing to commit hard money to the change effort?
- Are they willing to suspend current change efforts to provide the necessary space and resources?
- Are they willing to go to the public to ask for support?

Criterion 3: Change history of the school district
- How much money has been spent on change in the last five years?
- What types of professional development efforts have occurred?
- What were the driving forces for these expenditures and efforts?
- How willing are leaders to take risks and not punish "failures"?

Criterion 4: Scope of the change effort
- Are they interested in a districtwide effort or just school-based efforts?
- Are they willing to engage in a long-term effort?

Criterion 5: Flexibility of the board and administration
- How willing are they to engage in negotiations for release time for professionals?
- How willing are they to engage students and community people in the change effort?
- Will they be willing to allow shared decision making?
- Do they view leadership as helping or controlling?
- Are they willing to experiment with changes and forgive "failures"?
- How are problems handled?
- How willing are they to examine current district policy and develop/implement new policies aligned with a systemic change effort?

Criterion 6: Attitude toward outside facilitator(s)
- How willing are the school board and superintendent to allow external facilitators to become a part of their school community and have access to all people in it?
- How well do facilitators get along with the key leaders (e.g., board, superintendent, union leadership, business leaders)?
- What role do district leaders see the facilitators playing?

Table 12.2.   Criteria for Gauging System Capacity for Engaging in Transformational Change

Criterion 7: Attitude toward themselves and the community
- How well do the various stakeholder groups within the district (members and leaders) get along with each other?
- Are there serious conflicts that have a history?
- How harmonious are the relationships within each of those stakeholder groups (among members)?
- Who does the superintendent (or board) not want you to talk with, and why? And who does each want the external facilitator to talk with, and why?

Criterion 8: Stability of leadership in the community
- How long is the superintendent willing to stay and see this process through?
- How frequently do the other leaders change—the principals, other administrators, school board, teachers' union president, parents' organization leaders?

Criterion 9: Communications
- How extensive and frequent are the communications among the various groups in the school community, and what are the tone and quality of those communications?

Criterion 10: Resources and financial stability of the school system
- How sound is the system's financial standing?
- How good are the nonmonetary resources available to the external facilitators (e.g., specialized expertise, space)?
- Do they have a successful grant-writing officer?
- How successful has the school system been in obtaining grants?

Criterion 11: Business support for change in the schools
- How willing are the local chamber of commerce and local businesses and foundations in general to commit resources to a systemic change effort?

Criterion 12: Do-ability of the effort
- How big is the school system?
- How highly bureaucratized?
- How much time will the district require of you?

fined mind-sets that emerge from these educational activities are absolutely essential for the success of a district's transformation journey.

Following the activities for helping mind-sets to evolve, change leaders then design and implement a special large-group event for key external stakeholders (a Community Engagement Conference) and one for faculty and staff (a System Engagement Conference). These events are designed using tested principles for effectively engaging large groups of people in productive discussions about the future of their school system. The outcomes of both events provide a district's change leaders with the data they need to develop a *Framework of Ideal Beliefs* for the district that will guide the transformation of their system.

Table 12.3.   Ten Leadership Competencies for Leading Transformational Change

Leaders who want to facilitate systemic transformational change must:

1. Have strong interpersonal and group facilitation skills
2. Have a positive mind-set about empowering and enabling others to participate effectively in a transformation journey
3. Have experience in preK–12 education
4. Have an understanding of the dynamics of complex systemic change and how to create and sustain this kind of change
5. Have a personal presence and track record that commands respect
6. Have a likeable personality
7. Be organized
8. Be flexible and open-minded about how change occurs, with the ability to tolerate the messiness of the change process
9. Have a positive, can-do attitude
10. Be creative thinkers

Phase 3: Transform. Once the envision phase is near completion, the change process then flows into a set of transformation activities. The early transformation activities occur primarily within the units in the system targeted to begin the transformation journey. These "first to start" units are identified as high-leverage units that can stimulate and support subsequent change in other units.

Examples of some of the transformation activities that occur during phase 3 include:

- Aligning the district's transformation goals and *Framework of Ideal Beliefs* with external expectations;
- Designing new instructional and managerial paradigms for the units targeted to start the district's transformation journey;
- Training design teams to develop their capacity to engage in systemic transformation;
- Removing old programs, policies, and practices to make room for the new ones required by the new instructional and managerial paradigms (a principle derived from chaos theory; e.g., see Pascale, Milleman, & Gioja, 2000).

Phase 4: Sustain. One of the perplexing and enduring problems associated with creating change in school systems is the challenge of sustaining those changes. Sustaining change requires engaging in a set of specific activities designed to provide educators with formative evaluation data about the effectiveness of the transformation process and outcomes, retooling the district's reward system to reinforce desirable changes, institutionalizing the change process so it becomes a permanent part of the district's operations, and creating and rewarding strategic alignment among the various schools, programs, tasks, and activities within the school system. It is also helpful if school boards develop policies to protect the changes from the vagaries linked to the revolving door on the superintendent's office (i.e., many districts have high turnover in the superintendent's position, and each new superintendent often sweeps out his or her predecessor's changes and supplants those with his or her own change agenda).

Sustaining change also requires staff development and training to help educators continue to learn new knowledge and skills that are required by the changes. Then, educators need time to develop personal mastery in applying their new knowledge and skills. As educators engage in these learning activities, they will predictably move through a learning curve.

Without exception, the first movement in a learning curve is always down. This means that as educators begin learning new knowledge and skills, they will not be proficient in applying the knowledge and skills. Eventually, as they continue to learn and practice the new knowledge and skills, the downward slope of the learning curve will bottom-out and the educators will begin to increase their proficiency and move upward toward personal mastery of the new knowledge and skills. Because of the "first down, then up" learning curve, it is very important to design staff development activities that inform educators about that learning curve, and to help them understand the emotional cycle of change that is inextricably connected to that learning experience (e.g., as people start applying new knowledge and skills, they will not be proficient, and this experience often stimulates feelings of frustration, sadness, or anger).

Phase 5: Evaluate. Principles of formative evaluation are used in phase 4 to help educators sustain desirable changes in their system. In phase 5, educators apply principles of summative evaluation to assess the system's post-transformation performance.

There are several summative evaluation models in the field of education. One that is particularly suitable to the task of evaluating transformational change is Stufflebeam's (2000) Context, Inputs, Process, Product (CIPP) model. This model has elements of systems thinking built into it, which makes it appropriate for evaluating transformational change.

It is insufficient simply to conduct a summative evaluation of a transformation journey. The results of the evaluation must be reported to key external stakeholders and to faculty and staff. This need requires change leaders to use principles of strategic communication (see Duffy & Chance, 2007). Keeping the results secret is a dangerous political strategy that almost always backfires.

CONCLUSION

Our society has transformed into what sociologists call the Knowledge Age. Most of America's institutions are adjusting to the requirements of the Knowledge Age. The one institution lagging significantly behind in this transformation is education. School systems were designed for success in the preceding age—the Industrial Age. That design, which is focused on sorting students, is inappropriate for the requirements of the Knowledge Age, and this mismatch between organization design and environmental demands is, we believe, causing many of the teaching-learning problems associated with schooling in America (e.g., the achievement gap and low performance on achievement tests). Further, Bar-Yam (2004), drawing from complexity theory, tells us that systems can only be effective when their design matches the complexity of their external environment.

School districts are complex systems. Therefore, improving the performance of school districts requires change leaders to use principles of systems theory, systemic change, chaos and complexity theory, and organization theory and design to transform districts so they can educate students for success in the twenty-first century. However, the dominant and stunningly persistent approach to improving education—the school-based improvement paradigm—does not and cannot transform entire school systems. Instead, that approach unintentionally reinforces the old Industrial Age design of school systems by tweaking parts of the system (individual schools and programs) and maintaining the overall structure of the old paradigm by never transforming the core work (the teaching and learning process).

Despite the need for transformational change in school districts and despite the efforts of the early adopters to lead this kind of change, there is a lingering question in the dimly lit interstice between the articulation of an idealized vision for the future of schooling in America and the realization of that vision. The question is "How do we do this?" A more important question, however, is "Why should we do this?" This chapter answered the first question. The rest of the book addresses the second one.

NOTE

1. In a P–12 school district, a cluster is a high school and all the schools that feed students into that high school. The cluster contains the entire instructional program of the district. In school districts organized as high school districts or elementary districts, the clusters would still contain the districts' entire instructional program.

13

Seven Common Objections to Transformational Change and How to Respond

OVERVIEW

Whenever I make a presentation about transforming school systems, without exception one or more of seven common objections to transformational change are presented by some members of the audience. These objections more often than not come in the form of "Yes, nice idea, but . . ." What follows after the "but" is the objection.

I learned a technique for responding to these "buts" from family members who work in the business sales world. What they taught me is that when I am making a presentation to an audience of people who are unknown to me, I should anticipate key objections and address them *before* the objections are expressed. I have used this technique many times since I learned about it, and it works.

As change leaders, or aspiring change leaders, I strongly encourage you to learn to anticipate and respond to objections to transformational change before someone stands up and verbalizes them in front of your audience (which can be your peers and colleagues in a team, school, or district meeting). To help you anticipate key objections to transformational change, I highlight below seven common objections that I have encountered and the responses to those objections that I now use.

SEVEN COMMON OBJECTIONS TO
TRANSFORMATIONAL CHANGE

Objection #1: Yes, Nice Idea, but . . . Who Else Is Doing This?

This objection is often expressed by people who do not see the need to change or do not want to change. It may also come from people who are afraid of innovation or new ideas, and they are seeking comfort in knowing who else has gone before them. Unfortunately, this need for precedents can lead to change efforts based on imitation rather than created through invention.

In anticipation of hearing this objection, here are some examples of "who else."

- A school district that is engaged in systemic transformational change is the Metropolitan School District of Decatur Township in Indiana.
- The school districts that won the Baldrige National Quality Award in Education: Chugach School District, Anchorage, Alaska; Pearl River School District, Pearl River, New York; Community Consolidated School District 15 in Palatine, Illinois; Jenks Public Schools, Jenks, Oklahoma; Iredell-Statesville Schools, Statesville, North Carolina.
- The KnowledgeWorks Foundation and the Transformational Dialogue for Public Education in Ohio are engaging in conversations about using principles of systemic transformational change to transform school systems in Ohio.

Objection #2: Yes, Nice Idea, but . . . How Do We Pay for This?

This is a valid objection from those working in districts facing serious financial difficulties. Even those districts with sufficient operating budgets will express this objection because transformational change is expensive.

When this objection is expressed, the "economists" in the room take a seat at the head of the table. An unwavering concern for costs shuts down discussions about important changes that are needed but that are expensive. In their place, cheap, quick fixes are deliberated, approved, and implemented. "When we consider cost too early or make it the overriding concern, we dictate how our values will be acted upon, because the high-cost choices are eliminated before we start" (Block, 2003, p. 19).

In anticipation of hearing this objection, some possible responses are found in the strategies used by school systems to fund large-scale change (see Duffy, 2003a):

1. Reallocate existing dollars by identifying some money within the current operational budget that can be redirected to support transformational change.

2. Creatively use federal dollars.
3. Seek "extra" dollars (grant money).
4. Create a permanent budget line in the district's operational budget to support ongoing transformation efforts. Then this budget item is funded yearly as part of the district's budget cycle.

Objection #3: Yes, Nice Idea, but . . . We Can't Stop Doing What We're Doing to Engage in This Kind of Change Process.

This is also a valid objection rooted in the reality of school systems throughout the United States. Educators cannot tell students to stay at home for several months while they completely transform their school systems. They have to continue providing children with educational services while simultaneously engaging in transformational change.

Engaging in transformational change does not mean that you need to close down your school system until the transformation is complete. Rather, you engage in transformational change by creating a "parallel system" while continuing to educate students as you have done.

When planning to engage your school system in transformational change, you will have your current system (the one that has to keep working while you engage in transformational change) and a virtual system that you will create on paper and in your mind's eye. The "mind's eye" system is the parallel system.

The parallel system is created by teams of change leaders who engage in structured activities that create an idealized design for your system (see chapter 7 for more about principles of idealized design). As you implement the idealized design, the parallel system begins to displace the current system. At some point, the entire current system will be replaced by the idealized parallel system. This replacement process is illustrated in figure 13.1.

Objection #4: Yes, Nice Idea, but . . . We Don't Need to Do This. We Are Already a Good School System.

Jim Collins (2001) observed that "good is the enemy of great." The "we're already a good system" is a pernicious objection that prevents a school district from becoming even better than it currently is.

In anticipation of this objection, you could tell the following story followed by an explanation of the "S-curve."

Near the end of World War II, propeller-driven airplane engines had reached the upper limit of their performance capacity. Design engineers could not figure out how to make the engines go faster or fly farther. No amount of tinkering with the engines (i.e., the old system) could increase

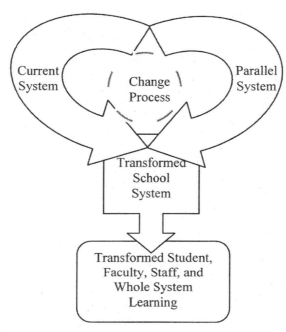

Figure 13.1.   Designing a Parallel System

the engines' capacity. So, what did the design engineers do? They started thinking outside the box and they created a brand new engine design—the jet engine; that is, they created a brand new system that was substantially different from the old system.

The jet engine system has now reached the upper limit of its performance capacity. Design engineers are now creating a brand new system for powering planes. It's the rocket plane. Design engineers envision planes taking off in one place, traveling through space, and then landing in another. Passengers will embark on a horizontal takeoff aboard a special rocket plane, climb to 40,000 feet before rockets fire, accelerate to 3,500 miles per hour, coast for a few minutes of weightlessness 62 miles above the Earth, flip over, and then return to ground—a feat that no current jet engine can achieve. Science fiction? A designer's dream? No, it's real.[1]

Like the airplane engines described in the story, all systems have life cycles and all systems eventually hit the upper limits of their performance capacity. System life cycles are graphically depicted as S-curves (Handy, 1995; Branson, 1987). An example of an S-curve is shown in figure 13.2 below. In the figure, the system's performance hits the upper limit of its performance (characterized as a "ceiling") and then starts to decline. Systems, however, can skirt along their performance ceilings for years, and while doing that they will be perceived as "good" systems. However, at some point they will start to decline, and no amount of tinkering with the old "good" system can prevent this decline in performance.

There is a way, however, to break through the performance ceiling to prevent system decline. It's called transformation. To avoid the downward slope of the S-curve, a different kind of intervention is required. The different intervention is to "reinvent"—to create a brand new system (like the design engineers did for airplane engines) that allows the system to break through its performance ceiling to achieve new levels of performance. This breakthrough is depicted in figure 13.3.

Our nation's school systems are functioning as "old" systems. No amount of tweaking, no amount of piecemeal change, no amount of restructuring of the old system, and no amount of "Band-Aid" quick fixes will significantly improve the performance of those systems, because they are either bumping up against the limits of their performance ceilings or they are on the slippery downward slope of the S-curve.

So, even though a school system may already be "good," there is a way for it to become significantly better by breaking through the performance ceiling that is pressing down on its performance capacity and that will eventually bend the system's performance curve toward the downward tail of the S-curve.

Objection #5: Yes, Nice Idea, but . . . It Will Take Too Much Time.

Transformational change does take time. In fact, it probably takes more time than we can ever imagine, and this time requirement forces educators

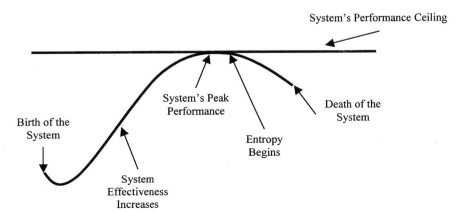

Figure 13.2. Performance Ceilings Block Breakthrough Performance

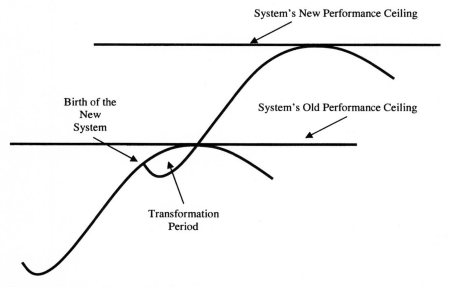

Figure 13.3.   Breakthrough Performance Requires a New S-Curve

to look for the quick fix. They want changes that can be made today, tomorrow, next week, and next month. When told that transformational change may take years, if people respond by saying that "it takes too long," that statement is a hidden "no, we don't want to do that."

Another problem associated with the desire for quick fixes is that almost without exception quick fixes do not permanently solve the problems to which they are applied. In fact, research on systems dynamics (Kim & Lannon, 1997) tells us that while a quick fix might create the illusion of problem dissolution, the original problem almost always returns and becomes worse.

Although whole-system transformational change takes more time than piecemeal, school-based reforms, the process should be expedited with as much speed as possible. Managing the process so that it proceeds at a reasonable rate of speed while simultaneously taking the time to make the necessary transformational changes requires change leaders who are masters of the art and science of transformation.

Objection #6: Nice Idea, but . . . We Don't Have the Right People Working in the System to Do This.

This objection seems to be rooted in a lack of confidence in one's vision for the future of a school system or a lack of confidence in one's ability to lead transformational change. But, who are the right people? I believe that *you are*!

- YOU become the person to "spread the word."
- YOU become the person to build political support for change.
- YOU become the person to seek out resources for change.
- YOU become the person to influence others to think about change.
- Don't wait for OTHERS to take the initiative—they may never.

Objection #7: Yes, Nice Idea, but . . . There's Nothing Really Different about the School System Transformation Protocol. It's Just Like TQM, Process Reengineering, the Baldrige Quality Process, and Other Quality Improvement Processes of the Past.

This objection appears to be based on a misunderstanding of the design and focus of the School System Transformation Protocol. When you describe the SST Protocol to your colleagues, please be sure to point out the following ways in which it is different from other change methodologies.

1. Traditional quality-improvement methodologies are designed to create piecemeal change; the SST Protocol is designed to create and sustain whole-system paradigm change.
2. Traditional quality-improvement methodologies tend to focus exclusively on the core work processes in an organization; the SST Protocol focuses on a school system's core and support work processes, the internal social infrastructure, and environmental relationships.
3. Traditional quality-improvement methodologies focus on tweaking the status quo, sometimes called continuous improvement; the SST Protocol aims to disrupt the status quo to help educators create and sustain a new paradigm for teaching and learning.
4. Traditional quality-improvement methodologies are driven from the top of an organization by directive; the SST Protocol is driven by broad stakeholder participation and ownership.

CONCLUSION

The language of objection uses sandpaper words that scour the luster off of bright ideas for change. Therefore, you must anticipate objections to transformational change and respond to them before they are expressed in writing or voiced. Although some objections are valid and should be addressed, if you know what the objections are and then wait until they are expressed, you run the risk of seeing the objections escalate to become a stinging swarm of almost insurmountable resistance to change.

NOTE

1. Visit www.daylife.com/article/0db3cwodQD8Az?q=Top+News to read about this new airplane engine.

V

THE FUTURE OF LEADERSHIP FOR TRANSFORMATIONAL CHANGE

Creating and sustaining transformational change in school systems requires sophisticated change leadership, yet the field of education does not have a set of professional standards to prepare these kinds of leaders, nor does it have very many graduate-level programs focusing on change leadership. This section provides information about an idealized future for preparing educators to serve effectively as change leaders in their districts.

Chapter 14 provides a broad overview of a new nationwide initiative sponsored by the Association for Educational Communications and Technology (AECT) called FutureMinds: Transforming American School Systems. This initiative was created to provide advice, guidance, and technical assistance for transforming school systems.

In chapter 15, you will learn about a set of research-based professional standards for preparing change leaders in education. An argument is made that state departments of education should use standards like these to create a professional license (or certification) for change leaders, and that schools of education in colleges and universities should use these standards to create graduate-level programs to prepare change leaders. The chapter also offers a description of an idealized design for a graduate-level change leadership program.

14

The AECT FutureMinds Initiative: Transforming American School Systems

OVERVIEW

This chapter presents highlights of a new nationwide initiative sponsored by the Association for Educational Communications and Technology (AECT) called FutureMinds: Transforming America's School Systems (www .futureminds.us). First, the purpose of the initiative is discussed. This is followed by a brief review of the environmental context for the initiative. Finally, the fundamental principles underlying the initiative are presented.

FUTUREMINDS: TRANSFORMING AMERICA'S SCHOOL SYSTEMS

The FutureMinds initiative was launched in 2007 by the Association for Educational Communications and Technology (AECT). Dr. Charles Reigeluth of Indiana University and I are the codirectors of the initiative.

The core purpose of FutureMinds is to provide unequivocal and substantial national-level leadership to facilitate the transformation of America's school districts to align with the requirements of four new paradigms (as described throughout this book). AECT furnishes professional direction,

An earlier version of this chapter appeared as the first article in a series of four articles on systemic transformational change as Reigeluth, C. M., & Duffy, F. M. (2008). The AECT FutureMinds Initiative: Transforming American School Systems. *Educational Technology*, 48(3), 45–49. Used with permission.

guidance, and follow-up support to help state education agencies and local school systems with the transformation process. The core methodology used by the FutureMinds initiative is the School System Transformation Protocol described in chapter 12.

THE CONTEXT FOR THE FUTUREMINDS INITIATIVE

Educational reforms increased dramatically during the 1960s, largely in response to Sputnik. Educational reforms redoubled in urgency with the "Nation at Risk" report in the 1980s and again with No Child Left Behind in the 2000s. Educational reforms have episodically focused on curriculum changes, consolidation of school systems, open classrooms, mastery learning, decentralization through school-based management, shared decision making, legislative mandates and controls, high expectations for student performance, integrated thematic instruction, professional development, technology integration, and standards with high-stakes assessments and accountability. Through all these waves of reforms, the educational system has remained resilient, and costs (human and financial) have increased dramatically while student learning has remained disappointing. Given all of these reforms, the diagnostic questions that beg to be answered are these: Why, after all of this change, has so little changed? And why hasn't spending more money solved the problems that the reforms were meant to solve?

Over the past two centuries, and especially since the latter part of the twentieth century, the United States' society has changed dramatically, as it evolved from the Industrial Age to the Knowledge Age. During this period of evolution, our society's needs have changed greatly. In response to these changes, organizations throughout the United States have coevolved to align with the requirements of the Knowledge Age—with one glaring exception: our school systems. Coevolution is a necessary process for any organization that wishes to remain relevant and successful in the Knowledge Age, and this is especially true of our school systems (Banathy, 1991; Bell, 1973; Reigeluth, 1994; Toffler, 1980). As systems thinkers know well, when a system's external environment changes dramatically, the system must undergo coevolutionary paradigm change to survive (Ackoff, 1981; Banathy, 1996; Capra, 1982; Checkland, 1984; Senge, 2000).

The FutureMinds initiative was created to respond to our society's need to create and sustain school systems designed to succeed in the twenty-first century.

FUNDAMENTALS OF THE FUTUREMINDS INITIATIVE

There are ten fundamental principles upon which the FutureMinds Initiative is based:

Principle 1—Transformation Requires Paradigm Change

The FutureMinds Initiative is founded on the understanding that there is a need to change four paradigms influencing the design and performance of school systems. These paradigm shifts were discussed in detail in earlier chapters.

- *Paradigm Shift 1:* Transform the core and support work processes.
- *Paradigm Shift 2:* Transform the system's social infrastructure.
- *Paradigm Shift 3:* Transform the system's relationship with its external environment.
- *Paradigm Shift 4:* Transform the way in which educators create and sustain change in their districts.

Principle 2—Transformation Focuses on the District as the Preferred Unit of Change

When paradigm change happens in only one part of a school system (e.g., in one school), that changed part becomes incompatible with the rest of the system, and the system exerts powerful forces to change it back. Therefore, paradigm change must view the whole school district as the unit of change.

Principle 3—Transformation Requires Mind-Set Change

Creating four different paradigms for designing and managing school systems requires entirely different mental models and mind-sets (see chapter 5) about education by *all* those involved with the system (its stakeholders), or else they will resist the change and be unable to perform the new roles required by the new paradigm. Therefore, the paradigm change process must place top priority on helping *all* stakeholders to evolve their mind-sets about education.

Principle 4—Transformation Requires an Invention Process

The Knowledge Age paradigm of teaching and learning is at the "Wright brothers" stage of development. Pieces of the new paradigm have been developed, but we still need to figure out how to put all the pieces together to work most effectively and efficiently. Furthermore, we expect aspects of the new paradigm to differ from one community to another. For both these reasons, it will not work to try to implement a "comprehensive school design" developed by other school districts. Instead, each school district must invent its own ways to implement the new paradigms. Only after a variety of designs have proven effective will it be possible for the paradigm change process to become an adoption process. One added benefit of inventing rather than adopting is that the invention process is a powerful tool for helping stakeholders to evolve their mind-sets about education.

Principle 5—Transformation Requires Broad Stakeholder Ownership

Because mind-set change is so important to successful paradigm change, stakeholders must be involved in the paradigm change process, for it is only through participation that mind-sets evolve. Furthermore, diverse perspectives enhance the creativity and effectiveness of the invention process. But it is wise to go beyond involvement to ownership of the change process, for that engenders true commitment and greatly reduces resistance to the new paradigm, enhancing sustainability. Also, the broader the ownership, the better the results (though the more time it takes to design the new paradigm).

Principle 6—Transformation Requires Consensus Building

Stakeholders have different values about, and views of, what is important in education. Empowering stakeholders can generate discord and increase divisiveness unless a consensus-building process is used, along with a consensus-sustaining process.

Principle 7—Transformation Requires Participatory Leadership

Stakeholder ownership and the consensus-building style of decision making both require a different paradigm of leadership from the common supervisory or "command-and-control" paradigm. They require a paradigm that empowers all stakeholders to be leaders, supports them in their work, and provides professional development whenever needed.

Principle 8—Transformation Requires an Experienced External Facilitator

The journey of paradigm change is a treacherous one, and stakeholders typically have a long history of disagreements, factions, animosities, rivalries, and such. Therefore, it is essential to have an external facilitator who is experienced in the systemic transformation process and has experience implementing the principles listed above. Furthermore, that facilitator must be viewed as neutral and impartial by all stakeholder groups. That person must also be available to facilitate all meetings in the school district until an internal capacity for engaging in transformational change is developed.

Principle 9—Transformation Requires Time

Mind-set change takes time, and the more mind-sets to be changed, the more time that is needed. This is because mind-sets change primarily through exposure to new ideas and plentiful small-group discussions. Unless individuals' time can be bought or otherwise freed up, the transformation process will take many years and be less likely to succeed. This makes external funding crucial.

Principle 10—Transformation Requires Capacity Building

Empowering educators to create and sustain transformational paradigm change is insufficient; they must also be enabled to engage in that kind of change process. Enabling educators to create and sustain transformational change means that they learn new knowledge, develop new skills, and expand their mind-sets (their attitudes) toward the four new paradigms that are required to create school systems that can provide children with a learner-centered educational experience. Empowering combined with enabling creates capacity, and capacity to launch a transformation journey and see it through to the end is absolutely necessary for successful transformation.

CONCLUSION

It has been well demonstrated that piecemeal reforms are not effective in meeting the educational challenges we face today in the Knowledge Age. There is clear need for school systems to transform to align with the requirements of our society's Knowledge Age. The four required paradigm shifts discussed throughout this book and reiterated in this chapter will result in fundamentally different roles for students, teachers, administrators, parents, and other community members. These four paradigm shifts, especially the shift that transforms the core work of school systems—teaching and learning—also require a much more central role for instructional technology (e.g. learning management systems to manage the learner-centered teaching and learning process). Fundamental paradigm change requires a very different approach to educational change—one founded in the district as the unit of change, mind-set change, invention, broad stakeholder ownership, consensus building, participatory leadership, experienced outside facilitation, time for participation, and capacity building.

Based on the fundamental principles presented above, the FutureMinds process requires external experts who train and coach state department of education-level and district-level personnel to facilitate district-wide paradigm change efforts using the SST Protocol (see chapter 12), which has a long history of development, improvement, and validation in the Metropolitan School District of Decatur Township, Indiana. The cost of external guidance is miniscule compared with the total expenditures states typically spend on school improvement, and the external guidance also results in building capacity within school districts to continue their transformation journeys without external facilitation. Can you imagine a better expenditure of public monies for education?

15

A National Framework of Professional Standards for Change Leadership in Education

OVERVIEW

In this chapter you will find a set of research-based professional standards for developing the requisite knowledge, skills, and dispositions of change leaders so they can facilitate the challenging and complex process of creating and sustaining systemic transformational change in their school districts. The standards were derived from research on effective change leadership and adjusted to apply to school systems.

The ten professional standards form what I call a *National Framework of Professional Standards for Change Leadership in Education*. Each standard has examples of the knowledge, skills, and dispositions that the research suggests are important for effective change leadership. It is my hope that this proposed national framework will result in (a) state departments of education creating a professional license for change leadership in school districts, and (b) schools of education in colleges and universities designing new graduate-level programs specializing in preparing educators to become change leaders.

Following the presentation of the proposed standards, I offer an innovative design for a graduate-level program to prepare teams of change leaders in education. This idealized program of study incorporates learning experiences that prepare educators at the education specialist degree level (alternatively, it could be designed as a master's of science or doctor of education program) to lead the process of creating and sustaining systemic transformational change in school districts. The learning experiences, in conjunction with the proposed standards, can then be used by state departments of education to create a professional license for change leadership in education.

THE NEED FOR SYSTEMIC TRANSFORMATIONAL CHANGE IN SCHOOL DISTRICTS

Throughout this book I have discussed how our society has undergone, and is still undergoing, a significant paradigm shift—one that is moving our institutions away from the requirements of the Industrial Age toward the requirements of the Knowledge Age. This societal paradigm shift is large and pervasive, and it is affecting most of our society's organizations as they coevolve to create more customized, personalized approaches to organization design, serving customers, and providing services. A few examples of changes in the design of organizations are shown in table 15.1 below. However, the organizations in our society that are lagging significantly behind our society's transformation curve are our school systems.

One of the hallmark characteristics of the Knowledge Age is a form of work called knowledge work, which has become the predominate form of work in our society. Knowledge work, a term coined by Peter Drucker (1959), is a work process whereby a worker manipulates information or develops and uses knowledge in the workplace. Knowledge workers are now estimated to outnumber all other workers in North America by at least a four to one margin (Haag, Cummings, McCubbrey, Pinsonneault, & Donovan, 2006, p. 4).

Now that knowledge work predominates in our society, America needs a system of education that has as its purpose to ensure that every individual who enters public education leaves having mastered a variety of important knowledge and skills. To achieve this purpose, some thought leaders in education believe that we need to transform the current profession-wide paradigm for teaching and learning to a new paradigm that is more closely

Table 15.1.   Examples of Paradigm Change in American Organizations

Industrial Age Organization Design Design	Shift to	Information Age Organization Design
Bureaucratic design	→	Team design
Autocratic leadership	→	Distributed leadership
Centralized control	→	Autonomy with accountability
Compliance by employees	→	Initiative by employees
Forced conformity	→	Managed diversity
Compartmentalization	→	Holism
(Division of labor, vertical communication)	→	(Integration, coordination, horizontal communication)

aligned with the requirements of the Knowledge Age. A paradigm of teaching and learning that meets the requirements of the Knowledge Age would not hold time constant, which forces achievement to vary; instead, it would hold achievement constant so that students can attain required learning standards. Within this new paradigm, each student would be given as much time as he or she needs to master mandated standards of learning. Further, to enrich their learning, students would benefit from having opportunities to select and study topics of their own choosing or to engage with others in community projects in which they would have opportunities to meet state-mandated standards of learning. The current reforms that predominate in education, however, fail to do this. Instead, these reforms leave the old education paradigm intact; therefore, these reforms cannot and will not meet the needs of our Knowledge Age society. We must transform rather than reform our school systems.

I feel strongly that it is a moral imperative for federal and state education officials, school system leaders, school board members, and other key stakeholders for school systems to: (a) understand that societal transformation is occurring; (b) recognize that the design and functioning of most current school systems are incompatible with our transforming society; and (c) recognize the kinds of key organization design features that would make school systems compatible with our changing society—features such as those displayed in table 15.2. I also think that individual state education agencies and local school systems must decide on what their transformed school districts should be like in response to the requirements of the Knowledge Age; that is, there is not a single one-size-fits-all ideal organization design for all school systems to replicate.

PARADIGM CHANGE REQUIRES SYSTEMIC TRANSFORMATION

Much has been written about the need for paradigm change in education (e.g., see Ackoff, 2001; Banathy, 1992b; Bar-Yam, 2003; Branson, 1987; Darling-Hammond, 1990; Duffy, 2003a; Duffy, Rogerson, & Blick, 2000; Egol, 2003; Elmore, 2004; F. E. Emery, 1977; Fullan, 2004; Kaufman, 2000; Pasmore, 1988; Reigeluth, 1994; Schlechty, 2002; Senge et al., 2000; Toffler, 1984; Tyack & Cuban, 1997). There is also a growing recognition that the Knowledge Age, with its predominance of knowledge work replacing the Industrial Age's predominance of manual labor, requires a shift from a standardized, sorting-focused paradigm of teaching and learning to a customized, learner-centered paradigm.

There is also substantial research supporting the efficacy of the customized, learner-centered paradigm of teaching and learning (see chapter 9). McCombs and Whisler (1997) summarize much of the research literature

Table 15.2. What a Paradigm Shift in Education Could Look Like

Current Paradigm for Schooling Is Suited to the Industrial Age	Shift to →	Desired Paradigm for Schooling Must Be Suited to the Information Age

Paradigmatic Principles

• Standardized, one-size-fits-all instruction • Autocratic classroom environment • Students assumed to learn by being told • Linear thinking	• Customized, tailored instruction • Democratic classroom environment • Students assumed to learn by doing • Systemic thinking

Practices Derived from the Paradigm

• Teacher doing *to* students • Teacher-directed student learning • Grade-level classes • Emphasis on discrete subjects • Teaching is content-oriented • Extrinsic motivation is used to encourage student learning • Age-based grouping • Large-group instruction in classes • Limited access to knowledge • Limited resources • Textbooks/teaching aids • Lockstep student progress	• Teacher doing *with* students • Self-directed student learning • Multi-age grouping • Interdisciplinary courses • Teaching is process/performance-oriented • Intrinsic motivation creates meaningful student engagement • Student readiness and interest grouping • Individual, small-group and large-group activities • Plentiful access to knowledge • Multiple resources of various kinds • Multimedia technologies • Customized student progress based on learning

Learning Outcomes within the Paradigm

• Norm-based, competitive assessment • Fixed response testing • Convergent learning with rote memory • Student unmotivated to learn • Student dependent on teacher for learning • Compliant learner	• Mastery assessment in progressive levels • Authentic testing • Convergent and divergent learning • Student motivated to learn • Student independence/interdependence for learning (self-actualization) • Engaged, life-long learner

Source: Adapted and modified from McBeath, R. J. (1969). Is Education Becoming? *AudioVisual Communication Review*, Spring, 36–40.

about learner-centered learning. Lambert and McCombs (1998) do an even more thorough review of the extensive research supporting the efficacy of learner-centered education. Finally, Bransford, Brown, and Cocking

(1999) also provide substantial research and theoretical support for learner-centered learning.

THE FAILURE OF PIECEMEAL CHANGE
TO TRANSFORM SCHOOLING

American school districts were designed to respond to the needs of the Industrial Age, but our society has evolved into the Knowledge Age, which has different requirements for education. This mismatch is what Banathy (1992b) calls "coevolutionary imbalance," and it places our country in peril because children are not being educated to succeed in our Knowledge Age society. To correct this coevolutionary imbalance, whole school systems must be transformed to provide children with a customized, personalized education.

As children receive a personalized, learner-centered education, fewer of them will be left behind. Actually, many of us who are advocates for learner-centered education believe that there will be a dramatic end to children being left behind in their pursuit of an education. Think about it. If children are receiving an education that is customized and personalized to meet their individual needs, interests, and abilities, and if they are given the time they need to master required knowledge and skills, how could they possibly be left behind? By contrast, the current approach to teaching and learning—the dominant paradigm—is designed to leave children behind and will continue to do so if left in place.

School systems, as I said earlier, are not making the required transformation journey. In fact, after many years of applying the traditional approach to improving education (one school, one program at a time), very little has changed in how America's children are educated in school systems. The old paradigm persists and is sustained by the one-school-at-a-time approach to improvement. This approach, although important and still needed if it is an element of a transformational change strategy, is inherently insufficient as a stand-alone change strategy because it disregards the nature of school districts as intact, organic systems governed by classic principles of system functioning. Further, the one-school-at-a-time approach often fails because changes to one part of a system make that part incompatible with the rest of the system, which then works to change it back to its prechange state. Therefore, the piecemeal approach to change is insufficient because it fails to transform an entire school district and it unintentionally maintains the system's status quo.

Given the insufficiency of the one-school-at-a-time approach to improvement, change efforts are now being scaled up to the level of the whole district, but the whole-district change methodologies currently being used are not creating and sustaining the paradigm shift in teaching and learning that is required for the Knowledge Age. This is because these approaches to whole-district change do not apply principles of systemic transformational change. Instead, many of these approaches to change are simply tweaking school systems in ways that maintain the status quo—the old paradigm.

One of the key reasons why current efforts to change whole districts are failing to create transformational paradigm change is because there is definitional confusion about the meaning of "system" and "systemic change" (see chapter 2 for a review of this confusion). Many approaches to change that are characterized as systemic are not; for example, high school reform is not systemic change, developing a new curriculum is not systemic change, and introducing new instructional technology is not systemic change. However, some of these approaches can be used as elements of a whole-system change methodology.

Further, not all systemic change efforts aim to create transformational, paradigm-shifting change. For example, some systemic change efforts aim to make systemic (system-wide) improvements to a system's current operations (its existing mental model for how to function). Making system-wide improvements to current operations is called continuous improvement, and this does not create transformational change. Transformational change, on the other hand, seeks organizational reinvention rather than simply trying to replicate best practices, discontinuity rather than incrementalism, and true innovation rather than periodic reordering of the system (Lazlo & Laugel, 2000, p. 184).

Transformational change also requires simultaneous changes along three change paths: Path 1—transform the system's core and support work processes; Path 2—transform the system's internal social infrastructure; and Path 3—transform the system's relationship with its external environment. Only one contemporary approach to improving school systems (Duffy & Riegeluth, 2008, presented in chapter 12) follows these three paths, and failure to create changes along these paths is part of the explanation of why so many contemporary change efforts failed or are failing to create systemic transformational change.

Despite the paucity of real-life examples of system-wide transformational change, there are many examples of schoolwide change that were very successful until the larger system that they were part of (i.e., the school system) changed them back to be compatible with the district's dominant, controlling mental model for teaching and learning. The power of the unchanged parts of a system to attack and destroy a changing part is not to be ignored or minimized. This phenomenon is real, it is common, and it is yet one more reason why whole districts need to be transformed, not pieces of them.

CHANGE LEADERSHIP COMPETENCIES

This section summarizes selected research on key competencies for leading change in organizations. The section concludes with an analysis of the reported research that identifies patterns within the data.

Charles Reigeluth and I (2008) identified ten change leadership competencies for the FutureMinds: Transforming American School Systems initiative that we codirect. These competencies are presented in table 15.3.

We also assume that very few current leaders in America's school systems have all the requisite technical knowledge and skills they need to guide a school district's transformation journey (characteristic 4, above). But we do believe that there are many current education leaders who have all of the other idiosyncratic characteristics and dispositions listed above (e.g., characteristics 5 through 10). Knowledge and skills can be taught, but the other dispositions probably cannot be taught because they are functions of a person's personality, personal style, and who they are as people. However, these nontrainable dispositions can be enhanced and refined through professional development opportunities.

Conner (1998) identified six distinct leadership styles related to change: antichange, rational, panacea, bolt-on, integrated, and continuous. Each leadership style "represents a unique set of perceptions, attitudes, and behaviors regarding how organizational disruption should be addressed" (Conner, 1998, p. 148). Stopper (1999, pp. 1–6) characterized each of Conner's leadership styles in this way:

The antichange leader. A leader embracing this style seeks to avoid as much change as possible. "The Anti-Change leader operates from an underlying

---

Table 15.3.   Ten Leadership Competencies for Leading Transformational Change

Leaders who want to facilitate systemic transformational change must:

1. Have strong interpersonal and group facilitation skills
2. Have a positive mind-set about empowering and enabling others to participate effectively in a transformation journey
3. Have experience in preK–12 education
4. Have an understanding of the dynamics of complex systemic change and how to create and sustain this kind of change
5. Have a personal presence and track record that commands respect
6. Have a likeable personality
7. Be organized
8. Be flexible and open-minded about how change occurs, with the ability to tolerate the messiness of the change process
9. Have a positive, can-do attitude
10. Be creative thinkers

assumption that organizational life should be a mostly calm experience; therefore, significant modifications of any kind are undesirable. Their message is, 'Stay the course. Keep adjustments small. No need to change in any major way'" (p. 3).

The rational leader. This leader focuses on how to constrain and control change with logic and linear, sequential, recipe-like execution. "Rational leaders tend to see life as a binary experience in which things are either good or bad, right or wrong, on track or off. They view organizational change as something to be implemented in as unemotional a fashion as possible. Good planning and carefully worded announcements are the keys to the rational leader's change strategy" (p. 3).

The panacea leader. The panacea leader believes that the way to respond to pressure for change is to communicate and motivate. "These senior officers have reconciled themselves to the fact that unforeseen, disconcerting transitions have become an inevitable part of their organization's life. It is their contention that negative emotions about change impede its progress and should, therefore, be either prevented or converted into positive feelings. These leaders place a high premium on a 'happy' workforce." One sign of this style is a high degree of emphasis on building enthusiasm for a change with little or no effort to address the deeper human issues" (p. 4).

The bolt-on leader. This leader strives to regain control of a changing situation by attaching (bolting on) change management techniques to ad hoc projects that are created in response to pressure for change. "The Bolt-on leader's approach to change recognizes the importance of addressing the human dimension of change 'whenever we have the time and resources to do so.' While these leaders see change management as an important component of the change initiative, they maintain the belief that only a cursory review of people issues may be necessary" (p. 4).

The integrated leader. The integrated leader searches for ways to use the structure and discipline of what Harding and Rouse (2007) called "human due diligence" (the leadership practice of understanding the culture of an organization and the roles, capabilities, and attitudes of its people) as individual change projects are created and implemented. "The cornerstone of this style of change leadership is the respect and emphasis placed on the psycho-social-cultural issues associated with accomplishing important initiatives. These leaders move beyond operating as if the intellectual power of their ideas alone can compensate for the lack of careful diagnosis and skillful navigation. Instead, they blend a balanced concern for both the human and technical aspects of orchestrating change into their decision-making process as well as their execution tactics" (p. 4).

The continuous leader. The continuous leader works to create an agile and quick-responding organization that can quickly anticipate threats and seize opportunities as change initiatives are designed and implemented. Continuous leaders believe that to drive success during turbulent times they "must deal with ongoing disruption. . . . For Continuous Leaders, what is paramount is not whether their organization can execute any current, singular change efforts, but whether it can sustain an endless avalanche of dramatic, overlapping alterations in its key success factors" (p. 5).

Conner also believed that the above leadership styles are related to two different types of organizational change: first-order change and second-order change. First-order change is incremental, piecemeal change that is common in the field of education. According to Conner, second-order change (which is what transformational change is) is "nonlinear in nature and reflects movement that is fundamentally different from anything seen before within the existing framework" (pp. 148–149).

Conner asserted that the first four leadership styles that he identified are appropriate for managing first-order change. However, he argues that the last two leadership styles are more appropriate for leading second-order change, because that kind of change process "requires shifting context; it represents a substantial variation in substance and form that discontinues whatever stability existed before" (p. 149). In other words, when an organization is engaging in discontinuous, transformational change, the Integrated and continuous leadership styles are more appropriate.

Stopper (1999) also identified what he believes are essential traits for change leaders. Those traits are:

Technical competence. Change leaders must have the technical knowledge and skills required to lead change.

Personal resilience. Stopper (1999, pp. 1–6) offered specific behavioral indicators for this characteristic:

- Positive—Resilient people effectively identify opportunities in turbulent environments and have the personal confidence to believe they can succeed.
- Focused—Resilient people have a clear vision of what they want to achieve and use this as a lodestar to guide them when they become disoriented.
- Flexible—Resilient people draw effectively on a wide range of internal and external resources to develop creative, pliable strategies for responding to change.
- Organized—Resilient people use structured approaches to managing ambiguity; they plan and coordinate effectively in implementing their change strategies.
- Proactive—Resilient people act in the face of uncertainty, taking calibrated risks rather than seeking comfort.

Cultural alignment. Change leaders must fit the culture, mission, and vision of their organizations.

Leadership approach to change. Change leaders use effective change leadership styles. Six leadership styles identified by Conner (1998) and characterized by Stopper (1999) were presented above. Both Conner and Stopper believed that only the last two styles (i.e., the integrated leader and the continuous leader) are suited to the challenges of discontinuous, second-order change, which is what systemic transformational change in school districts is.

The National Training Center (2008) identified a set of essential change leadership competencies. In addition to defining each competency, they also offered advice on how leaders can develop each one. The competencies they identified and examples of behavioral indicators for each one are presented below.

Vision

- Taking a long-term view and acting as a catalyst for organizational change.
- Collaborating with others to build a shared vision.
- Influencing others to translate vision into action.

External Awareness

- Identifying and keeping up-to-date on key policies and economic, political, and social trends that affect the organization.
- Determining how to best position the organization to achieve a competitive advantage.
- Anticipating potential threats or opportunities.

Creativity and Innovation

- Developing new insights into situations
- Applying innovative solutions to make organizational improvements.
- Creating a work environment that encourages creative thinking and innovation.
- Designing and implementing cutting-edge programs and processes.

Strategic Thinking

- Formulating effective strategies consistent with the organization's new mission, vision, and strategic direction.
- Examining policy issues that might constrain the strategic planning process.
- Determining short-term objectives and setting priorities.

Continual Learning

- Grasping the essence of new information.
- Mastering new knowledge and skills.
- Recognizing personal strengths and weaknesses.
- Pursuing self-development opportunities.
- Seeking feedback from others about their performance.

Resilience

- Dealing effectively with pressure.
- Maintaining focus and intensity.
- Remaining optimistic and persistent, even under adversity.
- Recovering quickly from setbacks.
- Balancing personal life and work.

Flexibility

- Remaining open to change and new information.
- Adapting behavior and work methods in response to new information, changing conditions, or unexpected obstacles.
- Adjusting rapidly to new situations.

Service Motivation

- Creating and sustaining an organizational culture that encourages others to provide the quality of service essential to high performance.
- Enabling others to acquire the tools and support they need to perform well.
- Influencing others toward a spirit of service and meaningful contributions to mission accomplishment.

Higgs and Rowland (2000) identified a set of change leadership competencies that I think are probably the most comprehensive and clearly articulated change leadership competencies available. They identified these competencies by benchmarking them against world-class best practices in the field of change management. The competencies are:

1. *Change Initiation*—ability to create the case for change and secure credible sponsorship
2. *Change Impact*—ability to scope the breadth, depth, sustainability and returns of a change strategy

3. *Change Facilitation*—ability to help others, through effective facilitation, to gain insight into the human dynamics of change and to develop the confidence to achieve the change goals
4. *Change Leadership*—ability to influence and enthuse others, through personal advocacy, vision, and drive, and to access resources to build a solid platform for change
5. *Change Learning*—ability to scan, reflect, and identify learning and ensure insights are used to develop individual, group, and organizational capabilities
6. *Change Execution*—ability to formulate and guide the implementation of a credible change plan with appropriate goals, resources, metrics, and review mechanisms
7. *Change Presence*—demonstrates high personal commitment to achievement of change goals through integrity and courage, while maintaining objectivity and individual resilience ("a non-anxious presence in a sea of anxiety")
8. *Change Technology*—knowledge, generation, and skillful application of change theories, tools, and processes

Kotter (1995) identified eight causes of failed transformational change. The opposites of those eight causes (described below) represent change leadership competencies. The derived competencies and sample behavioral indicators of those competencies are presented below.

1. Change leaders *increase urgency* by
   • assessing threats, opportunities, and trends in the external environment
   • collecting and interpreting data from outside the organization that demonstrate change is necessary

2. Change leaders *build a guiding team* by
   • assembling a group with enough power to lead the change effort
   • attracting key change leaders by showing enthusiasm and commitment
   • encouraging the group to work together as a team

3. Change leaders *get the vision right* by
   • creating a vision to help direct the change effort
   • developing strategies for achieving that vision

4. Change leaders *communicate for buy-in* by
   • using every means available to communicate the new vision and strategies
   • keeping communication simple and heartfelt
   • teaching new behaviors with the guiding coalition as role models
   • designing and executing a strategic communication plan

5. Change leaders *empower for action* by
   - eliminating obstacles to the change
   - revising or discarding managerial systems, policies, procedures, or structures that seriously undermine the vision
   - encouraging and rewarding risk-taking and nontraditional ideas, activities, and actions

6. Change leaders *create short-term wins* by
   - planning for visible performance improvements in the near term
   - creating those improvements quickly
   - recognizing and rewarding people who help create successful short-term wins

7. Change leaders *do not let up* by
   - planning for visible successful change in all areas of the organization
   - implementing action plans
   - recognizing and rewarding people who contribute to the success of the implementation
   - evaluating the change process and outcomes periodically and making necessary course corrections

8. Change leaders *make change stick* by
   - describing and reinforcing connections between the desirable changes that were made and the organization's ongoing and future success
   - creating and sustaining strategic alignment among all elements of the organization

EMOTIONAL INTELLIGENCE AND CHANGE LEADERSHIP

Emotional intelligence is a popular topic in the leadership literature. It is most often associated with Daniel Goleman (1995). However, there is a history of others who actually developed the concept before Goleman (please visit eqi.org/mayer.htm to see an annotated history of the concept).

Higgs (2002) commented on the fact that there is a lot of confusion, misunderstanding, and differences of opinion about the concept of emotional intelligence. It seems that there is also no agreed upon definition of the term. Dulewicz, Higgs, and Slaski (2001), for example, categorized several definitions of the term by grouping them as follows: definitions based on an interpretation of emotional intelligence as an ability (Salovey & Mayer, 1990); definitions of emotional intelligence as a set of competencies (e.g., Goleman, 1996); and definitions of emotional intelligence as a set of personal capabilities (e.g., Higgs & Dulewicz, 1999; Bar-On, 2000). According to Higgs, the personal capabilities approach is more easily operationalized, while retaining psychometric rigor. Using the personal capabilities characterization of emotional intelligence, Higgs and Dulewicz (1999, p. 20) offered the following definition:

> Achieving one's goals through the ability to manage one's own feelings and emotions, to be sensitive to, and influence other key people, and to balance one's motives and drives with conscientious and ethical behaviour.

In an extensive review of the literature on emotional intelligence, Dulewicz and Higgs (2000) identified the core elements of emotional intelligence that were subsequently validated in empirical studies. These elements are:

1. *Self-awareness*. The awareness of your own feelings and the ability to recognize and manage those feelings.
2. *Emotional resilience*. The ability to perform well and consistently in a range of situations and when under pressure.
3. *Motivation*. The drive and energy that you have to achieve results, balance short- and long-term goals, and pursue your goals in the face of challenge and rejection.
4. *Interpersonal sensitivity*. The ability to be aware of the needs and feelings of others and to use this awareness effectively in interacting with them and arriving at decisions impacting on them.
5. *Influence*. The ability to persuade others to change their viewpoint on a problem, issue, or decision.
6. *Intuitiveness*. The ability to use insight and interaction to arrive at and implement decisions when faced with ambiguous or incomplete information.
7. *Conscientiousness and integrity*. The ability to display commitment to a course of action in the face of challenge, to act consistently and in line with understood ethical requirements.

THE RELATIONSHIP BETWEEN EMOTIONAL INTELLIGENCE AND CHANGE LEADERSHIP COMPETENCIES

There is a relationship between emotional intelligence and change leadership competencies. Higgs (2002) compared the characteristics of emotional intelligence identified by Higgs and Dulewicz (1999) to the Higgs and Rowland (2000) change leadership competencies (identified above). Based on his review, Higgs concluded that it is feasible to hypothesize a number of relationships between the change leadership competencies and the emotional intelligence traits.

In reviewing the proposed relationships between emotional intelligence and change leadership competencies, Higgs asserts that there is an overarching hypothesis that there will be a clear and positive relationship between an individual's emotional intelligence and his or her overall change leadership competencies.

IDENTIFYING PATTERNS IN THE RESEARCH ON CHANGE LEADERSHIP COMPETENCIES

Below, I offer a comparative analysis of the various change leadership competencies and traits identified above, including emotional intelligence. To conduct the analysis, I used Higgs and Rowland's (2000) change competencies as a benchmark. I chose them as a benchmark because they have a substantial research base supporting them, and I think they are the most comprehensive change leadership competencies available.

Next, I created a matrix by listing all of Higgs and Rowland's change competencies in the left column of the matrix. Then, the authors of the five sets of change leadership traits and competencies described in this chapter were inserted across the top of the matrix (i.e., Duffy and Reigeluth, Conner, the National Training Center, Kotter, and Higgs and Dulewicz). Then, I sorted all of the change leadership traits and competencies described above into the cells created by the intersection of Higgs and Rowland's change leadership competencies and the authors of change leadership traits and competencies. The results are displayed in appendix A.

Duffy and Reigeluth's change leader traits were the only ones to align with all eight of Higgs and Rowland's change leadership competencies. All the traits and competencies identified by the remaining authors fit into the matrix, but not all of those competencies and traits aligned with Higgs and Rowland's competencies.

THE NEED FOR EFFECTIVE CHANGE LEADERSHIP STANDARDS AND PREPARATION PROGRAMS

It is clear that there is a stunning need for effective change leadership in America's school systems. If nothing else validates this need, the failure of piecemeal school reform to transform teaching and learning, the cynical characterization of proposed changes as "flavors of the month," and the astonishing inability to sustain change in school systems all stand as stark examples of why effective change leadership is needed. Yet this need is not being effectively responded to by the field of education leadership.

The Interstate School Leaders Licensure Consortium (Council of Chief State School Officers, 2008) and the Educational Leadership Constituents Council (National Policy Board for Educational Administration, 2002) share a set of high-quality standards for preparing future education leaders at the district and building levels. Their standards have subelements that expect future education leaders to possess knowledge of change models and processes. These elements are appropriately embedded within broader standards for preparing school-based and district-level education leaders. However, as long as change leadership competencies are subelements of other professional standards for leaders, the field of education will not meet the need for effective change leadership in school systems.

Given the need for effective change leadership and given the significant lack of response to that need, I propose that state departments of education should adopt a set of research-based change leadership standards and then create a professional license (or certificate) for change leadership based on those standards. Then, universities and colleges with graduate-level education leadership programs should create new graduate-level programs tailored to satisfy the change leadership standards—programs that specialize in educating change leaders about the how, what, and why of creating and sustaining systemic transformational change in school districts (e.g., the Education Specialist Degree Program in Change Leadership in Education at Gallaudet University in Washington, DC).

STANDARDS FOR PREPARING CHANGE LEADERS IN EDUCATION

The standards for preparing change leaders in education presented below are intended to define the practice of effective change leadership in school systems. The standards are derived from an analysis of the research and literature cited above, but adapted for the challenge of transforming school systems.

The formal development of change leaders' knowledge, dispositions, and skills, I believe, must occur within a rigorous team-based graduate-level preparation program that provides participants with learning experiences focusing on topics such as systems theory, systems thinking, systems dynamics, transformational change, change facilitation, interpersonal and group behavior in organizations, and organization theory and design, among others.[1] Although completing a change leadership preparation program will help professionals master the art and science of systemic transformational change, effective change leadership requires a career-long devotion to learning about systemic transformational change. The standards presented below also can be used to guide change leaders' ongoing professional development.

If teams of educators in change leadership preparation programs are to satisfy these standards, I believe it will be vitally important for these teams to become part of an organized nationwide "community of change leaders" that is endorsed and facilitated by state departments of education, local school systems, university faculty, and change partners from other sectors of American society. Being connected to an organized community of change leaders will also help each individual member of the change leadership teams to sustain his or her personal knowledge, skills, and dispositions for providing effective change leadership.

When implemented, the standards presented in appendix B and the related indicators should ensure high quality change leadership in education by:

- providing a clear vision of high-quality change leadership;
- providing a framework that focuses on the requirements of transforming school systems to align with the requirements of the Knowledge Age and beyond; and
- allocating resources to support change leadership priorities at the federal, state, and local levels of education.

Ten Standards for Preparing Change Leaders in Education

Ten standards for preparing change leaders in education are displayed in appendix B. Each standard has sample subelements, identified as knowledge, skills, and dispositions (all of which will need to be refined before adoption). The standards were developed by reviewing the research and literature on change competencies that was summarized above, and then adjusted to fit school systems.

Validation of the Standards Is Required

It is strongly recommended that the proposed standards and rubrics be validated. One validation design that could be used is a competency study. The ultimate outcome of this kind of study is a validated model of change leadership competencies.

Competencies are clusters of knowledge, skills, and dispositions required for job success. Job competency models are used to guide the professional development of employees. A competency model, according to Workitect (2008), is

> a description of those competencies possessed by the top performers in a specific job or job family. In effect, a competency model is a "blueprint for outstanding performance." Models usually contain eight to sixteen competencies with definitions, often grouped into "clusters" along with behavioral descriptors.

Boulter, Dalziel, and Hill (1998) described a six-stage competency development model. The six stages are:

1. Performance criteria—defining the criteria for superior performance in the targeted role
2. Criterion sample—choosing a sample of people performing the targeted role for data collection
3. Data collection—collecting sample data about behaviors that lead to success in the targeted role
4. Data analysis—developing hypotheses about the competencies of outstanding performers and how these competencies work together to produce desired results
5. Validation—validating the results of data collection and analysis
6. Application—applying the competency models in human resource activities

Bernthal and colleagues (2004, pp. 89–94) designed and conducted a competency study for the American Society for Training and Development (ASTD). Their study is an example of how to design and implement a competency study that results in valid competencies for guiding professional behavior. Their competency development methodology has four phases and specific tasks within each phase. The four phases and specific tasks are:

Phase 1: Needs Assessment and Data Collection
- Conduct a review of the literature
- Interview experts possessing the competencies you wish to identify
- Summarize and report phase 1 findings

Phase 2: Development of Competency Model
- Integrate the data collected from phase 1
- Develop a first draft of a competency model
- Invite groups of experts to review and offer input to the first draft of the competency model
- Use input from the groups of experts to develop a second draft of a competency model
- Invite groups of experts to review and offer input to the second draft of the competency model
- Use input from the groups of experts to develop a third draft of a competency model

Phase 3: Validate the Competency Model
- Design a survey asking questions about the third draft of a competency model and distribute it to experts and practitioners asking them to validate the competencies identified in the survey

Phase 4: Final Refinement of the Competency Model
- Review the results of the survey conducted in phase 3 and use the data to refine the competency model
- Disseminate final competency model to the field

The ten standards for change leadership presented in appendix B, I believe, satisfy the first stage of the Boulter, Dalziel, and Hill's six-stage competency development model, and the first phase of the ASTD competency modeling process. The implication of this conclusion is that further research is needed to validate the ten standards of performance.

A PROPOSED PROGRAM OF STUDY FOR PREPARING CHANGE LEADERS IN EDUCATION

Having validated standards for preparing change leaders in education is important, but insufficient. If the standards are to respond to the serious need for highly trained and competent change leaders in education, then state departments of education should develop a professional license (or certificate) for change leadership based on the standards. Then schools and colleges of education could use the standards to design graduate-level programs of study focusing on change leadership in education. Below, you will find an idealized mission, vision, and design for an innovative graduate-level program for preparing change leaders in education.

The Institute for Change Leadership in Education

In this section, I present an idealized design for a graduate-level program of study focusing on change leadership in education. While the design suggests that the program should lead to an education specialist degree, it could be modified to offer a master of science or a doctor of education degree in change leadership in education.

The Mission of the Institute

The Institute for Change Leadership in Education prepares teams of district-based change leaders to create and sustain systemic transformational change in their respective school systems.

The Vision for the Institute

Visualize community leaders, parents, students, and teachers working together in a large group, framing and defining their dreams, aspirations, and strategic goals for their school district. See all these participants energized by their productive collaboration and developing feelings of ownership for the dreams, aspirations, and goals. Where there is a need, envision participants becoming inspired to fill that need. Where there is an opportunity, hear others defining the goals for those opportunities

Imagine the excitement in the air as school administrators, principals, teachers, and support personnel use the outcomes of the earlier community gathering to redesign their district. Feel the palpable energy of school system transformation fueled by grassroots involvement, unleashed creativity, and, most of all, commitment from all the key players that contribute to a school system's success. Taste the sweetness of success as dreams, aspirations, and goals are realized as never before.

Sense the power of a school system in which teachers come together often in "communities of practice" to create more effective strategies for teaching and learning; where teachers, parents, and administrators collaborate on teams to find creative solutions to help students become more proficient in their learning; where students pool their learning to present knowledgeable presentations and documents on various topics.

Imagine a school system that cares as much for the adults who work in the system as it does for the students. See these professionals creating student, teacher, and system knowledge and then using that knowledge to move their district toward higher and higher levels of performance.

Observe a school district *not* engaged in yearly rapid-fire change. Instead, imagine that district having the capacity to sustain change over time. See that school district harnessing the collective power of its human, technical, financial, and time resources and focusing them on creating and sustaining a high-performing school system.

Note that this is the vision for *The Institute for Change Leadership in Education*—a vision that will create teams of highly trained and motivated change leaders who can facilitate the challenging and complex task of creating and sustaining systemic transformational change in their school districts.

Now, imagine this Institute in a school of education within a Department of Change Leadership in Education. Envision the faculty training teams of district-based change leaders about how to create and sustain systemic transformational change in their districts. Imagine that this training not only teaches these educators how to create and sustain transformational change, but actually expects them to go back to their districts to apply what they learn. Imagine faculty in the department providing coaching and technical assistance to those change leaders as they plan and implement a transformational change methodology.

Imagine the benefit to the school districts, the children they serve, and the educators working in those districts as the participating teams of change leaders begin applying cutting-edge principles for transforming their districts to enhance the quality of student, teacher, and system learning. Imagine these districts becoming communities of learners engaged in a never-ending journey of district-wide improvement.

If several colleges or universities adopt this institute design, then participating teams throughout the United States could be connected to create a virtual Change Leadership Community. Within this community of practice, team members could share their experiences, solicit ideas and suggestions to enhance their change leadership competencies, participate in collaborative problem-solving sessions, and so on.

Institute Design

A proposed design for this special institute is displayed in appendix C. The key characteristics of this institute design are:

1. It spans an academic year with two, two-week summer sessions on either end.
2. It is a thirty-credit post-master's program that leads to an education specialist degree in change leadership in education.
3. Training activities are designed to teach knowledge, develop skills, and refine dispositions for change leadership.
4. It is team-based; that is, individuals may not apply for admission to the program.
5. It expects participating teams to apply what they learned to transform their school systems.

CONCLUSION

I believe there is a striking need for effective change leadership in America's school systems. This need is not being addressed by state departments of education or graduate-level education leadership programs. Further, I believe that an effective and proactive response to this need is for state departments of education to adopt research-based standards to develop a professional license for change leaders in education, and for schools and colleges of education to design a graduate-level program specializing in educating change leaders about the why, what, and how of creating and sustaining systemic transformational change in school districts.

If America's school systems are to be transformed to meet the demands of the Knowledge Age, then they will need effective change leadership. Responding to this need will require courage, passion, and vision from state department of education leaders and university faculty if they are to do what's required to adopt a framework for preparing change leaders.

Some readers of this chapter will say, "Impossible, can't be done!" Call me a dreamer, a believer in the impossible becoming possible, but I think that once the proposed standards are validated, they can be applied to create a cadre of knowledgeable and highly skilled change leaders in education. I believe that university faculty who also have personal courage, passion, and vision can design and operate an institute like the one described in this chapter. Finally, in the words of Kris Kruger (a singer and songwriter), ". . . when we seek the unseekable, when we speak the unspeakable, when we think the unthinkable, when we achieve the unachievable, the impossible is possible."

NOTE

1. The team-based design is absolutely essential to the success of training programs. We are all too familiar with the failure of individuals who attend training programs to transfer their learning from the training context to their work context. Training teams of change leaders who then return to their systems to apply what they learned is a significantly more effective way to transfer learning from training environments to work environments. An excellent summary of the research about the transfer of learning is found in a National Science Foundation report titled "Transfer of Learning: Issues and Research Agenda," available at www.nsf.gov /pubs/2003/nsf03212/nsf03212_1.pdf.

Epilogue

A Call to Action: Join the Revolution to Transform America's School Systems

As you near the end of this book, I want to ask you five questions. Please consider your answers carefully and please answer them with an unqualified "yes" or "no." If you feel a need to qualify your answer, then that qualification is considered a "no."

1. Do you believe that our society has evolved into the Knowledge Age?
2. Do you believe that the field of education has not coevolved with our society?
3. Do you believe that entire school systems need to be transformed if we want the field of education to align with the requirements of the Knowledge Age?
4. Do you believe that America's school-aged children (present and future) deserve an education that prepares them for success in our nation's Knowledge Age society?
5. Do you believe that it is unethical, and perhaps immoral, for school systems to leave some children behind as they participate in the systems' teaching and learning processes?

If you answered "yes" to all of these questions then I have two more questions to ask you:

1. Given your answers, what are you going to do about it?
2. When will you start?

Before you take action, please be warned that you should not accept lightly this call to action. Leading or participating in a revolution against the four dominant paradigms controlling the field of education will require substantial courage, passion, and vision because you may be scorned, you may be ostracized, you may be ridiculed, and you may be punished for your heresy. Courage will help you to stand your ground in the face of predictable adversity. Passion will give you the emotional energy and resilience you need to persevere toward the goal of creating and sustaining paradigm change in your school system and in the field of education. And vision will be your North Star, guiding you toward an idealized future for your school system and for the field of education. And you must possess courage, passion, and vision all at the same time. If you do not possess these traits, please do not join the revolution I am advocating.

But . . .

If you do have courage, passion, and vision and if you answered "yes" to all of the first five questions, those of us who are advocates of a revolution to displace the four old paradigms need your help. We need you to join with us to revolt against the old paradigms.

Here's what you can do—right now—to become part of this revolution. Think of one person—just one—whom you believe shares your dream for transforming your school system for success in the twenty-first century. Call or e-mail that person and make an appointment to visit with him or her for thirty minutes or less. During the meeting, share highlights from what you learned in this book. Communicate your personal vision for transforming your school system. Ask for his or her support to help build a coalition for change. Then, do it! Make it happen! Start to prepare your system for a journey unlike any other it has experienced in the past—start dreaming, creating, and sustaining transformational change. Start moving toward an idealized design for your school system that educates students by providing them with a personalized, customized, learner-centered education experience; that provides the faculty and staff in your districts with a satisfying and motivating work life; that helps your district create and sustain proactive, opportunity-seeking relationships with its external environment; and that introduces into your district a methodology for creating and sustaining whole-system change.

If you are already engaging in a revolution to drive out the four dominant Industrial Age paradigms that influence the design and performance of school systems, or if you are intending to join the revolution, then I encourage you to consider joining the Division for Systemic Change within the Association for Educational Communications and Technology (AECT). That division is composed of professionals who recognize the need for systemic transformational change and the opportunities that paradigm change offers. To join the division, please go to www.aect.org/ and first join the association. After you join the association, you can then select the Division for Systemic Change as your preferred affiliation. The AECT annual conference happens every October, and the division membership meets at that conference.

Once you are affiliated with AECT and the Division for Systemic Change, then you can associate with the FutureMinds: Transforming American School Systems initiative (www.futureminds.us). That initiative is focusing on helping state departments of education and local school systems to create and sustain transformational change.

By taking the above three actions (talk with a colleague, join the AECT Division for Systemic Change, become associated with the FutureMinds initiative), you will be joining with colleagues who are striving to drive out the old paradigms influencing education and to create and sustain school systems designed to align with four new Knowledge Age paradigms.

A PARTING REFLECTION

Finally, I leave you with a parting reflection from a book by Olive Schreiner (1998, originally published in 1883), a South African peace and anti-apartheid campaigner. In her book titled *The Story of a South African Farm*, there is an allegory about "The Hunter." He has been hunting for the white bird of truth for his entire life. As part of his search he built a stone staircase into the sky. There is a point in the story where he is about ready to give up his search because of fatigue from the hunting and building, and he says,

> My strength is gone. When I lie down worn out, others will stand young and fresh. By the stairs I have built, they will mount. They will never know the name of the person who made them. At the clumsy work they will laugh, when the stones roll, they will curse me. But they will mount, and on my work, they will climb, and by my stair.

That staircase was the Hunter's legacy for future generations. What will your legacy be as a change leader who envisions transformational change in your school system? What will your "staircase" be? So, if you choose to dream, create, and sustain transformational change, if you are willing and able to join the needed revolution, then you must do so with courage, passion, and vision. Build that stair toward a desirable future for your district, and keep hope alive!

Appendix A: Comparative Analysis of Change Leadership Competencies and Traits

Table A.1

Higgs & Rowland's (2000) Change Leadership Competencies	Duffy & Reigeluth (2007)	Stopper (1999)	National Training Center (2008)	Kotter (1995)	Dulewicz and Higgs (2000) Emotional intelligence
Change Initiation—ability to create the case for change and secure credible sponsorship	Have an understanding of the dynamics of complex systemic change		External awareness	Change leaders increase urgency	Influence
			Service motivation	Change leaders communicate for buy-in	Conscientious-ness and integrity
Change Impact—ability to scope the breadth, depth, sustainability, and returns of a change strategy	Have an understanding of the dynamics of complex systemic change				
Change Facilitation—ability to help others, through effective facilitation, to gain insight into the human dynamics of change and to develop the confidence to achieve the change goals	Have strong interpersonal and group facilitation skills Have a positive mind-set about empowering and enabling others to Participate effectively in transformation	Leadership approach to change (integrated leader and continuous leader styles)		Change leaders build a guiding team	Interpersonal sensitivity
Change Leadership—ability to influence and enthuse others, through personal advocacy, vision, and drive, and to access resources to build a solid platform for change	Have a personal presence and track record that commands respect Have a likeable personality Have experience in K-12 education	Cultural alignment	Vision	Change leaders get the vision right Change leaders empower for action	

Competency	Behaviors				
Change Learning—ability to scan, reflect, and identify learning and ensure insights are used to develop individual, group, and organizational capabilities	Have an understanding of the dynamics of complex systemic change		Continual learning Flexibility		Self-awareness Intuitiveness
Change Execution—ability to formulate and guide the implementation of a credible change plan with appropriate goals, resources, metrics, and review mechanisms	Are organized Have an understanding of the dynamics of complex systemic change	Technical competence	Creativity and innovation Strategic thinking	Change leaders create short term wins Change leaders do not let up	
Change Presence—demonstrates high personal commitment to achievement of change goals through integrity and courage, while maintaining objectivity and individual resilience ("a nonanxious presence in a sea of anxiety")	Have a positive, can-do attitude Have a personal presence and track record that commands respect Have a likeable personality	Personal resilience	Resilience	Change leaders make change stick	Emotional resilience Motivation
Change Technology—knowledge, generation, and skillful application of change theories, tools, and processes	Have an understanding of the dynamics of complex systemic change				

Appendix B: A National Framework of Professional Standards for Change Leadership in Education

Performance Standards, Criteria, and Rubrics for the Graduate-Level Change Leadership in Education Programs

Standards of Performance	Sample Knowledge, Skills, and Dispositions for Each Standard
Standard 1.0—Systems Thinking: A change leader perceives school districts as intact, organic systems and explains how districts function as systems.	**Knowledge** . . . explains in detail the key features of school districts as systems. **Skill** . . . analyzes in detail the functional properties of school districts as systems. **Disposition** . . . fully accepts that school districts are intact, organic systems.
Standard 2.0—Focus of Systemic Transformational Change: A change leader understands that transforming an entire school district requires improvements in student, faculty and staff, and whole-system learning.	**Knowledge** . . . describes the importance of whole-system improvement in rich detail. **Skill** . . . collects and interprets data about the need for change. **Disposition** . . . accepts the importance of whole-district learning and can explain that importance in rich detail.
Standard 3.0—Initiating Change: A change leader creates the case for systemic transformation within school districts and in communities by providing data to support both the *need* for change and the *opportunities* that can be seized by engaging in change.	**Knowledge** . . . explains in rich detail a strong rationale for creating and sustaining whole-district change. **Skill** . . . explains in rich detail tools and processes for gaining and sustaining internal and external political support for change. **Disposition** . . . enthusiastically endorses the concept of whole-system change.

Standard 4.0—Assessing the Impact of Change: A change leader assesses the breadth, depth, sustainability, and anticipated positive outcomes of a systemic transformational change strategy.

Knowledge . . . can explain in rich detail the breadth, depth, sustainability, and expected returns from engaging in whole-system change.

Skill . . . able to conduct an in-depth analysis of the breadth, depth, sustainability, and expected returns from engaging in whole-system change.

Disposition . . . accepts the fact that whole-system change is complex and requires careful planning, and acts on this acceptance.

Standard 5.0—Facilitating Change: A change leader helps colleagues and community members gain insight into the human dynamics of system transformation and develops their confidence to achieve transformation goals.

Knowledge . . . possesses advanced level of knowledge of facilitation skills.

Skill . . . possesses advanced level of skill for facilitating interpersonal and group behavior.

Disposition . . . is a strong advocate for helping people understand the nature of change prior to launching a change effort.

Standard 6.0—Developing Political Support for Change: A change leader develops political support for systemic transformation through effective change leadership.

Knowledge . . . explains in rich detail strategies and tactics for building political support.

Skill . . . demonstrates sophisticated skills for developing political support.

Disposition . . . is a staunch advocate for acting in a political way to gain political support for change.

Standard 7.0—Expanding Mind-Sets: A change leader engages in and shares with colleagues personal learning to deepen and broaden personal mind-sets about why systemic transformation of school districts is necessary and about the best strategy for creating and sustaining transformational change.

Knowledge . . . provides a detailed and cogent rationale for engaging in personal learning.

Skill . . . develops a detailed and feasible plan to engage in personal learning.

Disposition . . . is a strong advocate for engaging in personal learning.

Standard 8.0—Planning Systemic Transformational Change: A change leader formulates and leads the implementation of a plan to create and sustain systemic transformation in school districts.

Knowledge . . . understands the complexity of planning for change and describes the key elements of change plans.

Skill . . . possesses advanced skills for planning for system-wide change.

Disposition . . . is a powerful advocate for engaging in good planning for change.

Standard 9.0—Demonstrating Disposition for Change Leadership: A change leader demonstrates high personal emotional intelligence while leading transformational change.

Knowledge . . . provides a powerful rationale for leading with a high level of emotional intelligence.

Skill . . . demonstrates advanced skills for emotional intelligence.

Disposition . . . is a strong advocate for the importance of leading change with a high level of emotional intelligence and teaches others how to develop their emotional intelligence.

Standard 10.0—Mastering the Art and Science of Systemic Transformational Change: A change leader is familiar with and skillful in using a variety of change theories, tools, and methodologies derived from interdisciplinary perspectives on change leadership and systemic transformation.

Knowledge . . . can explain in great detail at least one methodology for creating and sustaining whole-system change, including tools and processes that are part of that methodology.

Skill . . . can apply at least one methodology for creating and sustaining whole-system change, including tools and processes that are part of that methodology.

Disposition . . . is a vocal advocate for the importance of change leaders knowing, understanding, and applying change theories and tools.

Appendix C: An Innovative Design for a Thirty-Credit Education Specialist Degree Program in Change Leadership in Education

The Institute on Leading Transformational Change in School Systems

CURRICULUM

Summer 1 **(10 credits)**	A two-week residential workshop/seminar with the following topics:

- The need for a paradigm shift in education
- Customized, learner-centered teaching and learning
- Disposition for change leadership
- Emotional intelligence for change leadership
- Principles of systemic transformational change
- Systems thinking and system dynamics
- Principles of organization theory and design
- Interpersonal and group dynamics during times of change
- The School System Transformation Protocol
  - ☐ Phase 1: Prepare
  - ☐ Phase 2: Envision
  - ☐ Phase 3: Transform
  - ☐ Phase 4: Sustain
  - ☐ Phase 5: Evaluate
- Financing systemic transformational change
- Reshaping organization culture
- Expanding mind-sets
- Action planning for the one-year interim between summer sessions

**Fall and Spring
Interim
(10 Credits)**   Each team returns to its respective school system to apply learning from the first summer. This application requires them to conduct the SST Protocol "Phase 1: Prepare" activities that prepare their school system to
begin systemic transformation.

During the interim, teams from all universities offering
this institute will be connected through an Internet website that includes a virtual forum for everyone to talk to
each other and with the instructors about what they are
doing. An example of this kind of web site is www
.theworldcafe.com/

**Summer 2
(10 credits)**   A two-week residential workshop/seminar on the fol-
lowing topics:
• Review of Summer 1 concepts and principles
• Review and assessment of interim activities
• Managing and rewarding performance in transformed
  school systems
• Power and politics during times of change
• Creative thinking and problem solving
• Strategic communication
• Evaluating systemic transformational change
• "What do we do next?" action planning to transform
  the teams' school systems

Participating teams return to the Institute for their second summer to debrief their interim activities. Lessons
learned will be shared. Concepts and principles of systemic transformational change will be reviewed and reinforced, and new change leadership concepts and
principles will be introduced.

Each team will then design an action plan to implement fully the SST Protocol in their school systems. Each
plan will be shared with the other teams for their reaction and suggestions.

The teams will also evaluate the Institute and the
instructors' performance.

At the end of the second summer, participants who
have successfully completed the institute experience will

receive an education specialist degree in change leadership in education.

Capstone Experience/Product

The capstone product for the participants is an action plan to transform their school systems to align with the requirements of the Information Age. The capstone experience is the implementation of that action plan, but this experience will not commence until after teams complete the institute.

During the implementation period, teams of change leaders from throughout the United States who have completed this institute will remain connected through an online, virtual change leadership community.

OTHER SERVICES AND ADDED VALUES

The Institute will not just be a training program. It will also:

- Offer an Internet-based nationwide network to support participants during the interim between summers as they implement their action plans. Graduates of the program will be able to continue participating in the network after they graduate.
- Provide opportunities to graduate students in the department to do action research on systemic transformational change and then publish their findings.
- Provide department faculty with research, publishing, and consulting opportunities.
- Develop policy to influence state and federal policy on systemic transformational change in school districts.

GENERAL ADMISSIONS CRITERIA

- *Team participation*. Only teams of educators from a school system are eligible to apply for admission to the program.
- *Commitment to transform their systems*. To be accepted to the Institute each team must have a firm, written commitment from their key stakeholders to transform their school systems using what they learn in the Institute.
- *Work experience*. Each member of the team applying for admission to the Institute must have a minimum of five years of professional post-bachelor degree experience working in a school system.

- *Master's degree.* Further, a graduate-level program for preparing change leaders should be at the post-master's level. Each member of the team applying for admission to the Institute must have a master's degree or higher in an education field.
- *Disposition for change leadership.* Not everyone is cut out for change leadership. This challenging responsibility requires a special breed of leader with identifiable traits (see Duffy and Reigeluth's traits earlier in this chapter). Some of these traits are trainable, but others, like personality, are not. People either have those nontrainable traits, or they don't.

The disposition for change leadership should be a trait of the team applying for admission rather than traits held by each individual on the team. The disposition for change leadership can be assessed by surveying the attitudes of each member of a team applying for admission and then calculating a team profile. If the profile indicates that the team, as a whole, has a disposition for change leadership, then that team may be considered for admission to the Institute.

During summer 1, some of the learning activities will focus on refining and enhancing the team's disposition for change leadership. If individual members enter the Institute without a clearly defined disposition for change leadership, these learning activities will aim to help reshape their predispositions.

SPECIFIC ADMISSIONS CRITERIA

Criteria

Only district-based teams of five or more practitioners may participate in the Institute.

The teams must be staffed by teachers and administrators who meet the general admissions criteria, and the team membership must represent the entire instructional program in their district; for example, in a preK–12th grade district, members of the team must represent the early childhood, elementary, middle, and high school levels of schooling in that district.

Rationale for Each Criteria

Training teams of practitioners is critical for successful change.

Leading systemic transformational change requires representation of the whole system, thus the need for this kind of membership on the team.

One member of the team must be the superintendent of schools. If a district sends multiple teams, then the superintendent only has to be part of the first team.

School superintendents are key players for their districts' transformation journeys. They must be unequivocally committed to their districts' transformation if they want that journey to succeed. Their participation in the Institute sends a clear and powerful message about their commitment to lead this kind of change effort.

INSTITUTE MANAGEMENT

Institute Director: The institute should be based in a newly created Department of Change Leadership in Education. The department chairman will be coordinator of the Institute.

Financing the Institute: Participation in the Institute will be on a for-fee basis. Given the need for this kind of training, it is likely that federal or philanthropic grants to support it could be secured. A research component could also be designed into the Institute so that research grant money could be awarded.

ADJUNCT INSTRUCTORS AND TENURE-TRACK FACULTY

Adjunct instructors and tenure-track faculty will be selected and hired for their expertise in and experience with systemic transformational change.
  Possible adjunct instructors/guest speakers include:

- **Charles Reigeluth**, professor, Instructional Systems, Indiana University and codirector of the FutureMinds: Transforming American School Systems initiative
- **Tom Houlihan**, retired executive director for the Council of Chief State School Officers
- **Barbara McCombs**, director, Center for Human Motivation, Learning, and Development, University of Denver
- **Jack Dale**, superintendent, Fairfax County Public Schools, Virginia
- **Joe Simpson**, deputy state superintendent of schools, Wyoming
- **Michael Fullan**, professor emeritus of the Ontario Institute for Studies in Education of the University of Toronto

- **Stephanie Pace Marshall**, founding president and president emerita of Illinois Mathematics and Science Academy
- **Libia Gil**, senior fellow, American Institutes of Research
- **Don Stinson**, superintendent, Metropolitan School District of Decatur Township, Indiana

Note: The people identified above are listed as examples of the kind of professionals required to teach or make guest appearances in this Institute. None of them have expressed an interest in doing this.

Specialty areas needing tenured faculty include, but are not limited to:

- Systems thinking and system dynamics
- Systemic transformation and change leadership
- Interpersonal and group dynamics during times of change
- Power and politics during change
- Strategic communication
- Managing diversity during times of change
- Expanding mind-sets
- Learner-centered teaching and learning
- Emotional intelligence
- Creative thinking and problem solving
- Organization theory and design
- Strategic communication
- Personalized, student-centered learning
- Reshaping organization culture

Appendix D: Using Technology to Implement the Learner-Centered Paradigm of Teaching and Learning

Charles M. Reigeluth

The use of technology in education should be based on what we know about how students learn best and how we can best facilitate that learning. Tools should be selected based on purposes or functions to be served, not the other way around.

In our current educational system, student progress to a new topic is based on time, not on learning. If it is Monday, we move on to the next topic, in spite of some students not having attained the standards just taught. This system is sorting-focused (which was appropriate for the Industrial Age, when manual labor was predominant), not learning-focused (which is needed for the Information Age, when knowledge work is predominant). A learning-focused system would not allow a student to move on until she or he succeeded in attaining the current standard. And it would require each student to move on as soon as he or she succeeded in attaining the current standard. This requires a completely different paradigm of education, one that is customized to meet each student's needs and potential. This requires a different role for teachers, students, and technology.

Rather than integrating technology into the classroom (the current paradigm), we should be using technology to transform what goes on in the classroom. Technology allows us to customize education in a way that was not possible before. So how should technology be used? We currently see four main roles or functions for technology to make a customized, learning-focused educational system feasible and cost-effective. Each of these is described next.

RECORD-KEEPING FOR STUDENT LEARNING

Attainment-based progress for students requires a personal record of attainments for each student. This replaces the current report card, and it has three parts. First, it has a *standards inventory* that contains both required educational standards (national, state, and local) and optional educational standards for access by the teacher, student, and parents. It presents a list of things that should or can be learned, along with levels or standards or criteria at which they can be learned. Second, it has a *personal attainments inventory* that contains a record of what each student knows. In essence, it maps each student's progress on the attainments listed in the standards inventory (and perhaps some that are not yet listed there). It shows when each attainment was reached, which ones are required, what the next required attainments are in each area, and links to evidence of each attainment (in the form of summary data and/or original artifacts). Third, it has a *personal characteristics inventory* that keeps track of each student's characteristics that influence learning, such as learning styles, profile of multiple intelligences, student interests, and major life events.

PLANNING FOR STUDENT LEARNING

Customized education also requires a personal learning plan, or contract, for each student. It helps the student, parents, and teacher to (a) decide on *long-term goals*; (b) identify the full range of attainments that are presently *within reach* for the student; (c) select from those options the ones that they want to pursue now (*short-term goals*), based on requirements, long-term goals, interests, opportunities, and so on; (d) identify *projects* (or other means) for attaining the short-term goals; (e) identify *other students* who are interested in doing the same projects (if desired); (f) specify the roles that the teacher, parent, and any others might play in supporting the student in learning from the project; and (g) develop a contract that specifies goals, projects, teams, parent and teacher roles, and the deadline for each project.

INSTRUCTION FOR STUDENT LEARNING

Trying to "instruct" twenty-five students who are all learning different things at any point in time could be very difficult for teachers if they had to be the agent of instruction all the time, as is typical in the Industrial Age paradigm. However, we envision that learning will be primarily project (or problem) based, with both a project "space" and an instructional "space." In the problem space, technology offers an introduction to the project, resources for doing the project (including research tools and communication tools), and usually a place for working on the project. While working on the project, whenever the student encounters a deficiency in knowledge, skills, or understandings needed for doing the project, each student switches from the project space to his or her personalized instructional space, where highly efficient and appealing tools offer customized drill-and-practice, tutorials, simulations, and educational games, as appropriate, to foster the different kinds of learning in the most effective, efficient, and appealing way. The student continues to work in the instructional space until he or she reaches the criterion for mastery of the standard on authentic performances (based on appropriate amounts of transfer learning and automatization of skills), as described in the next section. In addition, technology provides tools for the teacher to monitor and support student progress on the project, and even provides tools to help teachers and others develop new projects and new instructional tools.

ASSESSMENT FOR (AND OF) STUDENT LEARNING

Conducting formative and summative assessments of students could be a nightmare for teachers, since students are not all taking a given test at the same time. And once again, technology can offer great relief. First, assessment is *integrated with instruction*. The plentiful performance opportunities that are used to cultivate skills and understandings are used for both formative and summative assessments. Second, the assessments present *authentic tasks* on which the students demonstrate their knowledge, understanding, and skill. Third, whether in a simulation or a tutorial or drill-and-practice, the technology is designed to evaluate whether or not the criterion was met on each performance and to provide *formative feedback* immediately to the student for the greatest impact. When the criteria for successful performance have been met on *x* out of the last *y* performances, the *summative assessment* is complete and the corresponding attainment is automatically checked off in the student's personal inventory of attainments. In the few cases where the technology cannot assess the performance, an observer has a handheld device with a rubric for assessment and personally provides the immediate feedback on student performances. The information from the handheld device is uploaded into the computer system, where it is placed in the student's personal inventory. Finally, technology provides tools to help teachers develop assessments and link them to the standards. Instructional-evaluation theory is critical for technology to reach its potential contribution to this role.

Note that these four roles or functions are seamlessly integrated. The record-keeping tool provides information automatically for the planning tool. The planning tool identifies instructional tools that are available. The assessment tool is integrated into the instructional tool. And the assessment tool feeds information automatically into the record-keeping tool. Also, please note that there are many other roles or functions for such a system. These secondary functions include communications (e-mail, blogs, websites, discussion boards, wikis, whiteboards, instant messaging, podcasts, videocasts, etc.), system administration (offering access to information and authority to input information based on role and information type), general student data (student's address, parent/guardian information, mentor-teacher and school, student's location/attendance, health information), school personnel information (address, certifications and awards, location, assigned students, tools authored, student evaluations that they have performed, teacher professional development plan and records, repository of teaching tools, awards their students have received), and more.

It should be apparent that technology will play a crucial role in the success of the Information Age paradigm of education. It will enable a quantum improvement in student learning, and likely at a lower cost per student per year than in the current Industrial Age paradigm. Just as the electronic spreadsheet made the accountant's job quicker, easier, and less expensive, the kind of system described here will make the teacher's job quicker, easier, and less expensive. But the use of technology must be theory-driven to realize its potential contribution.

References

Ackoff, R. L. (1974). *Redesigning the future: A systems approach to societal problems.* New York: Wiley & Sons.

———. (1981). *Creating the corporate future.* New York: John Wiley & Sons.

———. (1999). *Re-creating the corporation: A design of organizations for the 21st century.* New York: Oxford University Press.

———. (2001). A brief guide to interactive planning and idealized design. Retrieved from www.sociate.com/texts/ackoffGuidetoIdealizedRedesign.pdf (March 19, 2006).

Ackoff, R. L., Magidson, J., & Addison, H. J. (2006). *Idealized design: How to dissolve tomorrow's crisis . . . today.* Upper Saddle River, NJ: Wharton School Publishing.

Adleman, H. S., & Taylor, L. (2006). *The implementation guide to student learning supports in the classroom and schoolwide: New directions for addressing barriers to learning.* Thousand Oaks, CA: Corwin Press.

———. (2010). Creating successful school systems requires addressing barriers to learning and teaching. In F. M. Duffy & J. D. Dale (Eds.), *Creating successful school systems* (2nd ed.). Leading Systemic School Improvement. Lanham, MD: Rowman & Littlefield Education.

Alexander, P. A., & Murphy, P. K. (1993). The research base for APA's learner-centered psychological principals. In B. L. McCombs (Chair), *Taking research on learning seriously: Implications for Teacher Education.* Invited symposium at the Annual Meeting of the American Psychological Association, New Orleans, April 1994.

American Psychological Association Presidential Task Force on Psychology in Education. (1993). *Learner-centered psychological principles: Guidelines for school redesign and reform.* Washington, DC, and Aurora, CO: American Psychological Association and Mid-continent Regional Educational Laboratory.

American Psychological Association's Board of Educational Affairs, Center for Psychology in Schools and Education. (1997). Learner-centered psychological principles. Retrieved from www.apa.org/ed/lcp2/lcp14.html (December 26, 2007).

Anderson, J. R. (1983). *The architecture of cognition*. Cambridge, MA: Harvard University Press.

Arango, J. B. (1998). Helping non-profits become more effective. Retrieved from www.algodonesassociates.com/planning/Mental models.pdf (July 11, 2008).

Argyris, C. (1957). *Personality and organization*. New York: Harper Collins.

Argyris, C., & Schön, D. (1978). *Organizational learning: A theory of action perspective*. Reading, MA: Addison Wesley.

Armstrong, J. S. (1985). *Long-range forecasting: From crystal ball to computer* (2nd ed.). New York: John Wiley.

Augar, N., Raiman, R., & Zhou, W. (2004). Teaching and learning online with wikis. Paper presented at the Australian Society for Computers in Learning in Tertiary Education Conference, Perth, Australia.

Avolio, B. J., & Bass, B. M. (1988). Transformational leadership, charisma, and beyond. In J. G. Hunt, B. R. Baliga, H. P. Dachler, & C. A. Schriesheim (Eds.), *Emerging leadership vistas* (pp. 29–49). Lexington, MA: Lexington Books.

Avolio, B. J., Waldman, D. A., & Yammarino, F. J. (1991). The four Is of transformational leadership. *Journal of European Industrial Training, 15*(4), 9–16.

Baker, F. (1973). *Organizational systems: General systems approaches to complex organizations*. Homewood, IL: Irwin.

Baldrige National Quality Program. (2003). Education Criteria for Performance Excellence. Retrieved from www.quality.nist.gov/PDF_files/2003_Education _Criteria.pdf (September 4, 2003).

Banathy, B. H. (1991). *Systems design of education: A journey to create the future*. Englewood Cliffs, NJ: Educational Technology Publications.

———. (1992a). The prime imperative: Building a design culture. *Educational Technology, 32*(6), 33–35.

———. (1992b). *A systems view of education: Concepts and principles for effective practice*. Englewood Cliffs, NJ: Educational Technology Publications.

———. (1996). *Designing social systems in a changing world*. New York: Plenum Press.

Bandura, A. (1997). *Self-efficacy: The exercise of control*. New York: Freeman.

Barber, M., & Fullan, M. (2007). Tri-level development: It's the system. *The F. M. Duffy Reports, 12*(1), 1–4.

Barker, J. (1992). *Paradigms: The business of discovering the future*. New York: Harper Collins.

Bar-On, R. (2000). Emotional and social intelligence: Insights from the Emotional Quotient Inventory (EQ-i). In R. Bar-On & J. D. A. Parker (Eds.), *Handbook of emotional intelligence: Theory, development, assessment and application at home, school and in the workplace* (pp. 363–388). San Francisco: Jossey-Bass Publishers.

Bar-Yam, Y. (2003). *Dynamics of complex systems*. Boulder, CO: Westview Press.

———. (2004). *Making things work: Solving problems in a complex world*. Cambridge, MA: NECSI-Knowledge Press.

Bass, B. M. (1985). *Leadership performance beyond expectations*. New York: Academic Press.

Bass, B. M., & Avolio, B. J. (1993). Transformational leadership and organizational culture. *Public Administration Quarterly, 17*(1), 112–122.

Battino, W., & Clem, J. (2006). Systemic changes in the Chugach school district.

TechTrends, 50(2), 51–52.

Beckhard, R. (1983). Strategies for large system change. In W. L. French, C. H. Bell Jr., & R. A. Zawacki (Eds.), *Organization development: Theory, practice, and research* (pp. 234–242). Plano, TX: Business Publications, Inc.

Bell, D. (1973). *The coming of post-industrial society: A venture in social forecasting.* New York: Basic Books.

Bennett, D. A., & King, D. T. (1991). The Saturn school of tomorrow. *Educational Leadership, 48*(8), 41.

Bennis, W., & Nanus, B. (1985). *Leaders.* New York: Harper & Row.

Bernthal, P. R., Colteryahn, K., Davis, P., Naughton, J., Rothwell, W. J., & Wellins, R. (2004). *Mapping the future: New workplace learning and performance competencies.* Alexandria, VA: ASTD Press.

Beyer, J. M. (1981). Ideologies, values, and decision making in organizations. In P. C. Nystrom & W. H. Starbuck (Eds.), *Handbook of organizational design* (Vol. 2, pp. 166–202). New York: Oxford University Press.

Blake, R. R., & Mouton, J. S. (1964). *The managerial grid.* Houston: Gulf Publishing.

Block, P. (1987). *The empowered manager: Positive political skills at work.* San Francisco: Jossey-Bass Publishers.

———. (1991). *The empowered manager: Positive political skills at work.* San Francisco: Jossey-Bass.

———. (1993). *Stewardship: Choosing service over self-interest.* San Francisco: Berrett-Koehler Publishers.

———. (2003). *The answer to how is yes: Acting on what matters.* San Francisco: Berrett-Koehler Publishers.

Bloom, B. S., Krathwohl, D. R., & Masia, B. B., (Eds.). (1956). *Taxonomy of educational objectives, the classification of educational goals. Handbook I: Cognitive domain.* New York: David McKay.

Bolman, L. G., & Deal, T. E. (1997). *Reframing organizations: Artistry, choice, and leadership* (2nd ed.). San Francisco: Jossey-Bass Publishers.

Bonk, C. J. (2008). YouTube anchors and enders: The use of shared online video content as a macrocontext for learning. Paper presented at the American Educational Research Association Annual Meeting.

Bonk, C. J., & Cunningham, D. J. (1998). In C. J. Bonk & K. S. King (Eds.), *Electronic collaborators* (pp. 25–50). Mahwah, NJ: Lawrence Erlbaum Associates.

Boulter, N., Dalziel, M., & Hill, J. (Eds.). (1998). *Achieving the perfect fit.* Houston: Gulf Publishing Company.

Bransford, J., Brown, A., & Cocking, R. (Eds.). (1999). *How people learn: Brain, mind, experience, and school.* Washington, DC: National Academy Press.

Branson, R. K. (1987). Why the schools can't improve: The upper limit hypothesis. *Journal of Instructional Development, 10*(4), 15–26.

———. (n.d.). When all the quick fixes fail again, try R & D. Retrieved from www .icte.org/T01_Library/T01_257.PDF (May 18, 2009).

Braun, W. (2002). The system archetypes. Retrieved from wwwu.uni-klu.ac.at/ gossimit/pap/sd/wb_sysarch.pdf (May 31, 2008).

Bronfenbrenner, U. (1977). Toward an experimental ecology of human development. *American Psychologist, 32*, 513–531.

———. (1979). *The ecology of human development*. Cambridge, MA: Harvard University Press.

Brown, J. S., & Adler, R. P. (2008). Minds on fire: Open education, the long tail, and learning 2.0 [Electronic Version]. *EDUCAUSE Review, 43*, 16–32. Retrieved from connect .educause.edu/Library/EDUCAUSE+Review/MindsonFire OpenEducationt/45823.

Brush, T., & Saye, J. (2000). Implementation and evaluation of a student-centered learning unit: A case study. *Educational Technology Research and Development, 48*(3), 79–100.

Bunderson, C. V., Wiley, D. A., & McBride, R. (2009). Domain Theory for instruction: Mapping attainments to enable learner-centered education. In C. M. Reigeluth & A. A. Carr-Chellman (Eds.), *Instructional-design theories and models: Building a common knowledge base* (Vol. 3). New York: Routledge.

Burke, W. W. (2002). *Organization change: Theory and practice*. Thousand Oaks, CA: Sage Publications.

———. (2007). Organization change: *Theory and practice*. Thousand Oaks, CA: Sage Publications.

Burney, D. (2004). Craft knowledge: The road to transforming schools. *Phi Delta Kappan, 85*(7), 526–531.

Burns, J. M. (1978). *Leadership*. New York: Harper & Row.

Burns, T., & Stalker, G. M. (1961). *The management of innovation*. London: Tavistock.

Burton, R. M. (2006). *Strategic organizational diagnosis and design: The dynamics of fit* (3rd ed.). New York: Springer.

Caine, R. N. (2006). Systemic changes in public schools through brain-based learning. *TechTrends, 50*(2), 52–53.

Caine, R. N., & Caine, G. (1997). *Education on the edge of possibility*. Alexandria, VA: ASCD.

Caine, R. N., Caine, G., McClintic, C. L., & Klimek, K. J. (2005). *12 brain/mind learning principles in action: The fieldbook for making connections, teaching, and the human brain*. Thousand Oaks, CA: Corwin Press.

Capra, F. (1982). *The turning point: Science, society, and the rising culture*. New York: Simon and Schuster.

———. (1996). *The web of life: A new scientific understanding of living systems*. New York: Anchor Books.

Carr-Chellman, A. A. (1999). Systemic change: Critically reviewing the literature. *Educational Research and Evaluation, 4*(4), 369–394.

Cebrowski, A. Office of Force Transformation. Retrieved from en.wikipedia.org/ wiki/Office_of_Force_Transformation (November 21, 2009).

Checkland, P. (1981). *Systems thinking, systems practice*. Chichester, NY: John Wiley & Sons.

———. (1984). *Systems thinking, systems practice*. Reprinted with corrections. New York: John Wiley.

Christensen, C. M. (2003). *The innovator's dilemma: The revolutionary book that will change the way you do business*. New York: HarperCollins.

Christensen, C. M., Johnson, C. W., & Horn, M. B. (2008). *Disrupting class: How disruptive innovation will change the way the world learns*. New York: McGraw-Hill.

Clarke, J. (2003). Personalized learning and personalized teaching. In J. DiMartino, J. Clarke, & D. Wolk (Eds.), *Personalized learning: Preparing high school students to create their futures.* Lanham, MD: Scarecrow Press.

Collins, J. C. (2001). *Good to great: Why some companies make the leap . . . and others don't.* New York: HarperCollins.

Conner, D. R. (1998). *Leading at the edge of chaos.* New York: John Wiley.

Connolly, P. J. (2001). A standard for success. *Info World, 23*(42), 57–58.

Cook, W. J., Jr. (2000). *Strategics: The art and science of holistic strategy.* Westport, CT: Quorum Books.

Council of Chief State School Officers. (2008). Interstate school leaders licensure consortium. Retrieved from www.ccsso.org/content/pdfs/elps_isllc2008.pdf (January 24, 2008).

Craik, K. (1943). *The nature of explanation.* Cambridge: Cambridge University Press.

Csikszentmihalyi, M. (1990). *Flow: The psychology of optimal experience.* New York: Harper & Row.

Cummings, T. G., & Worley, C. G. (2001). *Organization development and change* (7th ed.). Cincinnati, OH: South-Western College Publishing.

Daft, R. L. (2001). *Organization theory and design* (7th ed.). Cincinnati, OH: South-Western College Publishing.

———. (2006). *Organization theory and design* (9th ed.). Cincinnati, OH: South-Western College Publishing.

Darling-Hammond, L. (1990). Achieving our goals: Superficial or structural reforms. *Phi Delta Kappan, 72*(4), 286–295.

Dede, C. (2005). Why design-based research is both important and difficult. *Educational Technology, 45*(1), 5–8.

Doblar, D., Easterling, W., & Reigeluth, C. M. (2009). Formative research on the school system transformation protocol: The development of transformational leadership capacity in a school district's systemic change process. Unpublished manuscript, Indiana University.

Dooley, K. (2004). Complexity science models of organizational change. In S. Poole and A. Van De Ven (Eds.), *Handbook of organizational change and development* (pp. 354–373). Oxford: Oxford University Press.

Drucker, P. F. (1959). *Landmarks of tomorrow: A report on the new "post-modern" world.* New York: Harper Colophon Books.

Duck, J. D. (2001). *The change monster: The human forces that fuel or foil corporate transformation and change.* New York: Crown Business.

Duffy, F. M. (2002). *Step-up-to-excellence: An innovative approach to managing and rewarding performance in school systems.* Lanham, MD: Scarecrow Education.

———. (2003a). *Courage, passion, and vision: A superintendent's guide to leading systemic school improvement.* Lanham, MD: Scarecrow Education / American Association of School Administrators.

———. (2003b). I think, therefore I am resistant to change. *Journal of Staff Development, 24*(1), 30–36.

———. (2004). *Moving upward together: Creating strategic alignment to sustain systemic school improvement.* Leading Systemic School Improvement, no. 1. Lanham, MD: Scarecrow Education.

————. (2006). Step-up-to-excellence: A change navigation protocol for transforming school systems. Connexions, June 9, 2006. Available from http://cnx.org/content/m13656/latest/.

————. (2007). Strapping wings on a caterpillar and calling it a butterfly: When systemic change is not systemic. *The F. M. Duffy Reports, 12*(3), 2.

————. (2008). Strategic communication during times of great change: strategies for bringing stakeholders together and creating buy-in for transforming a school system. *The School Administrator, 65*(4), 22–25.

————. (2009). A national framework of professional standards for change leadership in education, ISLLC Standard 6. *International Journal of Educational Leadership Preparation, 4*(1). Retrieved from http://ijelp.expressacademic.org/article.php?auto ID=249&issueID=68 (November 28, 2009).

Duffy, P., & Bruns, A. (2006). The use of blogs, wikis, and RSS in education: A conversation of possibilities. Paper presented at the Online Learning and Teaching Conference, Brisbane.

Duffy, F. M., & Chance, P. L. (2007). *Strategic communication during whole-system change: Advice and guidance for school district leaders and PR specialists.* Leading Systemic School Improvement, no. 9. Lanham, MD: Rowman & Littlefield Education.

Duffy, F. M., & Dale, J. D. (Eds.). (2001). *Creating successful school systems: Voices from the university, the field and the community.* Norwood, MA: Christopher-Gordon Publishers.

Duffy, F. M., & Reigeluth, C. M. (2007). *FutureMinds: Transforming American school systems.* Bloomington, IL: Association for Educational Communications and Technology.

————. (2008). The school system transformation (SST) protocol. *Educational Technology, 48*(4), 41–49.

Duffy, F. M., Rogerson, L. G., & Blick, C. (2000). *Redesigning America's schools: A systems approach to improvement.* Norwood, MA: Christopher-Gordon Publishers.

Dulewicz, V., & Higgs, M. (2000). Emotional intelligence: A review and evaluation study. *Journal of Managerial Psychology, 15*(4), 341–372.

Dulewicz, V., Higgs, M. J., & Slaski, M. (2001). Emotional intelligence: construct and concurrent validity. Henley Working Paper. Retrieved from www.henleymc.ac.uk/elibrary/hwpr02.nsf/papers/D9A0AF5F912C8F9E00256B170066E384 (June 11, 2008).

Duval, E., Hodgins, W., Rehak, D., & Robson, R. (2004). Learning Objects Symposium Special Issue Guest Editorial. *Journal of Educational Multimedia and Hypermedia, 13*(4), 331.

Eckel, P., Hill, B., & Green, M. (1998). On change: En route to transformation. An occasional paper series of the ACE project on leadership and institutional transformation. Washington, DC: American Council on Education. Retrieved from www.acenet.edu/bookstore/pdf/on-change/on-change1.pdf (April 25, 2008).

Education Commission of the States. (1996). *Bending without breaking: Improving education through flexibility & choice.* Denver, CO: Education Commission of the States.

Egol, M. (2003). *The education revolution: Spectacular learning at lower cost.* Tenafly, NJ: Wisdom Dynamics.

Eldredge, N., & Gould, S. J. (1972). Punctuated equilibria: An alternative to phyletic gradualism. In T. J. M. Schopf (Ed.), *Models in paleobiology* (pp. 82–115). San Francisco: Freeman, Cooper and Co.

Elmore, R. F. (2004). *School reform from the inside out: Policy, practice, and performance.* Cambridge, MA: Harvard University Press.

Elzen, B., Geels, F. W., & Green, K. (Eds.). (2005). *System innovation and the transition to sustainability: Theory, evidence and policy.* Cheltenham, UK: Edward Elgar Publishing

Emery, F. E. (1977). *Two basic organization designs in futures we are in.* Leiden, Netherlands: Martius Nijhoff.

Emery, F. E., & Thorsrud, E. (1976). *Democracy at work: The report of the Norwegian Democracy Program.* Leiden, Netherlands: Nijhoff.

Emery, M. (1996). *The search conference: A powerful method for planning organizational change and community action.* San Francisco: Jossey-Bass Publishers.

———. (2006). *The future of schools: How communities and staff can transform their school districts.* Leading Systemic School Improvement, no. 6. Lanham, MD: Rowman & Littlefield Education.

Emery, M., & Purser, R. E. (1995). *The search conference: A comprehensive guide to theory and practice.* San Francisco: Jossey-Bass.

Farson, R. (1996). *Management of the absurd.* New York: Simon & Schuster.

———. (2006). Decisions, dilemmas, and dangers. In F. M. Duffy (Ed.), *Power, politics, and ethics in school districts: Dynamic leadership for systemic change* (pp. 179–191). Leading Systemic School Improvement, no. 6. Lanham, MD: Rowman & Littlefield Education.

Fiedler, F. E. (1967). *A theory of leadership effectiveness.* New York: McGraw-Hill.

Fisher, W., & Brin, B. L. (1991). Parallel organization: A structural change theory. *Journal of Library Administration, 14*(1), 51–66.

Flood, R. L. (1990). Liberating systems theory: Toward critical systems thinking. *Human Relations, 43*(1), 49–75.

Flood, R. C., & Jackson, M. C. (Eds.). (1991). *Critical systems thinking.* New York: John Wiley & Sons.

Frederickson, J. R., & Collins, A. (1989). A systems approach to educational testing. *Educational Researcher, 18*(9), 27–32.

Fullan, M. (1993). *Change forces: Probing the depths of educational reform.* London: Falmer Press.

———. (2004). *Leadership & sustainability: System thinkers in action.* Thousand Oaks, CA: Corwin Press.

Gardner, H. (2004). *Changing minds: The art and science of changing our own and other people's minds.* Cambridge, MA: Harvard Business School Press.

Gardner, J. W. (1969). *No easy victories.* New York: Harper & Row.

———. (1990). *On leadership.* New York: Free Press.

Gibbons, A. S., Nelson, J. M., & Richards, R. (2002). The nature and origin of instructional objects. In D. A. Wiley (Ed.), *The instructional use of learning objects: Online version.* Available from www.reusability.org/read/.

Gibson, D., Levine, L., & Novak, W. E. (2006). Using system archetypes to identify failure patterns in acquisition. Retrieved from www.sei.cmu.edu/library/assets/archetypes.pdf (May 31, 2008).

Gleick, J. (1988). *Chaos: Making a new science*. New York: Penguin Books.

Gokhale, A. A. (1995). Colaborative learning enhances critical thinking. *Journal of Technology Education, 7*(1), 22–77.

Goldberg, R., Richards, J., & BBN Corporation. (1996). The co-NECT design for school change. In S. Stringfield, S. M. Ross, & L. Smith (Eds.), *Bold plans for school restructuring: The new American schools designs* (pp. 75–108). Washington, DC: Lawrence Erlbaum Associates, Inc.

Goleman, D. P. (1995). *Emotional intelligence: Why it can matter more than IQ for character, health and lifelong achievement*. New York: Bantam Books.

———. (1996). *Emotional intelligence*. London: Bloomsbury.

Goodlad, J. I. (1984). *A place called school: Prospects for the future*. New York: McGraw-Hill.

Greenleaf, R. K. (1973). *The servant as leader*. Peterborough, NH: Center for Applied Science.

Greenleaf, R. K., Spears, L. C., & Covey, S. R. (2002). *Servant leadership: A journey into the nature of legitimate power and greatness*. Mahwah, NJ: Paulist Press.

Grossman, L. 2006. Time's person of the year: You. *Time*. Retrieved from www.time.com/time/magazine/article/0,9171,1569514,00.html.

Haag, S., Cummings, M., McCubbrey, D., Pinsonneault, A., & Donovan, R. (2006). *Management information systems for the knowledge age* (3rd Canadian ed.). Whitby, ON: McGraw Hill Ryerson.

Habermas, J. (1973). *Theory and practice*. (J. Viertel, Trans.). Boston: Beacon.

———. 1984. *The Theory of Communicative Action: Reason and the Rationalization of Society*. (T. McCarthy, Trans.). Boston: Beacon Press.

———. (1987). *The theory of communicative action: Lifeworld and system: A critique of Functional reason*. (T. McCarthy, Trans.). Boston: Beacon Press.

Hammer, M., & Champy, J. (1993). *Reengineering the corporation: A manifesto for business revolution*. New York: Harper Business.

———. (2003). *Reengineering the corporation: A manifesto for business revolution*. New York: HarperCollins Publishers.

Handy, C. (1995). *The age of paradox*. Boston, MA: Harvard Business School.

———. (1998). *The age of unreason*. Cambridge, MA: Harvard Business School Press.

Harackiewicz, J. M., Barron, K. E., Tauer, J. M., Carter, S. M., & Elliot, A. J. (2000). Short-term and long-term consequences of achievement goals: Predicting interest and performance over time. *Journal of Educational Psychology, 92*(2), 316–330.

Harding, D., & Rouse, T. (2007). Human due diligence. *Harvard Business Review, 85*(4), 124–131, 142.

Harman, W. W. (1984). How I learned to love the future. *World Future Society Bulletin, 18*, 1–5.

Harrison, J. S., & St. John, C. H. (1996). Managing and partnering with external stakeholders. *The Academy of Management Executive, 10*(2), 46–60.

Head, S. (2005). *The new ruthless economy: Work and power in the digital age*. Oxford: Oxford University Press.

Heady, R., & Kilgore, S. (1996). The modern red schoolhouse. In S. Stringfield, S. Ross, & L. Smith (Eds.), *Bold plans for school restructuring: The new American schools designs* (pp. 147–178). Washington, DC: Lawrence Erlbaum Associates, Inc.

Heath, C., & Heath, D. (2007). *Made to stick: Why some ideas survive and others die.* New York: Random House.

Hersey, P., & Blanchard, K. H. (1988). *Management of organizational behavior: Utilizing human resources* (5th ed.). Englewood Cliffs, NJ: Prentice-Hall.

Higgs, M. (2000). *Do leaders need emotional intelligence? A study of the relationship between emotional intelligence and leadership of change.* Retrieved from www.usq .edu.au/extrafiles/business/journals/HRMJournal/InternationalChapters/Higgs6 .pdf (January 18, 2009).

———. (2002). Do leaders need emotional intelligence? A study of the relationship between emotional intelligence and leadership of change. *International Journal of Organisational Behaviour, 5*(6), 195–212.

Higgs, M. J., & Dulewicz, S. V. D. (1999). *Making sense of emotional intelligence.* Windsor, UK: National Foundation for Educational Research (NFER)-Nelson.

Higgs, M. J., & Rowland, D. (2000). Building change leadership capability: The quest for change competence. *Journal of Change Management, 1*(2), 116–131.

———. (2001). Developing change leaders: Assessing the impact of a development programme. *Change Management Journal, 2*(1), 47–66.

———. (2007). Leading change: What are the critical leader behaviours? Henley Working Paper Series, HWP 0711.

Hock, D. W. (1995). The chaordic organization: Out of control and into order. *World Business Academy Perspectives, 9*(1), 5–18.

Hodgins, H. W. (2002). The future of learning objects. In D. A. Wiley (Ed.), *The instructional use of learning objects: Online version.* Available from www.reusability .org/read/.

Holden, A. (1986). *Chaos.* Princeton, NJ: Princeton University Press.

Hoover, W. A. (2002). The importance of phonemic awareness in learning to read. *SEDL Letter, 14*(3). Retrieved from www.sedl.org/pubs/sedl-letter/v14n03/3.html (June 1, 2008).

Houlihan, G. T., & Houlihan, A. G. (2005). *School performance: How to meet AYP and achieve long-term success.* Rexford, NY: International Center for Leadership in Education.

Hoy, W. K. (1998). Self-efficacy: The exercise of control. *Education Administration Quarterly, 34*(1), 153–158.

Hurley, E. A., Chamberlain, A., Slavin, R. E., & Madden, N. A. (2001). Effects of success for all on TAAS reading scores—a Texas statewide evaluation. *Phi Delta Kappan, 82*(10), 750–756.

Jackson, M. C. (1985). Social systems theory and practice: The need for a critical approach. *International Journal of General Systems, 10*, 135–151.

———. (1991a). The origins and nature of critical systems thinking. *Systems Practice, 4*, 131–149.

———. (1991b). Post-modernism and contemporary systems thinking. In R. C. Flood & M. C. Jackson (Eds.), *Critical systems thinking* (pp. 287–302). New York: John Wiley & Sons.

Jackson, M. C., & Keys, P. (1984). Towards a system of systems methodologies. *Journal of Operations Research, 3*, 473–486.

Janis, I. L. (1972). *Victims of group-think*. Boston: Houghton Mifflin.

Jantsch, E. (1980). *The self-organizing universe*. Oxford: Pergamon.

Jenlink, P. M., Reigeluth, C. M., Carr, A. A., & Nelson, L. M. (1996). An expedition for change: Facilitating systemic change in public schools. *Tech Trends, 41*(1), 21–30.

————. (1998). Guidelines for facilitating systemic change in school districts. *Systems Research and Behavioral Science, 15*(3), 217–233.

Johnson-Laird, P. N. (1983). *Mental models: Towards a cognitive science of language, inference and consciousness*. Cambridge: Cambridge University Press.

Johnson-Laird, P. N., Girotto, V., & Legrenzi, P. (1998). Mental models: a gentle guide for outsiders. Retrieved from http://ICOS.groups.si.umich.edu//gentleintro .html (April 28, 2009).

Jones, B. B., & Brazzel, M. (Eds.). (2006). *The NTL handbook of organization development and change: Principles, practices, and perspectives*. San Francisco: Pfeiffer.

Kankus, R. F., & Cavalier, R. P. (1995). Combating organizationally induced helpless. *Quality Progress, 28*(12), 89–92.

Kaufman, R. (2000). *Mega planning: Practical tools for organizational success*. Thousand Oaks, CA: Sage Publications.

Keefe, J. (2007). What is personalization? *Phi Delta Kappan, 89*(3), 217–223.

Keefe, W., & Jenkins, J. (2002). A special section on personalized instruction. *Phi Delta Kappan, 83*(6), 440–448.

Kegan, R. (2000). What "form" transforms? A constructive developmental perspective on transformational learning. In J. Mezirow et al. (Eds.), *Learning as transformation: Critical perspectives on a theory in progress* (pp. 35–69). San Francisco: Jossey-Bass Publishers.

Kegan, R., & Lahey, L. L. (2001). *How the way we talk can change the way we work: Seven languages for transformation*. San Francisco: Jossey-Bass Publishers.

Kellert, S. H. (1993). *In the wake of chaos: Unpredictable order in dynamical systems*. Chicago: University of Chicago Press.

Kelly, K. (1998). *New rules for the new economy: 10 radical strategies for a connected world*. New York: Penguin Books.

Kim, D. H., & Anderson, V. (1998). *Systems archetype basics: From story to structure*. Waltham, MA: Pegasus Communications.

————. (2007). *Systems archetype basics*. Waltham, MA: Pegasus Communications.

Kim, D. H., & Lannon, C. P. (1997). *Applying systems archetypes*. Waltham, MA: Pegasus Communications.

King, K. S., & Frick, T. (1999). Transforming education: Case studies in systems thinking. Paper presented at the Annual National AERA Meeting, Montreal, Canada.

Kotter, J. P. (1995). Leading change: Why transformation efforts fail. *Harvard Business Review*, March–April, 59–67.

————. (1996). *Leading change*. Boston: Harvard Business School Press.

Krueger, K. (n.d.). Untitled lyrics. Retrieved from www.elyrics.net/read/k/kris-kruger -lyrics/untitled-lyrics.html (June 21, 2008).

Kuhn, T. S. (1962). *The structure of scientific revolutions* (1st ed.). Chicago: University of Chicago Press.

Lamb, B. (2004). Wide open spaces: Wikis, ready or not. *EDUCA USE Review, 39*(5), 36–48.

Lambert, N. M., & McCombs, B. (Eds.). (1998). *How students learn: Reforming schools through learner-centered education*. Washington, DC: American Psychological Association.

La Piana Associates. (2006). Leadership and management: Having a change-friendly mindset. Retrieved from www.lapiana.org/sr/tips/leadership/08_2004.html (August 15, 2006).

Lawrence, P. R., & Lorsch, J. W. (1967). *Organization and environment*. Boston: Harvard Business School Press.

Lazlo, C., & Laugel, J.-F. (2000). *Large-scale organizational change: An executive's guide*. Burlington, MA: Butterworth-Heinemann.

Lee, S., & Reigeluth, C. M. (2007). Community involvement in Decatur's journey toward excellence. In F. M. Duffy & P. Chance (Eds.), *Strategic communication during whole-system change: Advice and guidance for school district leaders and PR specialists*. Leading School Improvement, no. 9. Lanham, MD: Rowman & Littlefield Education.

Leithwood, K. (1992). The move toward transformational leadership. *Educational Leadership, 49*(5), 8–12.

Lewin, K. (1951). *Field theory in social science*. New York: Harper and Row.

Likert, R. (1961). *New patterns of management*. New York: McGraw-Hill.

Lorenz, E. N. (1995). *The essence of chaos*. Seattle, WA: University of Washington Press.

Lum, L. (2006). The power of podcasting. *Diverse: Issues in Higher Education, 23*(2), 32–35.

Manz, C. C., & Sims, H. P., Jr. (1995). Superleadership: Beyond the myth of heroic leadership. In J. T. Wren (Ed.), *The leader's companion: Insights on leadership through the ages* (pp. 212–221). New York: The Free Press.

Marcus, S. H., & Pringle, A. (1995). What competencies are needed in a changing environment? *The Human Resources Professional, 8*(3), 19–24.

Marzano, R. J. (2006). *Classroom assessment and grading practices that work*. Alexandria, VA: Association for Supervision and Curriculum Development.

Mayer, R. E. (1999). Designing instruction for constructivist learning. In C. M. Reigeluth (Ed.), *Instructional-design theories and models: A new paradigm of instructional theories* (2nd ed., pp. 141–159). Mahwah, NJ: Lawrence-Erlbaum Associates.

McCarthy, M. P. (2003). *Agile business for fragile times: Strategies for enhancing competitive resiliency and stakeholder trust*. New York: McGraw-Hill.

McCombs, B. L. (2008). From one-size-fits-all to personalized learner-centered learning: The evidence. *The F. M. Duffy Reports, 13*(2), 1–12. Available from www.thefmduffygroup.com/publications/reports.html.

McCombs, B. L., & Whisler, J. (1997). *The learner-centered classroom and school*. San Francisco: Jossey-Bass Publishers.

McDonald, P., & Gandz, J. (1992). Getting value from shared values. *Organizational Dynamics, 20*(3), 64–76.

McGrath, R. (1994). Organizationally induced helplessness: Antithesis of empowerment. *Quality Progress, 27*(4), 89–92.

Merrill, M. D. (2009). First principles of instruction. In C. M. Reigeluth & A. A. Carr-Chellman (Eds.), *Instructional-design theories and models: Building a common knowledge base* (Vol. 3). New York: Routledge.

Merrill, M. D., & ID2 Research Group. (1998). ID expert: A second generation instructional development system. *Instructional Science, 26*(3–4), 242–262.

Mezirow, J. (2000). Learning to think like an adult: Core concepts of transformation theory. In J. Mezirow et al. (Eds.), *Learning as transformation: Critical perspectives on a theory in progress* (pp. 3–33). San Francisco: Jossey-Bass Publishers.

Miller, D. L., Friesen, P. H., & Mintzberg, H. (1984). *Organizations: A quantum view.* Englewood Cliffs, NJ: Prentice-Hall.

Mirel, J. (2001). *The evolution of the new American schools: From revolution to mainstream.* Washington, DC: Thomas B. Fordham Foundation.

Mitchell, R. (1992). *Testing for learning.* New York: The Free Press.

Morgan, G. (1986). *Images of organization.* Beverly Hills: Sage Publications.

Murphy, R. (2002). Managing strategic change: An executive overview. Retrieved from http://handle.dtic.mil/100.2/ADA430599 (October 22, 2005).

Nadler, G. (1981). *The planning and design approach.* New York: John Wiley & Sons.

National Education Commission on Time and Learning. (1994). *Prisoners of time: What we know and what we need to know.* Washington, DC: United States Department of Education.

National Policy Board for Education Administration. (2002). *Standards for advanced programs in educational leadership for principals, superintendents, curriculum directors, and supervisors.* Retrieved from www.npbea.org/ELCC/ELCCStandards%20_5-02.pdf (January 24, 2009).

National Science Foundation. (2002). *Transfer of learning: Issues and research agenda.* Retrieved from www.nsf.gov/pubs/2003/nsf03212/nsf03212_1.pdf (June 21, 2008).

National Training Center. (2008). *Leadership competencies and developmental opportunities.* Washington, DC: U.S. Department of the Interior, Bureau of Land Management. Retrieved from www.ntc.blm.gov/leadership/27_frame_define.html (June 4, 2008).

Nevis, E. C., Lancourt, J., & Vassallo, H. G. (1996). *Intentional revolutions: A seven-point strategy for transforming organizations.* San Francisco: Jossey-Bass Publishers.

New Commission on the Skills of the American Workforce. (2007). Tough choices, tough times: The report of the new commission on the skills of the American workforce—executive summary. Washington, DC: National Center on Education and the Economy.

Nicholls, J. (1999). *What is leadership in depth?* Global Management 1999: Annual Review of International Management Practice (AMA International). London: Sterling Publications, Ltd.

Nonaka, I., & Takeuchi, H. (1995). *The knowledge-creating company: How Japanese companies create the dynamics of innovation.* New York: Oxford University Press.

Nowotny, H. (2005). The increase of complexity and its reduction: Emergent interfaces between the natural sciences, humanities and social sciences. *Theory, Culture & Society, 22*(5), 15–31.

Olson, E. E., & Eoyang, G. H. (2001). *Facilitating organization change: Lessons from complexity science.* San Francisco: Pfeiffer.

O'Sullivan, E. (2003). *Transformative learning.* Retrieved from http://tlc.oise.utoronto.ca/insights/integraleducation.html (April 30, 2009).

Owen, H. (2008). *Open space technology: A user's guide* (3rd ed.). San Francisco: Berrett-Koehler.

Pascale, R. T., Millemann, M., & Gioja, L. (2000). *Surfing the edge of chaos: The laws of nature and the new laws of business*. New York: Crown Business.

Pasmore, W. A. (1988). *Designing effective organizations: The socio-technical systems perspective*. New York: Wiley & Sons.

Pava, C. H. P. (1983a). Designing managerial and professional work for high performance: A sociotechnical approach. *National Productivity Review*, Spring, 126–135.

———. (1983b). *Managing new office technology: An organizational strategy*. New York: The New Press.

———. (1986). New strategies of systems change: Reclaiming nonsynoptic methods. *Human Relations*, 39(7), 615–633. Retrieved from http://hum.sagepub.com/cgi/content/abstract/39/7/615 (January 16, 2008).

Petroski, H. (1992). *To engineer is human*. New York: Vintage.

Pettigrew, A. (1987). Context and action in the transformation of the firm. *Journal of Management Studies*, 24(6), 649–670.

Pink, D. (2006). *A whole new mind: Why right-brainers will rule the future*. New York: Riverhead Trade.

Pogrow, S. (2000a). Success for all does not produce success for students. *Phi Delta Kappan*, 82(1), 67–80.

———. (2000b). The unsubstantiated "success" of success for all. *Phi Delta Kappan*, 81(8), 596–597.

———. (2002). Success for all is a failure. *Phi Delta Kappan*, 83(6), 463–468.

Purser, R. E., & Cabana, S. (1998). *The self-managing organization: How leading companies are transforming the work of teams for real impact*. New York: The Free Press.

Quinn, J. B., Anderson, P., & Finkelstein, S. (1998). Managing professional intellect: Making the most of the best. Harvard Business Review Series.

Quinn, R. E. (1996). *Deep change: Discovering the leader within*. San Francisco: Jossey-Bass Publishers.

Ranson, S., Martin, J., Nixon, J., & McKeown, P. (1996). Towards a theory of learning. *British Journal of Educational Studies*, 44(1), 9–26.

Reigeluth, C. M. (1993). Principles of educational systems design. *International Journal of Educational Research*, 19(2), 117–131.

———. (1994). The imperative for systemic change. In C. M. Reigeluth & R. J. Garfinkle (Eds.), *Systemic change in education* (pp. 3–11). Englewood Cliffs, NJ: Educational Technology Publications.

———. (1997a). Educational standards: To standardize or to customize learning? *Phi Delta Kappan*, 79, 202–206.

———. (1997b). Instructional theory, practitioner needs, and new directions: Some reflections. *Educational Technology*, 37(1), 42–47.

———. (1999). What is instructional-design theory and how is it changing? In C. M. Reigeluth (Ed.), *Instructional-design theories and models: A new paradigm of instructional theory* (Vol. 2, pp. 5–29). Mahwah, NJ: Lawrence Erlbaum Associates.

———. (2004). Chaos theory and the sciences of complexity: Foundations for transforming education. Paper presented at the American Educational Research Associates Special Interest Group, San Diego, CA. Retrieved from http://ccaerasig.com/mtngs/aera04.htm (February 6, 2005).

————. (2006a). The guidance system for transforming education. *Tech Trends, 50*(2), 42.

————. (2006b). A leveraged emergent approach to systemic transformation. *Tech Trends, 50*(2), 46–47.

————. (2007). Chaos theory and the sciences of complexity: Foundations for transforming education. In B. Despres (Ed.), *Systems thinkers in action: A field guide for effective change leadership in education* (pp. 24–38). Lanham, MD: Rowman & Littlefield Education.

Reigeluth, C. M., & Carr-Chellman, A. A. (Eds.). (2009). *Instructional-design theories and models: Building a common knowledge base* (Vol. 3). New York: Routledge.

Reigeluth, C. M., & Duffy, F. M. (2006). Trends and issues in P-12 educational change. In R. A. Reiser & J. A. Dempsey (Eds.), *Trends and issues in instructional design and technology* (2nd ed., pp. 209–220). Upper Saddle River, NJ: Merrill / Prentice Hall.

————. (2007). Trends and issues in P–12 educational change. In R. A. Reiser & J. A. Dempsey (Eds.), *Trends and issues in instructional design and technology* (2nd ed., pp. 209–220). Upper Saddle River, NJ: Merrill / Prentice Hall.

————. (2008). The AECT FutureMinds initiative: Transforming America's school systems. *Educational Technology, 48*(3), 45–49.

————. (2009). Criteria for assessing school district capacity for engaging in systemic transformational change. Unpublished manuscript.

Reigeluth, C. M., & Frick, T. W. (1999). Formative research: A methodology for creating and improving design theories. In C. M. Reigeluth (Ed.), *Instructional-design theories and models* (Vol. 2, pp. 633–651). Mahwah, NJ: Lawrence Erlbaum.

Reigeluth, C. M., & Garfinkle, R. J. (1994a). Envisioning a new system of education. In C. M. Reigeluth & R. J. Garfinkle (Eds.), *Systemic change in education*. Englewood Cliffs, NJ: Educational Technology Publications.

————. (1994b). *Systemic change in education*. Englewood Cliffs, NJ: Educational Technology Publications.

Reigeluth, C. M., & Joseph, R. (2002). Beyond technology integration: The case for technology transformation. *Educational Technology, 42*(4), 9–13.

Reigeluth, C. M., Watson, W. R., Watson, S. L., Dutta, P., Chen, C., & Powell, N. D. P. (2008). Roles for technology in the information-age paradigm of education: Learning management systems. *Educational Technology, 48*(6), 32–39.

Richter, K. B. (2007). Integration of a decision-making process and a learning process in a newly formed leadership team for systemic transformation of a school district. Unpublished doctoral dissertation, Indiana University.

Richter, K. B., & Reigeluth, C. M. (2007). Systemic transformation in public school systems. *The F. M. Duffy Reports, 12*(4), 1–24.

Rittel, H. W. J., & Webber, M. M. (1973). Dilemmas in a general theory of planning. *Policy Sciences, 4,* 155–169. Retrieved from www.uctc.net/mwebber/Rittel+Webber+Dilemmas+General_Theory_of_Planning.pdf (January 16, 2008).

Rogers, E. M. (1995). *Diffusion of innovations*. New York: The Free Press.

Salisbury, D. F. (1990). Cognitive psychology and its implications for designing drill and practice programs for computers. *Journal of Computer-Based Instruction, 17*(1), 23–30.

Salovey, P., & Mayer, J. D. (1990). Emotional intelligence. *Imagination, cognition, and personality, 9*, 185–211.

Sanders, W., & Rivers, J. (1996a). *Cumulative and residual effects of teachers on future student academic achievement.* Knoxville: University of Tennessee Value-Added Research and Assessment Center.

———. (1996b). Cumulative and residual effects of teachers on future student academic achievement: Tennessee value-added assessment system. Research progress report. University of Tennessee Value-Added Research and Assessment Center. Retrieved from www.mccsc.edu/~curriculum/cumulative and residual effects of teachers.pdf (July 8, 2007).

Savitz, A. W., & Weber, K. (2006). *The triple bottom line: How today's best-run companies are achieving economic, social and environmental success—and how you can too.* San Francisco: Jossey-Bass Publishers.

Schein, E. H. (1985). *Organizational culture and leadership.* San Francisco: Jossey-Bass Publishers.

Schlechty, P. C. (1990). *Schools for the 21st century: Leadership imperatives for educational reform* (1st ed.). San Francisco: Jossey-Bass Publishers.

———. (1997). *Inventing better schools: An action plan for educational reform* (1st ed.). San Francisco: Jossey-Bass Publishers.

———. (2002). *Working on the work: An action plan for teachers, principals, and superintendents* (1st ed.). San Francisco: Jossey-Bass Publishers.

———. (2005). *Creating great schools: Six critical systems at the heart of educational innovation.* San Francisco: Jossey-Bass Publishers.

Scholtes, P. R. (1992). *The team handbook.* Madison, WI: Joiner Associates, Inc.

Schreiner, O. (1998). The hunter's allegory. In *The story of a South African farm.* Mineola, NY: Dover Publications (Original work published 1883).

Schunk, D. H. (1990). Goal setting and self-efficacy during self-regulated learning. *Educational Psychologist, 25*(1), 71–86.

———. (1991). Self-efficacy and academic motivation. *Educational Psychologist, 26*(3), 207–231.

Schwartz, D. L., Lin, X., Brophy, S., & Bransford, J. D. (1999). Toward the development of flexibly adaptive instructional designs. In C. M. Reigeluth (Ed.), *Instructional-design theories and models: A new paradigm of instructional theory* (Vol. 2, pp. 183–213). Mahwah, NJ: Lawrence Erlbaum Associates.

Schweitz, R., Martens, K., & Aronson, N. (2005). *Future search in school district change: Connection, community and results.* Leading Systemic School Improvement, no. 4. Lanham, MD: Scarecrow Education.

Seligman, M. E. P. (1990). *Learned optimism: How to change your mind and your life.* New York: Pocket Books.

Senge, P. M. (1990). *The fifth discipline: The art and practice of the learning organization.* New York: Currency Doubleday.

Senge, P. M., Cambron-McCabe, N., Lucas, T., Smith, B., Dutton, J., & Kleiner, A. (2000). *Schools that learn: A fifth discipline fieldbook for educators, parents, and everyone who cares about education.* New York: Doubleday.

Senge, P. M., Kleiner, A., Roberts, C., Ross, R. B., & Smith, B. J. (1994). *The fifth discipline fieldbook: Strategies and tools for building a learning organization.* New York: Doubleday.

Simmons, J. (2006). *Breaking through: Transforming urban school districts.* New York: Teachers College Press.

Sirkin, H. L., Keenan, P., & Jackson, A. (2005). The hard side of change management. *Harvard Business Review,* October, 1–10.

Slavin, R. E., Madden, N. A., & Wasik, B. A. (1996). Roots & wings. In S. Stringfield, S. Ross, & L. Smith (Eds.), *Bold plans for educational reform: The new American schools.* Hillsdale, NJ: Erlbaum.

Smith, M. S., & O'Day, J. (1991). Systemic school reform. In S. H. Fuhrman, & B. Malen (Eds.), *The politics of curriculum and testing* (pp. 233–267). Politics of Education Association Yearbook. London: Taylor & Francis.

Spiro, D. (2006). *The creed room: A novel of ideas.* (1st Aegis Press ed.). Del Mar, CA: Aegis Press.

Squire, K. D., & Reigeluth, C. M. (2000). The many faces of systemic change. *Educational Horizons, 78*(3), 145–154.

Starbuck, W. H. (1996). Unlearning ineffective or obsolete technologies. *International Journal of Technology Management, 11,* 725–737.

Steckler, N., & Fontas, N. (1995). Building team leader effectiveness: A diagnostic tool. *Organization Dynamics, 23*(3), 20–36.

Sternberg, R., Torff, B., & Grigorenko, E. (1998). Teaching triarchically improves student achievement. *Journal of Educational Psychology, 90,* 374–384.

Stogdill, R., & Coons, A. E. (Eds.). (1957). *Leader behavior: Its description and measurement.* Research Monograph, no. 88. Bureau of Business Research, Ohio State University.

Stopper, W. G. (1999). Hiring to build change capacity: The human resource role. *Human Resource Planning,* 1–6. Retrieved from www.allbusiness.com/human -resources/294952-1.html (June 12, 2008).

Stringfield, S., Ross, S., & Smith, L. (Eds.). (1996). *Bold plans for school restructuring: The new American schools designs.* Mahwah, NJ: Lawrence Erlbaum Associates.

Stufflebeam, D. L. (2000). The CIPP model for evaluation. In D. L. Stufflebeam, G. F. Madaus, & T. Kellaghan (Eds.), *Evaluation models* (2nd ed.). Boston: Kluwer Academic Publishers.

Supovitz, J. A. (2006). *The case for district-based reform: Leading, building and sustaining school improvement.* Cambridge, MA: Harvard Education Press.

Szabo, M., & Flesher, K. (2002). CMI theory and practice: Historical roots of learning management systems. Paper presented at the E-Learn 2002 World Conference on E-Learning in Corporate, Government, Healthcare, & Higher Education, Montreal, Canada.

Tannenbaum, R., & Schmidt, H. W. (1957). How to choose a leadership pattern. *Harvard Business Review,* March–April, 95–101.

Tichy, N. M., & Devanna, M. A. (1986). The transformational leader. *Training and Development Journal, 41*(7), 27–32.

Toffler, A. (1980). *The third wave.* New York: Bantam Books.

———. (1984). *The third wave.* New York: Bantam.

Tomlinson, C. A. (1999a). *The differentiated classroom: Responding to the needs of all learners.* Alexandria, VA: Association for Supervision and Curriculum Development.

———. (1999b). Mapping a route toward differentiated instruction from personalized learning. *Educational Leadership, 57*(1), 12–16.

————. (2003). *Fulfilling the promise of the differentiated classroom: Strategies and tools for responsive teaching.* Alexandria, VA: Association for Supervision and Curriculum Development.

Trist, E. L., Higgin, G. W., Murray, H., & Pollack, A. B. (1963). *Organizational choice.* London: Tavistock.

Trist, E. L., & Murray, H. (1993). Volume II: The socio-technical perspective. In *The social engagement of social science, a Tavistock anthology.* Philadelphia: University of Pennsylvania Press.

Tushman, M. L., Newman, W. H., & Nadler, D. A. (1988). Executive leadership and organizational evolution: Managing incremental and discontinuous change. In R. H. Kilmann & T. J. Covin (Eds.), *Corporate transformation* (pp.102–130). San Francisco: Jossey-Bass.

Tushman, M. L., Newman, W. H., & Romanelli, E. (1986). Convergence and upheaval: Managing the unsteady pace of organizational evolution. *California Management Review, 29*(1), 29–44.

Tyack, D. B., & Cuban, L. (1995). *Tinkering toward utopia: A century of public school reform.* Cambridge, MA: Harvard University Press.

————. (1997). *Tinkering toward utopia: A century of public school reform.* Cambridge, MA: Harvard University Press.

Ulrich, W. (1983). *Critical heuristics of social planning: A new approach to practical philosophy.* Bern, Switzerland: Haupt.

Vaill, P. (1991). *Managing as a performing art: New ideas for a world of chaotic change.* San Francisco: Jossey-Bass Publishers.

Vygotsky, L. (1986). *Thought and language.* (A. Kozulin, Trans.). Cambridge, MA: MIT University Press (Original work published 1926).

Waldersee, R. (1997). Becoming a learning organization: The transformation of the workforce. *Journal of Management Development, 16*(4), 262–274.

Walter, G. M. (1995). Motivating for superior performance. *HR Executive Review: The High Performance Enterprise, 3*(1), 6–7.

Watson, S. L., & Reigeluth, C. M. (2008). The learner-centered paradigm of education. *Educational Technology, 48*(5), 39–48.

Watson, S. L., Watson, W. R., & Reigeluth, C. M. (2008). Systems design for change in education and training. In J. M. Spector, M. D. Merrill, J. J. G. van Merrienboer, & M. P. Driscoll (Eds.), *Handbook of research on educational communications and technology* (3rd ed.). Mahwah, NJ: Lawrence Erlbaum Associates.

Watson, W. R., Lee, S., & Reigeluth, C. M. (2007). Learning management systems: An overview and roadmap of the systemic application of computers to education. In F. M. Neto & F. V. Brasileiro (Eds.), *Advances in computer-supported learning.* Hershey, PA: Information Science Publishing.

Watson, W. R., & Watson, S. L. (2007). An argument for clarity: What are learning management systems, what are they not, and what should they become? *Tech Trends, 51*(2), 28–34.

Wheatley, M. J. (1999). *Leadership and the new science: Discovering order in a chaotic world.* San Francisco: Berrett-Koehler Publishers.

————. (2001). Bringing schools back to life: Schools as living systems. In F. M. Duffy & J. D. Dale (Eds.), *Creating successful school systems: Voices from the university, the field and the community.* Norwood, MA: Christopher-Gordon Publishers.

Whetzel, D. (1992). *The secretary of labor's commission on achieving necessary skills.* Washington, DC: ERIC Clearinghouse on Tests, Measurement, and Evaluation. Retrieved from www.eric.ed.gov:80/ERICDocs/data/ericdocs2sql/content_storage_01/0000019b/80/23/60/f0.pdf (June 5, 2006).

Wiggins, G. (1998). *Educative assessment: Designing assessments to inform and improve student performance.* San Francisco: Jossey-Bass Publishers.

Wiley, D. (2002). Connecting learning objects to instructional design theory: A definition, a metaphor, and a taxonomy. In D. A. Wiley (Ed.), *The instructional use of learning objects: Online version.* Available from www.reusability.org/read/.

Williams, J. B., & Jacobs, J. (2004). Exploring the use of blogs as learning spaces in the higher education sector [Electronic Version]. *Australasian Journal of Educational Technology, 20,* 232–247. Retrieved from www.ascilite.org.au/ajet/ajet20/williams.html (October 15, 2008).

Workitect. (2008). *Competencies.* Retrieved from www.workitect.com (June 20, 2008).

Wright, C. E. (2004). Making schools work: Creating service-oriented, performance-driven school systems. Retrieved from www.k12sems.com/images/MakingSchoolsWork_SEMSWP(Mar 2004).pdf (February 20, 2007).

Yasuo, Y. (1993). *The body, self-cultivation, and ki-energy.* (S. Nagatomo & M. S. Hull, Trans.). New York: State University of New York Press.

Zegart, A. (2007). Our clueless intelligence system. *Washington Post,* July 8.

Zimmerman, B. J. (1990). Self-regulated learning and academic achievement: An overview. *Educational Psychologist, 25*(1), 3–17.

Zimmerman, D. (1998). A Fissure in the second order: A new look at change and school reform. Paper presented at the annual meeting of the American Educational Research Association, San Diego, CA, April 13–17. ERIC Document Reproduction Service No. ED420080.

Index

About the Author and Contributors

Francis M. Duffy is a professor of change leadership in education at Gallaudet University in Washington, DC. He is the founding editor of Rowman & Littlefield Education's Leading Systemic School Improvement Series and has written numerous books. He is also the codirector of the FutureMinds: Transforming American School Systems initiative sponsored by the Association for Educational Communications and Technology. He may be reached at duffy@thefmduffygroup.com.

CONTRIBUTORS

Zengguan Chen is associate instructor at Indiana University, Bloomington (e-mail: chen22@indiana.edu).

Pratima Dutta is associate instructor at Indiana University, Bloomington (e-mail: pdutta@indiana.edu).

Nathan D. P. Powell is associate instructor at Indiana University, Bloomington (e-mail: powellnd@indiana.edu).

Charles M. Reigeluth is professor, Instructional Systems Technology Department, School of Education, Indiana University, Bloomington (e-mail: reigelut@indiana.edu).

Sunkyung Lee Watson is assistant professor of educational studies at Ball State University, Muncie, Indiana (e-mail: slwatson@bsu.edu).

William R. Watson is assistant professor of curriculum and instruction at Purdue University, West Lafayette, Indiana (e-mail: brwatson@purdue.edu).